Also by Curt Weeden

CORPORATE SOCIAL INVESTING

with Forewords by Paul Newman and Peter Lynch

HOW WOMEN CAN BEAT TERRORISM

CURT WEEDEN

QUADRAFOIL PRESS, INC.

MOUNT PLEASANT, SOUTH CAROLINA

Copyright © 2003 by Curt Weeden

Published by Quadrafoil Press, Inc.
1150 Hungryneck Blvd., Mount Pleasant, SC 29464

Library of Congress Control Number 2003094925

ISBN: 0-9743714-0-8

Cover and text design: Jonathan Gullery

Printed in United States of America

A CHAQUE FEMME

Destiny is not a matter of chance;
it is a matter of choice.
It is not a thing to be waited for;
it is thing to be achieved.
—William Jennings Bryan

If nonviolence is the law of our being,
the future is with women.
—Mahatma Gandhi

TABLE OF CONTENTS

Part VI: Negative Envy

Part VII: The Solution

ACKNOWLEDGEMENTS

Most of this book is based on lessons learned from women. My wife has been and continues to be an invaluable instructor about what really matters in life. My daughters, daughter-in-law, sisters-in-law and nieces have taught me how to face hardships with courage, perseverance, dignity and humor. Another woman, my late mother, helped me grasp the fact that a simple life can be abundantly rich. A long list of other inspirational women have added to my understanding and appreciation – from Sister Isolina Ferre (a tiny Catholic nun who received the Medal of Freedom for being a giant in Ponce, Puerto Rico) to Helen Hayes, the "First Lady of American Theater," who taught me that caring about people is far more important than fame or fortune.

I am especially grateful to the many people who reviewed earlier drafts of *How Women Can Beat Terrorism* and then helped me turn a fledgling manuscript into a book that I sincerely hope will make a difference to the world. Joan Ganz Cooney, the co-founder of Sesame Workshop, offered good advice and encouragement. So did Dr. Steven Schroeder, the former President & CEO of the Robert Wood Johnson Foundation and now a distinguished professor of health and health care at the University of California San Francisco.

My business associate, Don Greene (formerly President of the Coca-Cola Foundation) provided ongoing direction. Just as helpful were my long-time friends Paul Ostergard (President and CEO of Junior Achievement International), Robert Beggan (President and CEO of United Way International), Dr. Sheldon Rovin (Wharton School faculty member and co-author of *Redesigning Society)*, and Dr. Reed Whittle (international management consultant). Family friends including Walter Covell kept me on track with helpful comments about both content and style.

Many corporate executives associated with the Contributions Academy (the principal management education resource for corporate contributions and community relations professionals in the U.S. and abroad) have been extraordinary in their willingness to share their thoughts and suggestions about *How Women Can Beat Terrorism*. David Nasby, vice president of the General Mills Foundation, opened a number of important doors – as did Eileen Walter, manager of community relations and contributions at Rockwell Automation. Karen Davis, the director of the Hasbro Charitable Trust, introduced me to her chairman, Alan Hassenfeld, who is a remarkable man committed to helping women in many parts of the world. Ronnie Gunnerson, senior vice president for corporate affairs at Turner Broadcasting, presented me with numerous useful suggestions – as did a long list of others including Gil Llanas, manager of philanthropic programs and operations for the Northwestern Mutual Foundation; Bess Stephens, a Hewlett-Packard vice president; and my friend, Ed Wallace, manager of community affairs at Sony Electronics.

At different Academy programs, several contributions managers agreed to take part in "focus groups" and were asked to challenge the content of *How Women Can Beat Terrorism*. Among those who provided help and direction: Cal Lockett, vice president for public affairs at Wellpoint; Tricia Lawrence Savane, grants manager for Credit Suisse First Boston; Brandi Robinson, executive director, philanthropy and community development for Novartis Pharmaceuticals; Alice Lull, manager of community relations, Ortho-McNeil Pharmaceuticals; Lori Quartermain, assistant administrator, Dana Corporation; Sarah Brelvi, community giving director, AT&T; Joan Cronin, formerly with the Hasbro Charitable Trust; and Judy Ann Christison, manager, community and contributions for Deere & Company. The Academy's program coordinator, Karen Hart, has devoted many long hours to this effort.

Others who have been important to this book include friends and former colleagues at the Johnson & Johnson Family of Companies – among them, Robert Wilson (vice chairman), Roger Fine (general counsel), Gary Gorran (executive director for administrative services), William Dearstyne (company group chairman – retired), and Conrad Person (director of international and product contributions).

Jonathan Gullery excelled in the design and formatting of this book. Michael Derr used a keen editorial eye to help shape its text.

Finally, I recruited both my sons to serve as a sounding board for parts of *How Women Can Beat Terrorism*. They convinced me that the recommendations in this book are equally as important to men as they are to women.

PROLOGUE

This book is about hope.

Keep this opening sentence close at hand as you read *How Women Can Beat Terrorism*. There will be moments when you will need it as a lifeline – to yank you out of what may seem to be an inescapable vortex that is pulling civilization in the wrong direction.

This is a book about how to deal with terrorism – not by ferreting out sleeper cells or by duct-taping your doors and windows; not by punishing al Qaeda or rogue regimes like the deposed dictatorship in Iraq; but rather by doing something about the *conditions* that too often foster and encourage terrorism.

Mostly, this book is about *women*.

It is about women in poor, underdeveloped regions of the world who, when given the latitude and resources, have proven that they can hose down the embers of discontent and hatred before they flame into a firestorm.

This book is also for and about women in the United States, Western Europe and other well-to-do, industrialized nations. Hope hinges on whether these women are willing to kick-start a process that can quite literally change the world.

How Women Can Beat Terrorism is a rallying cry to every adult female living in more-developed countries to do what has to be done to empower women in the poorest regions. If that happens, all of us – women, men, children – get handed an extraordinary two-pronged payoff:

- An improvement in the quality of life for billions of people whose lives are defined by poverty and hopelessness.

- And the establishment of a global climate where terrorism is less of a threat to developed nations than is the case today.

Liberate, Educate, Motivate, Celebrate, Elevate

In a nutshell, here is the main message running through this book: We need to *liberate, educate, motivate, celebrate* and *elevate* women in places where they are more often repressed than respected. They offer us our best chance of venting the buildup of socioeconomic pressure that is hazardous to all of us – and there are two reasons why:

First, women have an admirable track record when it comes to curtailing poverty and improving quality of life in those parts of the world where life is the hardest.

Second, women generally make better choices than men about when to have children – reproductive decisions that can ultimately determine the economic fate of families, communities and society as a whole.

These two facts, which have been around for a long time and are well substantiated, will not come as revelations to policy makers and others engaged in "nation building." Even so, for a lengthy list of political, religious and cultural reasons, women too frequently are denied the freedom or the resources to help their communities, families or themselves.

This needs to change.

Fast.

And the way to turn things around is for *women* in relatively affluent nations to start the ball rolling. They constitute such a huge, influential group of people that they have the potential to compel their respective governments to "think women" when making foreign-assistance decisions. If they are successful, they will shake up the "same old, same old" system of tossing currency and supplies at foreign governments and their representatives (usually men) who simply can't – or won't – deliver the goods the way women can.

Sure, there are places on earth where men have done and continue to do a good job in wringing out extraordinary humanitarian benefits from small amounts of foreign assistance. But in many countries and regions, men have faltered. In these locations, there are isolated cases where women have become instrumental in leveraging foreign aid in a way that has improved the basic living conditions of their families and communities. While few and far between, these success stories offer an important ray of hope.

One would think countries that dole out foreign assistance would look for a maximum return on their investments by making sure such aid ended up: (a) at the grass-roots level, where it has the greatest chance of alleviating poverty; and (b) in the hands of women, who are far more likely to use the money to enhance quality of life. Unfortunately, this isn't what happens. Few developed nations direct any significant amount of foreign assistance to women-oriented grass-roots programs.

Those nations that spend a portion of their budgets on foreign aid need to turn their funding spigots in a different direction. Of course, getting that to happen is easier said than done. Unless women in these more economically advanced countries push hard to change the way foreign aid decisions are made, the status quo will probably prevail. Why will it take women rather than men to get the job done? *Because no one can better understand or appreciate the unmet potential of a woman than another woman.* Yes, some men are equally tuned in to how women can be more helpful in resolving problems that serve to encourage terrorism and other kinds of conflicts. However, not enough men choose to wave that flag. Consequently, it is left mainly to women to put the world on a new heading.

The Big Three

How Women Can Beat Terrorism contends that there are three significant "core" problems that can help incubate terrorism or can turn half the world into a cheering section for terrorists: (1) poverty, (2) hopelessness and (3) population growth in population-stressed parts of the world. Given the bloodshed and turmoil in the Middle East as well as other global conflicts and tensions, it may seem a little late to be worrying about the "Big Three." This book comes to a different conclusion. It argues that if we *don't* do something about the "Big Three," then we are destined to confront their unpleasant, expensive effects, including more-frequent and more-lethal terrorist attacks backed by armies of terrorist sympathizers.

It costs a lot to pay for homeland security, missile-defense systems and the search for weapons of mass destruction. While these attempts to keep us safe may offer partial protection, they can't give total security. Certainly, those of us in the United States and other developed countries should do what we can to make ourselves less vulnerable. However, our defense portfolio needs to include another strategy. By using foreign aid more effectively than we have in the past, it can become a kind of pre-emptive weapon – one that can ward off trouble by doing something now about the miserable state of human affairs in half the world.

The "Big Three" problems are the starting point for *How Women Can Beat Terrorism*. The book opens with this unnerving speculation: If we don't enlist women to help attack the conditions that foster terrorism, here is what is likely to happen between now and 2030:

- As many as *100 million* people may die worldwide as a result of terrorism and other mankind-induced conflicts.

- Death and destruction will not be confined to the lesser-developed countries of the world. Highly developed nations will bear their "fair share" of the carnage. In the U.S., for example, that could mean *4 million* or more people will lose their lives.

Sound improbable? The statistics are based on extrapolations and projections from credible sources. Even more disconcerting – it may not take 30 years to reach those numbers.

Rocky Road Ahead

Before reading Part I of this book, remember that there is a caveat to much of the depressing information you are about encounter: *The future is not carved in stone.* We have the capacity to chart a different course. The world is filled with underutilized resources called *women* who could steer us into waters that are far less turbulent.

Part I tells us something we already know. Mankind has managed to create a hazardous world, one that is far more dangerous than many might assume. Aside from what's going on in headline-making countries such as Iraq, North Korea and Iran, lethal technologies are increasingly accessible to many other poor regions of the globe. "Dirty" bombs,[1] sarin or VX nerve gas, anthrax, smallpox, tularemia and dozens of other deadly agents or devices are, in many areas, available for the asking.

Part I warns of impending events that could dwarf horrifying acts of destruction that have occurred in recent history. During the next 30 years, some of us may witness catastrophes worse than what America experienced on September 11, 2001— or even worse than the single most destructive day in history (Aug. 6, 1945), when the B-29 *Enola Gay* dropped a nuclear explosive that took the lives of 140,000 residents of Hiroshima, Japan.[2]

How Women Can Beat Terrorism reminds us that while wide-scale war will always be a concern, it will be the "small" actions (mostly defined as terrorist attacks) that are more likely to inflict the most serious wounds in the days and years ahead. Even though the number of worldwide terrorist attacks has not risen sharply,[3] it isn't the frequency of these acts that is so worrisome. As the Center for National Security Studies predicted long before the collapse of the Twin Towers: "The lethality of [terrorism] incidents has been increasing."[4] That *"lethality"* trend is – for sure – going to continue. Regrettably, the prospect of biological, chemical and nuclear devastation has leap-frogged the realm of science fiction and is now very much a part of the 21st century.

As if it isn't enough that the U.S. and other developed countries have to worry about mass destruction being imported in shipping containers and suitcases from abroad, Part I also reminds us that a danger also lurks inside national borders. In the United States, for example, there are native sons (and daughters) who could easily be provoked to act if provided with the right materials:

> Domestic extremist groups appear to have just as much, if not more, interest in unconventional weapons as their Middle Eastern counterparts. In the mid-1980s, a Christian survivalist group known as The Covenant, the Sword and the Arm of the Lord hatched a plan to carry out a mass-casualty attack on major American cities by poisoning water supplies with potassium cyanide. In the early 1990s, members of an anti-government militia group, the Minnesota Patriots Council, acquired the deadly toxin ricin.[5]

The opening salvo of *How Women Can Beat Terrorism* paints a picture that is anything but pretty. However, it is reassuring to know that if we are smart enough to access the untapped capabilities of women in many parts of the world, there is still time to add brighter colors to the canvas. But before reaching for our palette, let's make sure we have a firm understanding of the three most critical elements that need to be fixed: poverty (Part II), hopelessness (Part III) and population growth (Part IV).

Poverty and Hopelessness

Most of us would probably define poverty as a term that describes how much one *owns* (or, alternatively, how much one *doesn't* own). Part II contends that ownership has a close relative: control. What you *control* or *could* control also comes into play when judging just how well off or disadvantaged you happen to be.

Abraham Maslow's famous hierarchy of needs (eating and drinking; safety and security; belongingness and love; esteem) provides us with an insight into human behavior.[6] Part II presents a different kind of hierarchy based largely on ownership and control, which are described as the rebar of any human social system. Having little or no ownership and little or no control equates to genuine poverty. And even worse than being truly poor is having no realistic *hope* of improving one's ownership or control.

Part III shows what happens when ownership and control get squashed and hopelessness takes over. This is the social condition that makes a fanatic drool. After all, no one is more open to being persuaded to do or support something extreme than someone who has nothing to lose.

Think about this:

Right now, more than half the people on earth live in developing nations where economic and social gaps are so wide that they give rise to frustration, desperation and feelings of vengeance among those on the bottom of the pile.[7] Remarkably, in spite of hardships and difficult living conditions, the vast majority of people in these locations pose no serious threat to the more-developed world. However, things are likely to change.

How Women Can Beat Terrorism looks long and hard at a socioeconomic gap that has become canyon-like in size. Without a doubt, the gap is in and of itself a potentially fatal sinkhole for much of humanity. However, as Part III notes, it's what people now *know* about the gap that makes the problem even more serious. Thanks to far-reaching *information technology,* poor people are now getting the message about just how unbalanced living circumstances are. This awareness about who has or doesn't have *control,* and about who *owns* or doesn't *own* goods, services or intellectual property, can sometimes lead to ugly, hostile resentment.

Population Growth

Part IV puts a finger on the link between hopelessness and population growth in certain regions of the world – and by doing so, moves this book into touchy territory. Whenever the term *population* becomes a topic of conversation, it usually triggers a spectrum of reactions. The three most common points of view, and their supporting arguments, are:

1. *Don't worry, be happy.* Because worldwide reproduction rates are slowing down, "overpopulation" is no longer a big deal. In fact, according to some forecasters, the number of births will equal the number of deaths at or before the middle of this century. In other words, the world's population will be in perfect balance at around 7.9 billion people.[8] What's more, even though our population will continue to grow between now and 2050, we have the resources and wherewithal to handle the hundreds of millions of people who are yet to make their appearance. So any talk one hears about how humans are reproducing themselves into oblivion should be disregarded.

2. *The sky is definitely falling.* In spite of a gradually reduced reproduction rate, there are 210,000 more births than deaths in the world every day. And the world's projected population of 7.9 billion that is occasionally bandied about, well, that's the *low end* estimate of the total population by 2050. The *high-end* prediction is 10.9 billion.[9] The planet simply cannot withstand this additional influx of people. The earth is already feeling the effects of too many humans – *and terrorism is one of those effects.*

3. *We're not breeding fast enough.* It's not population growth that's the problem, stupid, it's *under-reproduction.* There are 20 or so countries where women are simply not producing enough babies to replace their respective national populations.[10] Big problems stem from this fertility falloff. As one United Nations ambassador warned, fertility reduction could spell misfortune for many societies.[11] A serious drop in reproduction rates can destabilize a country, open the doors to a huge incursion of immigrants and erode the cultural underpinnings of a society. We need *more* births, not fewer.

After reading Part IV of *How Women Can Beat Terrorism*, you will understand why *consensus* is not in the vocabulary of those who hold differing opinions about population. Each would give you different responses to such nagging questions as:

Are people really reproducing at a rate that is genuinely dangerous to the environment? Is environmental degradation one of the causes of terrorism?

Is the population-growth scare just overblown nonsense being peddled by a bunch of paranoid eco-nuts?

Are we committing economic suicide if we allow population growth to slow down?

These questions lead to speculation – and what is terrifying about speculation is that your guess about what's going to happen tomorrow is as good as anyone else's. You may come to the conclusion that the world can easily tolerate another two billion to five billion people and that such a population load has no significant bearing on terrorism. That contention is as valid as another point of view that says we're one step (or baby) away from catastrophe. Only time will tell who is right. Hence, *all* of the theories about population growth deserve some thought and attention. One of them is going to be correct.

That's the problem with guesswork. Conjecture can make you a hero or a goat. The crowd who backed the world-is-flat theory went from smart to dumb in a hurry. The astronomers who were absolutely certain that the sun traveled around the Earth lost any chance of getting into the science hall of fame. Paul Ehrlich, who in 1968 wrote *The Population Bomb*, collected a lot of royalty checks from his bestselling book, but he also ended up with an ample amount of egg on his face.[12]

Ehrlich, who became a fixture on NBC's *Tonight Show* during the 1970s, predicted that by 1985 all kinds of bad things were going to happen: world famine, a falloff in life expectancy, even a transition of America's Midwest into a desert. Here's an excerpt from his book that illustrates the tone of his message:

> "A minimum of 10 million people, most of them children, will starve to death during each year of the 1970s. But this is a mere handful compared to the numbers that will be starving before the end of the century..."[13]

The population "bomb" never exploded quite the way Ehrlich predicted. A couple of million people (a lot of them kids) did die as a result of famine-related causes during the past two or three decades. However, Ehrlich's 10 million-starvations-a-year forecast was not even close. *The Population Bomb* was a publishing success, but many of its predictions were duds. The skeptics who love to put down the overpopulation mavens cackle that there are a lot of Ehrlichs out there who are nothing more than scare-mongering Chicken Littles.

The usual "we're overpopulating the planet" beef goes something like this: Mankind is in jeopardy because we are running out of – or completely befouling – our life-supporting resources. *How Women Can Beat Terrorism* argues that population growth is much more dangerous for another reason: *If we continue to jam more people into already overloaded parts of the world, we up the odds that we will kill a lot of our own long before we have a chance to completely ruin our land, water and air.*

We know that women tend to make better choices about reproduction – the number of children they produce, the spacing between children, and so forth. *Educating* women about what size family makes the most sense, and then *liberating* and *motivating* women to limit reproduction, is high on the list of "things to do" over the next three decades.

Three Forces

Part V examines three forces that weigh heavily on poverty, hopelessness and population growth in population-stressed areas of the world. These forces are:

- Definitions of death – as influenced by religion.

- Organizations.

- Technology.

Our beliefs about what happens after we die have a remarkable impact on decisions we make while we're alive. Those beliefs divide us into an incredible number of denominations, orders, cults and cells. Depending on our *definition of death,* our beliefs can sometime help soften the sting of poverty and hopelessness (for example, suffer in life and get rewarded in heaven). Just as easily, however, our beliefs can incite us to do damage in the name of something we can't comprehend.

People who are like-minded about what happens after death are generally ripe for being *organized.* Religious institutions are classic examples of how powerful and influential organizations can be. There are, of course, many other kinds of groups that chisel and shape society. Clubs, teams, corporations, unions, political parties, armies – mankind loves to be organized. The massing of humans can be a platform for great achievement or – as Part V acknowledges – can be a catalyst for disaster.

How Women Can Beat Terrorism devotes many pages to the third force, *technology*. And for good reason. Like fire, technology can give us immeasurable comfort, but it also can turn us into a pile of cinders. Technology provides us with creature comforts that were inconceivable a couple of generations ago, but it also threatens to wipe out every last man, woman and child on earth.

Technology has the capacity to help close the societal and economic cracks that exist throughout the world. However, because some people reap the benefits of technology and others don't, it can also be a divisive force that turns those cracks into crevices. Take the technology used to purify water, for instance. Those of us living in industrialized nations have the assurance, thanks to technology, that we can get a contaminant-free drink of water any time. But the U.N. says that 1.1 billion people reside in less-developed locations with no access to safe drinking water and no technology that can be easily called upon to correct the problem.[14]   One way of looking at those 1.1 billion people is to see them as only 17 percent of the globe's population. A much higher percentage of the world was in dire need of clean water only a few decades ago. As far as this example is concerned, then, technology has been a tremendous asset. Maybe so. But try telling that to the 1.1 billion people who still have to worry each time they go to the well.

Part V also takes a hard look at technologies that have given mankind an ever-expanding menu of deadly tools. The list of lethal technologies is getting longer, and the ability to acquire or make munitions, biological agents or poison gasses is getting easier, thanks to information technology (particularly the Internet). Individuals and small cells of people are becoming technologically empowered. And there, as Hamlet once said, is the rub.[15]

Nations such as North Korea, Syria and other rogue countries[16] may indeed pose a threat to the "civilized" world. Today, however, nation states are not the only players on the mass-destruction playing field. Now, individuals (remember the Unabomber?) and not-so-large groups, including Al-Fatah, the Japanese Red Army, the Basque Fatherland & Liberty and more than 100 other terrorist cells,[17] pose a serious threat to larger and larger populations of people. While those of us who watched the 1972 Olympics in Munich were stunned by the terrorist attack that ended the lives of several Israelis, that incident paled in comparison with the 1995 Oklahoma City bombing – and *that* incident paled in comparison with the September 11, 2001, tragedy.

Inch by inch, technology is taking us down a treacherous road.

Definitions of death, organizations and technology – three formidable forces that have a huge bearing on three daunting problems: poverty, hopelessness and population growth in certain parts of the world.

Negative Envy

The combination of these problems and forces can produce a disquieting offspring called *negative envy*. As laid out in Part VI, negative envy is a feeling imbedded in too many people around the world, a feeling that is often behind acts of violence directed at the developed world.

Unlike "jealousy" which is more a yearning to own or control something that someone else has, "negative envy" is all about taking away or destroying what others have. It is the old thinking of "if I can't have it (because I don't have the resources to buy it or because my religious leaders tell me I am not allowed to partake of it), then I'll make sure you can't have it, either."

Negative envy is all too evident in the way humans interact with one another. All of us have seen it at work among a group of children. All of us have, regrettably, seen what it can do in a child-custody dispute gone wrong. When it creeps into world affairs, the harm that negative envy can do when coupled with lethal technology is nearly beyond comprehension.

Part VI makes a case for lessening negative envy by giving half the world the *hope* that *ownership* and *control* are not impossible dreams, that quality of life for the planet's most deprived can actually be improved. To make that happen, it means fighting poverty. And that brings us full circle to those who have the best chance of eliminating poverty: *women.*

It all comes back to women.

Does Poverty Cause Terrorism?

This book calls on women to become chief combatants against poverty – an undertaking that will ultimately erode terrorism's underpinnings. But is it logical to assume that if global poverty is beaten back, the world will be less threatened by terrorism?

There are contrary lines of thought about whether poverty has any significant bearing on terrorism. We know that at least some terrorists are more affluent and better educated than average citizens in their home countries.[18] Osama bin Laden, the multimillionaire poster boy for terrorism, is a case in point.

On the other hand, most world leaders, ranging from the president of the World Bank to the secretary general of the United Nations and even the president of the United States, contend that poverty has at least *some* bearing on terrorism. U.N. chief Kofi Annan says poverty is a "root cause" of terrorism.[19] World Bank head James Wolfensohn observes that terrorism is just symptomatic of a much more insidious disease: "The disease is the discontent seething in Islam and, more generally, in the world of the poor."[20]

How Women Can Beat Terrorism ends up accepting both lines of reasoning much the way George W. Bush did when he said that terrorist organizations are "hateful groups that exploit poverty and despair."[21] Terrorists themselves may not be poor, but often point to the downtrodden as one of the raison d'êtres for their actions. The complaints that al Qaeda had about the Jewish control of Jerusalem and Americans standing on Saudi Arabian soil got a lot of publicity, but another one of its big grievances was the poverty and suffering in Iraq largely attributed to U.N. economic sanctions.

Few terrorists seem to be modern-day Robin Hoods who are mainly out to make the world better for the poor. They tend to use poverty as a cover to advance a different agenda – one that is frequently based on religious fanaticism. Still, certain terrorist groups get big approval ratings from poor people around the world. How do you spell terrorist in many underdeveloped nations? "Hero."

In the eyes of the poor – perhaps as many as *three billion* poor people – a terrorist is David going up against a well-fed, overindulged Goliath. As difficult as it may be to accept, high-profile terrorists that take on the U.S. and other Western countries may have the biggest fan club on earth. It is a fan club that, at the very least, will give moral support and safe harbor to those who have the moxie to take a swing at the big guys.

Poverty may not *cause* terrorism (although some will argue that it does), but poverty is frequently used to legitimize terrorism. In return, terrorists give poor people something they usually don't get: serious attention. Look what happened after September 11, when many world leaders began talking about world poverty as something other than an afterthought.

Poverty and terrorism *are* linked. Start closing the global economic "wealth gap" and the fan club shrinks. Terrorists find fewer safe havens. Terrorism loses favor as poor people see it as an impediment to their own ability to own and control.

Terrorism in some form or another has always been with us. And it won't go away in the 21st century. The goal has to be to minimize terrorist incidents. By lessening worldwide poverty, we move a lot closer to that objective. All well and good, but with half the world just about running on empty, is it realistic to think that anything truly consequential can be done to put a serious dent in global poverty?

Part VII tells us that there is.

Women on the Front Line

We can take full advantage of the proven ability of women who live in hard-pressed countries to improve the quality of life for themselves, their families and their communities. How? By doing two things:

First, use foreign aid to offer incentives to grass-roots, women-focused initiatives.

Pouring foreign aid into a central government's coffers is a time-honored method of trying to bring about economic reform in a poor country. In too many cases, the approach doesn't work. Bureaucracy and corruption are often clots in the funding artery that keep foreign aid from getting to where it will do the most good.

Government and nongovernment-organization (NGO) assistance that avoids this top-down filtration process and manages to find its way to effective grass-roots projects and programs has a much greater chance of scoring high marks in the battle against poverty. And when that assistance is aimed at educating and motivating women, the odds are even greater that good things are going to happen.

The objective, Part VII says, is not to get women to work more. In many developing countries, in fact, women are already the heavy machinery in the work force. In Asia, women work an average of 13 hours more each week than men.[22] Worldwide, women make up more than half of the agricultural work force.[23] Much of the work that women do is labor intensive (for example, in Southeast Asia, women are responsible for 90 percent of rice cultivation).[24] Thus, the problem isn't getting women *into* the work force. The challenge is to educate and motivate women so that the work they perform yields more positive benefits for their families, their communities and themselves.

Second, work to drastically reduce birthrates in poverty-stricken locations.

Mull over this projection: *Some 96 percent of the world's population increase will take place in the developing regions of Africa, Asia and Latin America.* The worldwide census is going to climb from 6.2 billion in 2003 to somewhere between 7.9 billion and 10.9 billion in 2050 (see Chart 1). *Billions* of new lives will be jammed into countries that already are being crushed by poverty. Unless we can stem reproduction rates where they are the most harmful, it will be extremely difficult to significantly improve living standards in the most impoverished parts of the globe.

Chart 1

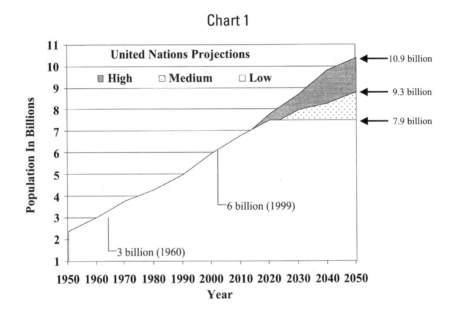

World Population Growth, Actual and Projected, 1950-2050
Source: United Nations Population Fund, 2001

The key to curtailing the population surge in these hard-pressed countries gets back, once again, to *women*. We know that in places where women are oppressed, birthrates stay high. Where women have the latitude to make more of their own decisions, birthrates go down.[25] We know that in male-dominated societies, family planning is shunned or discouraged.[26] We know that when women have enough control of their lives so as not to fear reprisals, their child-bearing decisions are often different from those in patriarchal societies. Some population experts state that if women had their way in the world, *the global population growth would be 20 percent lower than it is today.*[27]

Of course, we also know something else. Any attempt to influence another country's stand on reproduction can prove to be a messy business. Culture, religion and even politics can be immense barriers. Nevertheless, this is a job that needs doing and needs doing *now.*

It Starts With Women in the United States, Europe and Other Developed Nations

With few exceptions, getting enough foreign aid aimed at the right programs and projects in developing nations just isn't happening. And the situation isn't going to change unless decision makers in the U.S., Europe and other developed countries shift gears.

If we stay on the same road we're traveling now, *How Women Can Beat Terrorism* predicts the current approach to foreign assistance will have little positive effect on poverty, hopelessness or population growth in developing countries. As lethal technology becomes more accessible to these regions, all of the ingredients are in place for a violent concoction that could claim the lives of 100 million people between now and 2030.

The world is at a crossroads. We can follow the avenue we're on now and continue racking up 27 major armed and increasingly deadly conflicts per year,[28] along with a slew of lesser bloodletting clashes politely called "other violent crises" which often involve religious, political or social factions.[29] Or we could put ourselves on a new track. We could use foreign aid to wage a *real* war on poverty and hopelessness in areas where that war desperately needs fighting. We could liberate, educate, motivate, celebrate and elevate women in a way that will make them front-line soldiers in carrying out such a war. If we head in this new direction, the future will look brighter.

Moving us to the road less traveled will require more than a nudge. It requires pressure – a lot of it. Part VII's "The Solution" calls on women's organizations and women-oriented media to urge female constituents and audiences in highly industrialized nations to put all candidates for national office to a test. Under the plan, each and every incumbent or aspirant looking to sit at the table where national policy decisions are made would be pushed hard to give clear, unequivocal answers to these questions:

- Will you support allocating at least 0.7 percent of your country's annual budget for helping developing countries combat poverty at the grass-roots level? (0.7 percent is the minimum agreed-upon level of foreign assistance targeted by the Organization of Economic Cooperation and Development, and many developed countries, including the U.S., fall well short of that percentage.)

- Do you agree that such grass-roots programs should be aimed at helping women wherever it is practical and possible?

- Will you assign the highest possible priority to curbing reproduction rates in those parts of the world already under stress because of population growth?

- Will you support signing the Convention for the Elimination of All Forums of Discrimination Against Women (CEDAW)? (Note: Although 169 countries have backed this convention since it was adopted by the United Nations in 1979, the United States and a handful of other nations have refused to sign the convention.)

Current and prospective public policy makers who answer "yes" to these questions are the people we desperately need in government today – representatives who have the will and the smarts to grasp the concept that strategically placed foreign aid is as much a health-insurance policy for the more-developed world as it is a way to counter poverty in the underdeveloped world.

How do we find out if present and future government leaders are "pro women" when it comes to making foreign-assistance policy decisions? How do we get them to give straightforward answers to our four questions?

Part VII gives us the answer: By applying a *lot* of pressure.

No group of people is better positioned to exert that kind of pressure than women living and voting in the U.S., Europe and other developed nations. They represent a formidable power block that can get the attention of any government office holder or candidate. No one can empathize more with a woman who is virtually imprisoned by repressive cultures or governments than another woman. No one can make a more compelling case for *liberating* women in places where their influence is badly needed than other women.

How Women Can Beat Terrorism is, more than anything else, a call for action issued to women throughout the industrialized world. It is a plea for women in wealthy countries to demand that their governments revamp the way rich countries deal with poor countries; to implore that all of us deal differently with women in places where their subjugation is a risk to the entire planet.

PART I

THE PROBLEM

CHAPTER 1

WHERE WE'RE HEADING

I believe that man will not merely endure: He will prevail.
He is immortal, not because he ... has an inexhaustible
voice, but because he has a soul, a spirit capable of compas-
sion and sacrifice and endurance.[1]

The usually taciturn William Faulkner delivered these words as part of his 1950 Nobel Prize acceptance speech in response to charges that his literary work was overly pessimistic. Taking a lesson from Faulkner, Part I of this book begins with these few words offered as a counterbalance to a great deal of bad news packed into the next three chapters: whether because, as Faulkner contends, each person has a soul, or whether humans simply possess extraordinary staying power – Homo sapiens are unlikely to disappear from the face of the earth. And *women* in particular will play a large role in the survival of mankind because they have an incredible potential to resolve some of the nastiest problems the world is facing.

Of course, depending on how we elect to deal with terrorism and conflict, survival could prove to be a most unpleasant exercise. There is a better than even chance that over the next two or three decades, Faulkner's contention that mankind has a hefty supply of compassion will be sorely tested. As *How Women Can Beat Terrorism* will point out, there are ways for us to avoid at least some of this imminent pain. The question looms: Will we be wise enough to choose a path that bypasses some of this turbulence?

Rich rewards await mankind if we can circumvent major global upheavals over the next 30 years. There will be a gene-based medicine for virtually every disease, augurs one biochemist.[2] Nature will continue to astound us with mind-boggling performances – for example, a spectacular total solar eclipse will roll over Africa and Australia late in 2030.[3] In 30 years, "cancer will get absolutely whipped," insists a biotech executive.[4] And if a scenario based on a Japanese Rocket

Society report proves accurate, space tourism will become a $100 billion-a-year enterprise with millions of jobs connected to the industry.[5]

However, 2030, and the decades leading up to that date, will hardly be trouble free. The U.S. Geological Survey says the San Francisco Bay Area will be hit by an earthquake with at least a 6.7 magnitude by 2030.[6] The U.S. Social Security Trust will go belly up if changes are not made between now and 2030.[7] Standards of living will start to plummet within the next 30 years unless humans stop depleting the earth's natural resources, says the World Wildlife Fund.[8]

All of these developments, though, are likely to pale by comparison to other events poised to ambush us during the same time period.

A few years ago, *Atlantic Monthly* correspondent Robert Kaplan wrote a compelling article called "The Coming Anarchy."[9] That essay quoted foreign-policy and military experts who foresaw the advent of fuzzy centers of power that have the ability to penetrate nearly any country with idealistically greased tentacles. These same experts predicted that nebulous clumps of people bound together by common beliefs or religious convictions would become more dangerous to the world than full-scale wars between or among nations.

Kaplan's article also warned that "environmental scarcity will inflame existing hatreds and affect power relationships." His comment is a reminder that *scarcity* and *shortage* are not necessarily one and the same. Scarcity can mean natural resources and goods exist in one place, but are not accessible to people living in another location. However, if such resources and goods are out there and are being denied to some people because of distribution issues, politics or sheer selfishness, then the stage is set for trouble.

Apply Kaplan's theory to a population-pressured country or region of the world and the prospects of what could happen over the next three decades become a major concern. China is a good example. By 2030, that nation's population will reach 1.6 billion, with 44 percent of its citizens living north of the Yangtze River Valley.[10] The problem: Only 14 percent of the country's water resources service this huge area. This will lead to a "serious water crisis" by 2030, according to the Chinese Ministry of Water Resources.[11] The struggle to find water for hundreds of millions of people may prove to be one of China's biggest headaches in the years ahead. The country recently announced plans to spend billions for a massive engineering project that will move some water to where it is (and will be) desperately needed – a project akin to rerouting the water in the Mississippi River to the East Coast of the U.S.[12] However, that long and expensive project may solve only part of the problem. The country may also be forced to look beyond its borders and take whatever steps are necessary to keep a large percentage of its population from dehydrating.

Human population growth and an uneven distribution of the earth's resources are creating conditions where perilous actions are more and more possible. Drop another evolving factor into the stew pot and the future looks even bleaker. It seems that information technology is seeding the storm clouds by making lethal technology ever more accessible and usable. At least that's what Bill Joy, the chief scientist for Sun Microsystems and former co-chair of the Presidential Information Technology Advisory Committee, thinks. He says that computing will get cheaper and more powerful so that "by 2030, we should have inexpensive personal computers that are about a million times as powerful as they are today."[13] This mind-boggling forecast along with predictions about other technological advances brings Joy to this gut-churning conclusion:

> *I don't think it is an exaggeration to say that we're on the course to the perfection of extreme evil, basically allowing evil to spread well beyond that which the weapons of mass destruction bequeath to the nation-states.*[14]

Those incredible tools of knowledge and convenience that are sitting on our laps or nestled in our palms have nearly incalculable destructive power. That's disquieting news for two reasons. First, it gives even small *organizations* (such as terrorist cells) a networking capacity that greatly increases their chances of creating havoc. Second, it opens the door even wider for disgruntled loners to do major damage. Joy speculates that if just 1 percent of society has a delusional disorder, we need to ask ourselves: "Are we going to give the people in our society who are clearly crazy – and we can't deny that they're out there – illimitable power?"[15]

If Joy's forbidding prophecy isn't worrisome enough, consider what else will be going on between now and 2030. Although alternative energy sources will be scouted out and developed, there still will be a growing dependency on nuclear power in many parts of the world over the next three decades. Russia, for instance, will rely on nuclear energy for a third of its power needs by 2030.[16] Thirty-one more nuclear reactors that are now being built in different parts of the world will be up and running, and several others are likely to be constructed over the next two decades, bringing the number of nuclear-power plants in operation to more than 470.[17] Because there will be a vast increase in the amount of plutonium and enriched uranium produced for these plants, the risk of nuclear-material diversion and misuse (particularly in nations where security measures are far inferior to those in more-developed countries) grows greater and greater.

In the U.S. alone, the amount of nuclear waste scattered throughout the country is staggering. More than 40,000 tons are stored at facilities in 34 states, and the stuff is piling up at a rate of 2,000 tons a year. Granted, the U.S. has stringent standards in place to keep the waste secure. However, much of the radioactive material will be moved to a central storage area over the next several years.[18] There is nothing like the thought of used reactor-fuel rods being shipped from point A to point B to stir up concern.

While we look at and worry about countries such as North Korea that make no bones about producing, and possibly selling, materials needed to fabricate nuclear weapons, developments that rarely hit the radar screen could be more troublesome. In Russia, for example, there have been (according to the *Bulletin of Atomic Scientists*) "hundreds of attempted smuggling transactions involving radioactive materials" since 1991.[19] If there is a bright side to that revelation, it is the Russian disclosure that "only" 18 smuggling operations that were broken up involved the theft of weapons-grade uranium or plutonium.[20] How many other nuclear smuggling activities are going on undetected throughout the old Soviet commonwealth is anyone's guess.

With so much radioactive material in circulation or storage and with so much more that will be produced over the next several years, some is bound to end up in the wrong hands. It takes only a small amount of nuclear material combined with conventional explosives to produce a "dirty" bomb. And while most experts think radiological dispersion devices would be lethal to only a few people (but would do enough damage to create psychological chaos), others contend that a powerful, strategically placed dirty bomb could kill 2,000 people and leave thousands of others with radiation poisoning.[21]

Of much greater consequence would be the detonation of a box-size atomic bomb, which now, thanks to technology, seems quite feasible. Getting the bomb-grade fissile material needed to make one of these weapons is still a challenge, but far from impossible. Large enough quantities exist, and in places like North Korea or the remnants of the Soviet Union, the material appears to be obtainable if enough money is put on the table. Should one of these small atomic devices be detonated, a group called the Center for Defense Information figures that about 100,000 people would be killed outright and another 100,000 would die not long after from radiation and other problems linked to the explosion.[22] If that doesn't keep you awake at night, consider the simultaneous explosion of two, three or more of these weapons in densely populated urban areas.

Physicians for Social Responsibility (see more about this organization in Chapter 16) theorized what would happen if eight U.S. cities were "nuked" with missile-delivered 100-kiloton warheads.[23] According to the projection, the explosions would kill about 6.8 million Americans. The anti-missile defense system that the U.S. is developing may keep this kind of airborne threat to a minimum. And since stuffing such nuclear explosive power into suitcases isn't currently plausible, perhaps we shouldn't get the jitters over the prospect of such a devastating event actually occurring. However, over the next decade or two, mankind may chalk up another perilous achievement by finding ways to miniaturize these types of weapons so that they are more easily transportable.

So much for radioactive explosives. As the anthrax-laden letters of 2001 reminded us, there are other effective ways of killing and disabling. In spite of efforts to ban biological and chemical weapons, we are now face to face with a kind of terrorism that is nearly certain to leave an extraordinary mark on humankind over the next few years. We can get a hint of things to come by reflecting on what happened in 1995 when a religious sect called Aum Shinrikyo released sarin gas in a Tokyo subway station. "Only" 12 commuters died in the attack, but 5,000 were injured. It was later reported that the gas used in the attack was of poor quality and that the dispersion method was largely ineffective.[24] Had the sect been able to produce a more lethal gas and design an improved delivery system, the number of dead and injured would have skyrocketed.

Existing biological weapons are truly frightening, but other pathogens we might encounter are even more horrifying. When Matthew Meselson, a Harvard biologist, looks to the future, he sees the possibility of germs being designed not just to kill, but possibly to alter how we think, reproduce and develop. He wonders whether "designer pathogens" could be used as part of a Hitler-like initiative to enslave certain members of yet-to-be-born generations.[25] We could dismiss the idea as pure whimsy, but given technology's awesome velocity, the notion is far from fantasy. In fact, some experts predict that the explosion of knowledge about how to produce customized pathogens is so accessible that even modestly skilled scientists could shortly have the ability to turn out products capable of resisting antidotes and vaccines.[26]

The 21st century has introduced us to a world where "war" has been redefined. Conflict is not limited to a "theater of operations" or a battlefront. It is anywhere and everywhere. Defending one's homeland becomes exceedingly difficult, if not impossible, since no national border is completely impervious to the kinds of lethal technology that humanity has developed.

What do we do?

Option A: We could rely on the old "the best defense is a good offense" approach. Wiping out or crippling a known enemy's ability to harm may make sense in some cases, but that strategy runs into trouble when an enemy is elusive or when potential enemies are scattered in different locations. "Operation Iraqi Freedom," carried out by the U.S. and a few allies, was billed as a war waged to defend America and its "coalition of the willing." As we will eventually learn, what happened in Iraq was not a war. It was a battle that will likely prove to be a relatively small event in a much larger and possibly much deadlier conflict. Operation Iraqi Freedom may have squelched one country's ability to do harm to other nations, but it has done little to ensure the safety of America and other more-developed countries. In fact, the argument that Operation Iraqi Freedom was a kind of Boston Tea Party for billions around the world is not farfetched. The point is that trying to subdue every country perceived to be a threat just isn't workable in a world where there is a growing list of nations and transnational groups that have, or soon will have, weapons of mass destruction.

Option B: We could build the right kind of shield. Although a sophisticated missile-defense system, border patrols and an internal security program will discourage some acts of terrorism, no nation can live in a protective bubble that assures total safety. If those days ever existed, they are now history.

Option C: We could get a lot more serious about prevention. The next chapter points out that conditions are right in a *lot* of places for turning out a large crop of terrorists. The U.S., Western Europe and other developed nations can continue trying to swat at these antagonists as they swarm out of these breeding grounds – or those countries could work to change the conditions that encourage, protect and sometimes perpetuate terrorism.

If option C prevails and if prevention becomes the ultimate homeland defense for developed countries, then the primary defenders need to be *women*.

CHAPTER 2

FIVE-CLUSTER ANALYSIS

The awesome power of lethal technologies and the information channels that are pathways to those technologies do not give us much hope that we can get through the next three decades without running into at least a few serious problems. Even if women end up playing a larger role in heading off a firestorm, trouble spots still will exist. Pinpointing where those problems will occur and how deadly they are likely to be comes down to guesswork – and guessing is always a gamble. Still, *How Women Can Beat Terrorism* takes a chance with a few predictions based largely on what we know about (a) mankind's intrinsic characteristics, (b) the widening societal gaps that have cropped up in different parts of the world and (c) the powerful influence technology is having on our lives.

Chapter 2 breaks the world into five "clusters" and then forecasts what may happen to all or some of the countries included in each cluster. The main intent of this forecast is to outline a cluster-by-cluster "damage appraisal report" for the future.

Cluster 1: Least-Developed Nations

Sixty-two of the 63 countries designated as "low income" by the World Bank fall in this category (Yemen has been moved to Cluster 3 – the Middle East).[1] These are the poorest of the poor nations, where human suffering and desperation are as commonplace as high human reproduction rates.

This category includes hotspots that continue to make the news – Afghanistan, India, North Korea, Pakistan, Somalia and Zimbabwe, among others. Many of the nations are still wrestling with ways to blend historically incompatible tribal structures. Others are so poor that the line between life and death is paper thin.

In recent times, more blood has been spilled in this cluster than in any other. The death toll in places like Vietnam and Cambodia over the past few decades has been staggering. Poverty and violence have gone hand-in-hand in Bangladesh, Georgia, Haiti and Indonesia. However, no place has been so ravaged by human conflict than Cluster 1 countries located in Africa.

Chart 2A

Afghanistan	Guinea	Niger
Angola	Guinea-Bissau	Nigeria
Armenia	Haiti	Pakistan
Azerbaijan	India	Rwanda
Bangladesh	Indonesia	São Tomé and Príncipe
Benin	Kenya	Senegal
Bhutan	Korea, Democratic Republic of	Sierra Leone
Burkina Faso	Kyrgyz Republic	Solomon Islands
Burundi	Lao, People's Democratic Republic	Somalia
Cambodia	Lesotho	Sudan
Cameroon	Liberia	Tajikistan
Central African Republic	Madagascar	Tanzania
Chad	Malawi	Togo
Comoros	Mali	Turkmenistan
Congo	Mauritania	Uganda
Côte d'Ivoire	Moldova	Ukraine
Eritrea	Mongolia	Uzbekistan
Ethiopia	Mozambique	Vietnam
Gambia, The	Myanmar	Yemen, Republic of
Georgia	Nepal	Zambia
Ghana	Nicaragua	Zimbabwe

Countries by Income
Low Income
Source: The World Bank, World Development Indicators 2001

   In Sudan, a war that spanned two decades was responsible for the deaths of 2 million people. In 1999, 11 major conflicts occurred across Africa. Aside from the dead and wounded, battles have left the continent with more than 8 million refugees.[2]

   Whether in Africa or elsewhere, the nations in Cluster 1 are replete with people who are truly poor – defined in Part II as being void of ownership and control. Ample anecdotal evidence indicates that a lot of animosity is building in these poverty-stricken corners of the globe. Nowhere are the conditions better suited for confrontations of major proportions than in Cluster 1.

Aside from a couple of notable exceptions, we might be lulled into thinking that as bad as things can sometimes get in Cluster 1, at least most countries in this group don't have access to super-lethal technology. Granted, Pakistan and India (both are in this cluster) are well-known nuclear powers. However, their radioactive saber rattling is so much in the open that it attracts and gets international mediation. The world keeps a steady eye on these two adversaries, but it has a more difficult time figuring out what's really happening inside places like Libya. As will be pointed out later in this book, it would be naive to believe that many (perhaps even all) of these nations are going to be denied access to "weapons of mass destruction" by 2030.

Cluster 1 also has a high quotient of perceived hopelessness (see Part III). When that condition exists, the benefits of dying can outweigh the few advantages of existing in a constant state of deprivation or danger. And that, in turn, makes for a hazardous environment.

While there are countries inside Cluster 1 that could make life miserable for nations categorized in better-off clusters, it is the intra-cluster hostilities that could more easily spin out of control. Two African countries, Eritrea and Ethiopia, are good examples. Eritrea is about the size of Pennsylvania. Ethiopia is its much larger neighbor. To conclude that the two countries don't get along would be an understatement. Not only do they battle one another, but also their clashes are so ferocious that in just one three-day firefight, as many as 10,000 soldiers were killed.[3]

Both Eritrea and Ethiopia are extremely poor, but even so, they somehow manage to find money to buy weapons. When U.N. Secretary-General Kofi Annan recently talked about the problems and frustrations of peacekeeping initiatives in Africa, thoughts of Eritrea and Ethiopia had to be whirling through his mind:

> There are many places in Africa where governments
> persist in spending money on weapons they can ill
> afford for wars they should not fight; where conflicts
> are seen as business opportunities for arms merchants
> and rebel groups alike.[4]

Suppose either Eritrea or Ethiopia comes to the conclusion (much the way Iraq did during the Iraq-Iran war) that biological weapons, or BWs, could be a far more effective way of taking care of business than firing bullets or planting land mines. Suppose either country went shopping for "BWs." If push came to shove (particularly relevant if one country had its back against the wall), would those agents be used?

Best guess: yes.

Will at least one country inside this cluster of 62 nations be the site of a biological or nuclear incident between now and 2030?

Best guess: yes. Probably more than one, and probably on more than one occasion.

Chart 2B

Albania	Guyana	Peru
Algeria	Honduras	Philippines
Belarus	Iran, Islamic Republic of	Romania
Belize	Iraq	Russian Federation
Bolivia	Jamaica	Samoa
Bosnia and Herzegovina	Jordan	Sri Lanka
Bulgaria	Kazakhstan	St. Vincent and the Grenadines
Cape Verde	Kiribati	Suriname
China	Latvia	Swaziland
Columbia	Lithuania	Syrian Arab Republic
Costa Rica	Macedonia	Thailand
Cuba	Former Yugoslav Republic of	Tonga
Djibouti	Maldives	Tunisia
Dominican Republic	Mali	Turkey
Ecuador	Marshall Islands	Vanuatu
Egypt, Arab Republic of	Micronesia, Federated States	West Bank and Gaza
El Salvador	Morocco	Yugoslavia, Federal Republic
Equatorial Guinea	Namibia	(Serbia-Montenegro)
Fiji	Papua New Guinea	
Guatemala	Paraguay	

Countries by Income
Lower Middle Income

Source: The World Bank, World Development Indicators 2001

Cluster 2: Lower-Middle-Income and Upper-Middle-Income Nations

Ninety-six countries are categorized by the World Bank as lower-middle income or upper-middle income. Eleven of those nations have been moved to Cluster 3 (Middle East) for purposes of this analysis. That leaves 85 countries in Cluster 2, and they are a mixed bag. Although living conditions are substandard for many living in Cluster 2 countries, chances are that most people are better off than those in Cluster 1 countries. A majority of people in Cluster 2 have at least a wisp of optimism that things are going to get better. In other words,

Cluster 2 comes with a higher level of hope for its huge population. Even so, this does not mean countries in Cluster 2 are exempt from conflicts that may involve the use of weapons of mass destruction.

A few longstanding international disputes between Cluster 2 countries could erupt with such intensity as to bring into play either biological or nuclear weapons. However, strife *inside* some of these nations may be what triggers the use of highly lethal technologies. Here are just a few examples of the strife some countries face internally:

- Colombia – continued violent insurgencies by rebel forces, including the Revolutionary Armed Forces of Colombia (FARC) and the National Liberation Army (ELN).

- Egypt – anti-government and anti-foreigner violence by the Muslim Brotherhood.

- Guatemala – ongoing guerilla disturbances.

- Philippines – Muslim insurgency in parts of the nation.

- Turkey – continued struggle with the Kurdish-rebel separatist movement complicated by the dismantling of the Hussein regime in Iraq.

A number of countries in Cluster 2 have enormous societal gaps within their own boundaries. Although there may not be a widespread sense of absolute hopelessness in these nations, such immense economic and social breaches are mixing bowls for dissatisfaction. The problems that Mexico (another Cluster 2 country) has had in Chiapas is just one of many examples of internal national conflict that could be a hatchery for trouble down the road. These cells of discontent are catch basins for extremism that can lead to the use of lethal technology, including bioweapons and nuclear devices.

While the know-how to construct weapons of mass destruction may be scarce in Cluster 2, the materials to make such weapons are not. Fifteen nuclear-power reactors are in operation in Cluster 2 (only four countries in Cluster 1 have reactors in operation).[5] The reliance on nuclear-power generation in this cluster means there are large supplies of uranium, spent nuclear waste, and other radioactive materials that are potential sources for weapons development.

Chart 2C

American Samoa	Grenada	Panama
Antigua and Barbuda	Hungary	Poland
Argentina	Isle of Man	Puerto Rico
Bahrain	Korea, Republic of	Saudi Arabia
Barbados	Lebanon	Seychelles
Botswana	Libya	Slovak Republic
Brazil	Malaysia	South Africa
Chile	Malta	St. Kitts and Nevis
Croatia	Mauritius	St. Lucia
Czech Republic	Mayotte	Trinidad and Tobago
Dominica	Mexico	Uruguay
Estonia	Oman	Venezuela, Republica Bolivariana de
Gabon	Palau	

Countries by Income
Upper Middle Income
Source: The World Bank, World Development Indicators 2001

Other countries in Cluster 2 do not have nuclear-power plants but operate research reactors or conduct activities that use radioactive materials for medical and industrial purposes. A few nations – Chile and Colombia, for example – even received highly enriched uranium from the United States for research purposes.[6] It is conceivable that spent fuel from these activities could be used to produce crude, but still deadly, dirty bombs.

What about biological weapons in Cluster 2? The U.S. claims it has "broad and deep" evidence that Cuba (a Cluster 2 nation) is producing offensive biological weapons under the shield of its well-developed biomedical operations.[7] Because so many biological and chemical agents are relatively easy to produce, it would be foolish to think that no Cluster 2 countries are in the BW game.

Because the raw materials for making devices that can kill large numbers of people are so widespread and relatively accessible in Cluster 2, it is also probable that weapons of mass destruction have been, or will be, developed. As will be pointed out in the next few pages, some of these devices are bound to find their way to countries in other clusters. However, incidents will crop up inside Cluster 2 countries that will drive organizations (governments, insurgents, religious groups and so forth) to employ whatever lethal technology is at their disposal.

Will Cluster 2 be ground zero for one or more incidents that include a biological or nuclear weapon between now and 2030?

Best guess: yes. There are simply too many lethal resources too close at hand for this cluster to escape use of these weapons over the next three decades.

Cluster 3: Middle East

Perhaps the most dangerous trouble spot on earth is about to become a lot more dangerous.

The countries that make up the jigsaw puzzle called the Middle East (see Chart 2D) have extraordinary histories of conflict and violence. While Jewish-Arab issues may be at the heart of many Middle Eastern problems today, the region was beset by battles long before Theodore Herzl's publication of *The Jewish State* in 1896 – widely considered to be the launchpad for Zionism and the impetus for the establishment of a Jewish homeland in Palestine.[8] The notion of jihad is centuries old and has been a prime mover for many a bloodbath in this intersection of the world, where belief systems keep running into each other like bumper cars.

This proclivity to battle over religious or ethnic differences in the Middle East is not going to go away. In fact, the differences are going to become much more pronounced as the population continues to build rapidly in the predominantly Arab nations of the Middle East.

To some in the region, reproduction itself is a weapon. Palestine's Yasser Arafat once labeled Palestinian mothers as his "biological bomb."[9] That bomb is getting more powerful by the day – the birth rate in the Palestinian territories is 6.1 per 100 residents; by comparison, the birth rate in Israel is 2.6 per 100.[10] This incredible difference in reproduction rates is a major issue in Israel – a country about the size of New Jersey. Taking into account the West Bank and Gaza territories that Israel occupies, the nation's residents are being pulled apart by different definitions of death (a.k.a. religion), while at the same time being pushed together by a rapidly growing population. In just the West Bank and Gaza alone, the number of people jammed into these small areas will reach 9 million in 2030 – up from 3.1 million in 2000 – a threefold increase.[11] The population explosion will widen societal gaps that are already enormous. As the Conference Board looks ahead at the region, here is what it sees:

The demographic pressures on the labor force in this region will intensify. Not only does the Middle East have one of the fastest population growth rates in the world, but the overall population is very young. The under-14 population group accounts for almost 40 percent of the total population... Over the next 15 years, the region will add more than 60 million new workers to a labor force that is already substantially underemployed.[12]

Societal gaps can be found throughout the Middle East. Negative envy and hopelessness are cousins in too many pockets throughout the region. In those locations, people are prone to listen carefully to a message that says "sacrifice your unpleasant life on earth for the guarantee of great rewards that will be yours if you die right." This willingness to become a martyr has been – and continues to be – a driving force in the region. The Iran-Iraq war should have taught us just how powerful this concept is:

Imbued with the conviction that their deaths could bring honor and paradise to themselves, their families, and Muslims everywhere, thousands of Iranian men eagerly slaughtered themselves. Even among hard-core Sunni Muslims, who usually look askance at, if not detest, their Shiite brethren, the imagery of martyrdom and jihad that Iran's Ayatollah Ruhollah Khomeini unleashed became irresistibly magnetic.[13]

The Iran-Iraq war claimed an estimated 1 million lives. It took that many casualties, some experts contend, to burn out the spirit of martyrdom. The world looked on like the referee who lets two hockey players go at it in the center of the ice rink until the combatants get too exhausted to keep throwing punches. That "let 'em fight it out" strategy may be an acceptable way to settle a hockey dispute, but it could be a mistake in dealing with future slugfests between two or more countries. The reason: There is a good chance that the combatants will use nuclear or biological weapons – weapons that can be as dangerous to spectators as to those locked in battle.

Chart 2D

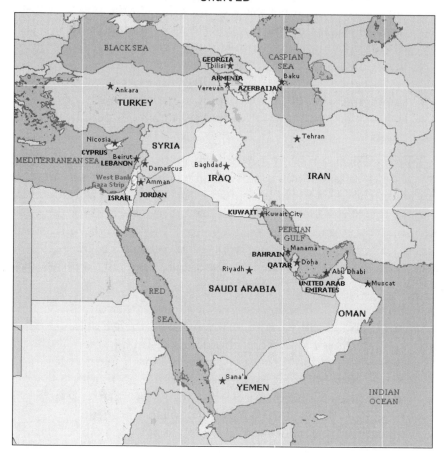

Map of the Middle East
Source: 1800-Countries.com

It is important to keep in mind that the Middle East is not short on weapons of mass destruction. A group called the Federation of American Scientists thinks Israel has enough plutonium to produce up to 200 nuclear bombs.[14] The Carnegie Endowment disagrees, speculating that the country has enough nuclear material for between 98 and 172 bombs.[15] Regardless of which estimate is right, Israel has a lot of firepower. Other Middle East countries that have resident nuclear scientists and engineers (Iran, for example) are not far away from developing their own nuclear arsenals – especially if fissile material can be obtained from foreign sources.[16] As for biological weapons, they may be stockpiled in any or all of the nations in Cluster 3.

For decades, the Middle East has been the flash point for the kind of trouble that could have worldwide implications. Given the advances made in weapon technology and the wider access to biological weapons, chemicals and nuclear devices, the prospects that any kind of uneasy peace will keep this region from unraveling are slim. Add to that the religiously inspired extremism that takes advantage of the overly wide societal gaps in the area, and the word "inevitable" creeps into any discussion about the eventual use of weapons of mass destruction.

Question: Will nuclear or biological weapons be used in the Middle East by the year 2030?

Answer: yes – long before that date.

Cluster 4: Higher-Income Nations – Except U.S.A.

Less than 20 percent of humanity lives in this cluster, and for them, life is comparatively good. As well it should be. People have sufficient control of their immediate environment, or at least think they do. People generally own more than they need. As one Oxford professor reminds us: "in the 1960s, the richest fifth of the world's population had a total income 30 times greater than the poorest fifth; in 1998, the ratio was 74:1."[17]

By comparison with the rest of the world, things are not only good in Cluster 4, but they're also getting better. By leaving the lesser-developed world in the dust, however, Cluster 4 creates some serious public-relations problems for itself. The same Oxford scholar says: "There can be little doubt that the lopsided nature of economic globalization – the fact that capital flows mainly within the developed world, that trade and migration are still restricted in many ways – is leading to unprecedented levels of inequality around the world."[18]

Chart 2E

Andorra	Germany	New Caledonia
Aruba	Greece	New Zealand
Australia	Greenland	Northern Mariana Islands
Austria	Guam	Norway
Bahamas, The	Hong Kong, China	Portugal
Belgium	Iceland	Qatar
Bermuda	Ireland	San Marino
Brunei	Israel	Singapore
Canada	Italy	Slovenia
Cayman Islands	Japan	Spain
Channel Islands	Kuwait	Sweden
Cyprus	Liechtenstein	Switzerland
Denmark	Luxembourg	United Arab Emirates
Faeroe Islands	Macao, China	United Kingdom
Finland	Monaco	United States
France	Netherlands	Virgin Islands (U.S.)
French Polynesia	Netherlands Antilles	

Countries by Income
High Income

Source: The World Bank, World Development Indicators 2001

Some individuals and groups living inside Cluster 4 countries have become so agitated by this inequality that they could become a threat to their own nations. Much more dangerous, though, are the nations and organizations in Clusters 1, 2 and 3 that perceive themselves to be the victims of this inequality. So, for Cluster 4, the greatest danger is from other clusters – from people filled with envy and resentment and from organizations that know how to capitalize on those deep feelings.

Will there be one or more nuclear or biological attacks in Cluster 4 by the time 2030 arrives? It is a virtual certainty.

Where will these attacks take place? Given the objectives of those who use weapons of mass destruction (to kill or disable as many people as possible using a single or small number of strikes), the most likely targets are locations where people are packed together: cities. Chart 2F lists the 15 largest metropolitan areas in both Clusters 4 and 5. Consider it a terrorist's menu.

Chart 2F

Metro Area	Population in Millions
Tokyo	34.9
New York	21.6
Osaka	18.0
Los Angeles	16.8
London	11.8
Paris	9.8
Chicago	9.4
Washington	7.8
San Francisco	7.2
Hong Kong	6.9
Philadelphia	6.3
Boston	5.9
Detroit	5.8
Dallas	5.5
Madrid	5.2

15 Largest Metro Regions in Zones 4 and 5
(Populations are for central city and neighboring communities)
Source: Th. Brinkhoff: The Principal Agglomerations of the World.
http://www.citypopulation.de/Country.html?E+World

September 11, 2001, gave us good insight into the tactical thinking of modern-day terrorists. Hit multiple sites concurrently. Pick out targets that have symbolic, governmental or economic importance. Get media coverage in order to create a shock wave of fear within a targeted location.

If a terrorist organization is out to cripple the global economy by creating a major disruption in the international marketplace, a nuclear or biological assault on Tokyo, London or Paris, along with two or three cities in the U.S., might be judged as the best way to reach that goal. Although such an undertaking would be ambitious and difficult to orchestrate, we live in a time when technology is making the difficult quite doable.

Cluster 5: United States

> We must move the battle to the enemy's grounds to
> burn the hands of those who ignite fire in our own
> countries... The only language understood by the West
> is maximum casualties.[19]

Egypt's Ayman al-Zawahri leads a small but ferocious Islamic terrorist group called the Qaeda-al Jihad. To him, the West's greatest
culprit is the United States. He makes no effort to hide his objective:
inflict as much damage as possible on America and its people. If "maximum (American) casualties" is Qaeda-al Jihad's principal mission,
and if the organization can get its hands on the right nuclear or biological tools to get the job done, isn't it logical to assume that the
group will use those weapons?

The U.S. has become the prime target for organizations that
have been carrying around a sack full of bitterness for a long time. With
a porous border and an inclination to beat back any heavy-handed
government imposition on individual rights, the U.S. is a great stomping ground for these unhappy organizations. What happened on
September 11 is far from the end of America's confrontation with
imported terrorism, and some of the incidents that lie ahead will
involve the use of nuclear or biological weapons.

Terrorists learned from the September 11 calamity. First, they discovered a "bounce back" quality among Americans that even sur-
prised those living in the U.S. The events that took place in New
York, Washington and Pennsylvania on Sept. 11 were certainly disruptive and caused much pain and suffering for thousands. However,
the terrorist acts hardly brought America to its knees. An argument
could be made that September 11 actually helped strengthen the
nation on many fronts.

The second lesson learned came about seemingly more as a matter of coincidence than planning. Not long after September 11, anthrax
showed up like a blood clot in one of the country's most important
circulation systems: the network of post offices. This "double
whammy" set off a nationwide ripple effect. Combining *two* potentially devastating threats (one by air and the other by envelope) created notable, although relatively short-lived, fear. It would be foolhardy
to think that those whose greatest aspiration is to scare a country into
paralysis did not take note of the fear. This all leads to an obvious conclusion:

America will most certainly experience chemical or biological attacks during the next 30 years. In addition, there is a high probability that the U.S. will also feel the sting of nuclear devices within its borders. Even with new safeguards, it is still relatively easy to smuggle nuclear materials into the U.S. An article in *Scientific American* made this observation about the illegal trafficking of radioactive substances into the U.S.:

> Police seize at the most 40 percent of the drugs coming into the U.S. and probably a smaller percentage of those entering Western Europe. The supply of nuclear materials is obviously much smaller, but law-enforcement agents are also less experienced at stopping shipments of uranium than they are in seizing marijuana or hashish. To believe that authorities are stopping more than 80 percent of the trade would be foolish.[20]

Stepped-up security measures introduced by the U.S. under its Homeland Security program may deter some nuclear smuggling operations. However, a few of the most dangerous isotopes (uranium 235 and plutonium 239, for example) are not easily detected by Geiger counters and other inspection devices. This suggests that if nuclear materials have not already made an illegal entry into the U.S., they are probably going to slip into the country within the next few years.

Whatever mass destruction tools will be used, the terrorist objective will be, of course, to evoke as much fear as possible. Still unknown is just how much resolve Americans actually have. Will Americans rebound from such attacks as they did after September 11? Or will radioactive contamination and the threat of new waves of bioterrorism fracture the economic, political and social systems that hold the U.S. together?

Within the next 30 years, we will know the answer.

CHAPTER 3

THE ROAD TO 2030

As depressing as the prospect may be, Chapter 2 brings us to this plausible conclusion: By 2030, nuclear and/or biological weapons will be employed in *every one of the five clusters*. Unfortunately, we have entered an age when the self-imposed constraints regarding the use of these weapons will be pushed aside in many parts of the world.

The use of nuclear or biological weapons in lesser-developed countries will prompt a fair amount of hand wringing and diplomatic jawboning on the part of the more-developed world but not much else. It is doubtful that more-developed nations will have an interest in getting too close to a nuclear or bioweapon shootout in any of the countries in Clusters 1 and 2. One reason: Developed countries in Clusters 4 and 5 are going to have to confront a host of their own radioactive and biological problems (or at least the threat of those problems). Then there's Cluster 3 – the Middle East has a well-earned reputation for being the epicenter of global trouble. Before we celebrate the arrival of 2030, that trouble will turn both radioactive and biological.

Of all the unfortunate events likely to take place in the next two or three decades, none could be more tragic than those occurring within the borders of the United States (Cluster 5). The U.S. is in the cross hairs of many of the world's poor who are looking to assign blame for the ever-widening worldwide societal gap. To many, the United States is the prime mover when it comes to making the rich richer and the poor poorer. As the director of International Security Studies at Yale puts it, disenfranchised people feel that "the U.S., its companies, and its citizens are … to be blamed for the social and political cost of economic integration."[1]

Thus, while there may be inter- and intra-cluster nuclear or biological conflicts in other parts of the world, it will be the U.S. that probably will take the brunt of the worst attacks – at least in the immediate future. It will happen because, as another Yale professor notes, "the geographical position and the military power of the U.S. are no longer sufficient to ensure its security."[2] Even with a defense budget that is larger than the defense spending of one-third of 190 other countries combined, the U.S. is still vulnerable.[3]

If lessons have been learned from recent events, terrorists will simultaneously strike a few targets that are thought to be vital to American economic and government interests. Consider this scenario:

Nuclear devices explode in Los Angeles and Chicago. A combined 300,000 people are killed or left with life-threatening injuries. At least 100,000 more require immediate medical attention. There is no way of knowing what the long-term radiation effects will be on those living or working in either city.

At the same time, sarin gas is discharged in Atlanta, Dallas and Boston. The overall loss of life in the three cities is estimated at more than a million. Dirty bombs explode at container ports in New York and Long Beach, California, virtually shutting down the country's shipping system. Conventional car bombs go off in five other urban areas, resulting in a limited loss of life, but since it is unclear if the explosions were caused by radiological dispersion devices or were filled with biological agents, people evacuate the cities in a panic.

What would the response be in different parts of the United States?

Ideally, the country would spring back as quickly as it did after the September 11 attacks. However, the World Trade Center and Pentagon attacks gave an inkling of other kinds of reactions that could be detrimental to a national recovery:

- Huge yachts leave their berths carrying the megarich as far away as possible from populated centers that could be future terrorist targets – or away from whatever radioactive fallout or germs that might still be blowing in the wind. Ridiculous assumption? Yacht sales hit new highs in late 2001 following the World Trade Center and Pentagon bombings.

- Supply and demand systems break down. Businesses can't or don't operate because the market for goods and services shrinks to nothing. Workers stop working because they are too fearful or too shocked to leave their families – or because employers shut down operations. A lack of raw materials and employees forces plants to close their doors.

- Hoarding instincts kick in. People sense that social systems are unraveling and stock up on food, water, medicine, other basic necessities and, of course, money. There is a run on grocery stores, pharmacies and banks.

- Urban territories become danger zones. People avoid highly congested areas because the areas are a potential target for terrorists, or because they have already been contaminated. There is a swift move to relocate to more rural locations. The migration pattern ruins businesses and industries dependent on access to centralized manpower.

- Rule of law is overrun by the need to protect the most basic social unit of all – the nuclear family. People fall back to the Maslow triangle's "safety" plank (see Chart 3) – we do what we need to do in order to survive, even if it means violating lawful codes of conduct.

Chart 3

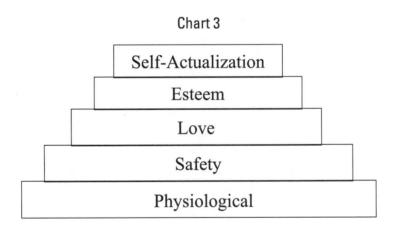

Maslow's Hierarchy of Needs
Source: Abraham H. Maslow, Robert Frazer, James Fadiman,
Movtivation and Personality (New York: Addison-Wesley, 1987).

Clearly, these are the outcomes terrorists want to see. Are these projections realistic following concurrent attacks that might take the lives of around 1.5 million Americans?

Hard to say.

What if nuclear and biological weapons used in U.S. cities killed 15 million? We know that the technology exists to achieve this kind of death toll. Would that body count be enough to shock America into paralysis?

We don't know.

While the prospect of losing 15 million U.S. citizens is nearly incomprehensible, once again we have to remember that such a tragedy would still leave 95 percent of Americans walking around. Dazed and demoralized, perhaps, but still walking around.

Casualty Count

The 20th century won the dubious-achievement award for being the bloodiest in history. War and atrocities claimed the lives of more than 100 million people.[4] While it is pure speculation, it would appear that mankind is poised to break that record within the first 30 years of the 21st century.

It is staggering to think that we could be teetering on the edge of a three-decade period when nuclear and biowarfare could wipe out as many as 100 million humans. However, put this looming possibility in perspective.

The elimination of 100 million people equals less than 2 percent of our current worldwide population. Assuming reproduction rates continue at their current pace, it would take about a year and four months to replace those who may lose their lives as a result of conflicts in different parts of the world.

If future casualties were to be concentrated only in one or two countries, the loss of 100 million people certainly would be devastating. If limited to the United States, for instance, a third of the nation would be wiped out. As our "cluster analysis" in Chapter 2 noted, however, every cluster will probably experience nuclear or biological incidents, or both, in the near term. As a result, the casualty count will be spread out and, in turn, many countries will be affected.

Especially noteworthy is the nature of the destruction – and who will be among the casualties. Instead of long, protracted battles designed to capture and hold territory, fewer but far more lethal attacks will be carried out in the name of ideals (mainly under the "definition of death" banner). The victims of these assaults will be mostly civilian men, women and children – an appalling prospect, but necessary to think about.

The rules and practices of warfare have changed over the past 100 years. Carnage used to be largely restricted to the battlefield in the old days. Uniformed military slugged it out, while collateral damage to civilians was kept to a minimum. The Food and Agriculture Division of the U.N. makes the point that, in recent times, 90 percent of war casualties have been civilians compared with only 10 percent at the beginning of the 20th century.[5] "War has become civilianized rather than civilized," the FAO contends.[6]

One rarely discussed incident in the Western world that illustrates how civilians have become fair game during wartime occurred on March 9, 1945. On that day, the U.S. used 300 aircraft to firebomb Tokyo. Between 80,000 and 100,000 people (civilians for the most part) died, which made the event even more deadly than the A-bomb attack on Nagasaki.[7] While America's president called civilian bombings "inhuman barbarism" at the outbreak of World War II, the country resorted to the same tactic as a means of convincing the Japanese to surrender during the final phase of the war. Although the firebombing has never been given much exposure in the U.S., here is what Jonathan Rauch says about the incident in an *Atlantic Monthly* column: "The firebombing of Tokyo should be considered a war crime, a terror bombing, if those terms are to have any meaning at all."[83]

The United States has civilian blood on its hands, as do most countries or organizations that are engaging in modern warfare. The line between civilians and the military has always been blurred, and that line will be completely erased between now and 2030 as the terms "warfare" and "terrorism" become one and the same. Today's rules of engagement cover every person in every corner of the globe. It doesn't matter if you are a 20-year-old in uniform or a 2-month-old in diapers. Under the new rules of conflict, you are a target. No person – whether young or old, male or female – gets an exemption.

The Lone Ranger Factor

The heavy-duty violence that awaits us over the next decades will be a product of organized planning and execution. However, lesser but still deadly incidents will dot the same timeline, courtesy of those who may act alone or in concert with a few other like-minded people.

The next time you are flying in a Boeing 767, look around at your 200 fellow passengers and think about this:

- More than 430 million people worldwide are estimated to be mentally ill.[9]

- About 12 percent of the world's population will have mental-illness problems at any time during the next 20 years.[10]

- 5.4 percent of American adults have a serious mental illness.[11]

- Countries where poverty and hopelessness are serious problems often have a higher-than-average percentage of people who are mentally ill (in Pakistan, for example, more than 16 percent of the country's population is suffering from some form of mental disorder).[12]

The more people conceive, the more the population of mentally ill expands. In fact, one could argue that the pressures of population growth actually lead to an increase in mental illness. Why? Because, as the director general of the World Health Organization points out, poverty and violent conflict are two of the three major factors that thrust people into mental illness (the other is aging).[13] At least in some parts of the world, population compression is the seedbed for both poverty and violence.

Much is written about the mentally ill being no more of a danger to society than those who are of sound mind. That's probably true in respect to most mental illnesses. However, for people unfortunate enough to be inflicted with the most severe types of mental illness – schizophrenia or manic-depression – violent occurrences are not uncommon.[14] Let's use a real-life example in a highly industrialized nation to make the point.

A man named Mamoru Takuma invaded an elementary school in Osaka, Japan, and killed eight children (15 others were injured). Takuma pleaded guilty to the crime, but lawyers claimed the incident was the result of his schizophrenia. During the course of the trial, the prosecution profiled Takuma as a man who felt everyone was out to get him and murdering children was his way of causing a wide circle of people to suffer as much pain as he had endured during his lifetime.[15]

Suppose Mr. Takuma had been privy to a packet of anthrax or some other biological agent provided to him by others who could capitalize on his alleged demented state. Would he have taken full advantage of the killing power of these biological weapons even if it meant losing his own life? Since Takuma had attempted suicide in the past (another failure that contributed to his anger at the world, according to the prosecution), this possibility surely cannot be ruled out.

Takuma attacked the Japanese school using conventional weapons, but schizophrenics or other mentally unbalanced people may have much more powerful tools at their disposal in the future. Many schizophrenics are highly intelligent (read *A Beautiful Mind*, by Sylvia Nasar),[16] and some certainly have the capacity to access or even produce extremely destructive weapons.

Just as terrorist organizations learned how to convert a seemingly benign conveyance called a commercial airliner into a bomb, such groups have also learned that suicide-prone, paranoid schizophrenics can be another type of effective delivery system for weapons of mass destruction. The World Health Organization estimates that between 10 million and 20 million people (most of whom are classified as mentally ill) attempt suicide each year.[17] Most have no interest in killing anyone other than themselves. There are a few, however – like Mamoru Takuma – who would seem to be excellent recruits or dupes for organizations eager to erase large numbers of people from the planet.

Of course, not all suicide bombers can be clinically diagnosed as mentally ill. Not all who murder themselves, as a means of murdering others, are insane. Seemingly mentally competent people have been sacrificing themselves in this way for a long time. Muslim fighters in northern Persia, for instance, practiced suicidal terrorism in the 11th century.[18] Today, the media regularly report on acts of suicide that result in multiple deaths and injuries. This excerpt from *Foreign Policy* magazine attempts to explain the link between this kind of suicide and martyrdom:

> Suicide terrorism, both ancient and modern, is not
> merely the product of religious fervor, Islamic or other-
> wise. Martha Crenshaw, a leading terrorism scholar at
> Wesleyan University, argues that the mind-set of a sui-
> cide bomber is no different from those of Tibetan self-
> immolators, Irish political prisoners ready to die in a
> hunger strike, or dedicated terrorists worldwide who

wish to live after an operation but know their chances of survival are negligible. Seen in this light, suicide terrorism loses its demonic uniqueness. It is merely one type of martyrdom venerated by certain cultures or religious traditions but rejected by others who favor different modes of supreme sacrifice.[19]

Whether spurred on by opportunists, motivated by religious zeal, driven by nationalistic fervor or twisted by insanity, an individual can do extraordinary damage – far more than what Timothy McVeigh managed to "achieve" in Oklahoma City when he murdered 168 people (19 of them children) and injured more than 500. Far more than the 329 passengers killed when a suspected Sikh militant blew up an Air India Boeing 747 in 1985. Far more than the 259 who died, thanks to a Libyan terrorist, in the Pan Am airliner crash over Lockerbie, Scotland, four days before Christmas 1988.[20] Each of these incidents sent shock waves throughout the world. However, those shock waves would have been tsunami-like if the individuals responsible for the terrorist incidents had been able to get their hands on biological, chemical or nuclear weapons. Technology has given the next crop of demented or fanatical individuals who act alone or in concert with others the capability of doing unprecedented damage to people and property.

Still, as ominous as all of this may sound, the lone ranger (or small group of lone rangers) is not our greatest worry. Much more dangerous are larger, more organized groups of people who are not averse to using weapons of mass destruction. Glued together by extreme beliefs and motivated by a determination to do away with massive segments of present-day civilization, these organizations are poised to cause inordinate harm, thanks to the availability of information and lethal technology.

What's Ahead?

How does this all add up? What's lying in wait for us over the next 25 to 30 years?

This chapter ends with assumptions that combine technology, poverty and population growth. It is not a healthy mix. The timeline running through *How Women Can Beat Terrorism* stretches to 2030, when, according to the United Nations Population Division, birthrates in the least-developed countries of the world finally will decline to where they equal death rates.[21] If the U.N. forecast is accurate, we may be experiencing an unpleasant journey over the next three decades. Too many signs are warning us that anticipated population growth is going to create havoc in those countries where people are already adversely affected by widened societal gaps.

If nothing is done to curb poverty and slow down reproduction rates in these already overpopulated areas of the world, all indications are that everyone will pay a price. Just how high that price tag will be is in question. We can, however, propose what may happen if predictions about worldwide demographics prove to be accurate. Just as some of Paul Ehrlich's prophecies in *The Population Bomb* were off the mark, this chapter's predictions may also prove to be false. One can only hope that they are, because here are the disturbing images showing up in the crystal ball:

- Nuclear or biological weapons, or both, will be used in all five of the clusters described in Chapter 2.

Particularly in less-developed countries, we can expect to see much greater use of biological agents than other types of weapons of mass destruction. Bioweapons are not only becoming easier to access, but they also are unbelievably cost effective. A NATO report in 2001 stated that the same casualty rates per square kilometer could be obtained by spending $9,000 for conventional weapons – or just $5 for bioweapons.[22]

Nuclear and chemical weapons will also come into play throughout the world. In addition, low-yield nuclear bombs and radioactive dispersion devices will be used in certain parts of the world. Why? Because there are simply too many weapons-grade nuclear materials circulating around the world and too much talent willing and able to convert that material into terrorist tools.

- More than 100 million people worldwide will die as a result of terrorist acts and war.

At first reading, the reaction to this statement has to be: *This can't be right – not even close.* After all, if more than 100 million people were wartime victims during the last century, how can we assume that the death toll in just the next 30 years will be equal to or greater than that figure?

Actually, it is feasible – and here's why:

First, human conflict is likely to be as much a part of this century as the last. The difference is that by the middle of the 21st century, we will have at least three times as many people on earth than in 1950. All things being equal (which, of course, they often are not), that could translate into 300 million victims by the end of 2099. Proportionately, that would mean 100 million people killed by around 2030.

Second, although we may not see the type of world wars that accounted for so many of the battle casualties during the 20th century, we will see regional conflicts that are just as deadly. Case in point: The U.S. estimates that if Pakistan and India were to engage in a nuclear conflict, 12 million people would die and 5 million would be injured in South Asia.[23] In other parts of the world that have endured protracted conflicts, we will almost certainly see the use of some types of nuclear weapons. The casualty count grows quickly when armies and terrorists begin detonating radioactive material as part of their assault strategies.

Third, biological weapons will make a bold appearance in different parts of the world. We need to remember that it takes very little biological "ammunition" to kill a lot of people. The World Health Organization concluded that 110 pounds of anthrax released from an aircraft along a small stretch of land upwind of a population center of 500,000 would kill 95,000 people and incapacitate another 125,000.[24] To date, finding effective ways of dispensing agents like anthrax, tularemia, typhus and the like has been a deterrent to bioweapons use. Technology will eliminate that problem long before we reach 2030.

- The United States will incur between 1.5 million and 10 million casualties as a result of international and domestic terrorism.

The U.S. is not accustomed to homeland terrorism. Between 1995 and 2000, there were more than 2,000 international terrorist attacks (this excludes domestic terrorism such as the Oklahoma City bombing), and only 15 of them occurred in the U.S.[25] The tragic events of September 11 killed nearly five times as many Americans as terrorist incidents of the previous 30 years combined.[26]   This staggering projection – that between 1.5 million and 10 million people will die on U.S. soil between now and 2030 – is bound to produce skepticism. But consider the following:

In a 1958 *Emergency War Plans* document, the U.S. government estimated an all-out nuclear war with the then-Soviet Union would kill 25 million Americans outright and injure another 25 million.[27] The report was produced when the U.S. population was only 140 million people. In a nuclear war today, casualty estimates would be a lot higher because the population has doubled since the mid-'50s. *How Women Can Beat Terrorism*, however, is not predicting a full-scale nuclear attack on the U.S. Instead, the projection is based on the use of mass-destruction weapons strategically placed in locations with high concentrations of civilians.

We probably will not see the day when a 20-megaton nuclear detonation ruins an American city – an event that the Physicians for Social Responsibility think would kill 1 million people if exploded in a city of 2.8 million.[28] Also not factored into this projection is the deliberate or accidental destruction of a nuclear-power plant. What we are much more likely to see are several smaller nuclear explosions designed to cripple crucial economic and government centers throughout the U.S.

As damaging as a series of nuclear attacks might be, the United States is even more vulnerable to biological assaults. According to the Brookings Institution, a million people could die if terrorists use anthrax, Ebola or other pathogens as their weapons of choice.[29] That's in the short term. As biological-dispensing techniques improve over the next decade or two, bioagents represent an even greater threat to the United States.

It needs to be stressed again – biological weapons are not that difficult to produce and use. The U.S. Centers for Disease Control states that even rank amateurs could use pathogens to inflict heavy casualties.[30] The CDC goes on to say that for every $1 million made available to a private or state-sponsored terrorist group, bioweapons could be used to kill up to 100,000 people – and for every 1,000 casualties, another 100,000 to one million people would be in need of prophylactic attention.[31] We have yet to come to grips with just how horrifying BW attacks could be. The time for that reckoning is not far away.

The U.S. is singled out from other countries and cluster categories because it is viewed as the world's terrorist high bar. The country will be increasingly under pressure as external and even some internal groups test the nation's capacity to take a punch. Just how the country elects to defend itself (for example, by shrinking individual rights in exchange for more national security) will – in part – determine how high the casualty count will go between now and 2030.

If the U.S. were to bear its "fair share" of the 100 million people who are projected to die as a result of conflict over the next three decades, about 4 million Americans would be killed (the U.S. accounts for about 4 percent of the world's population). However, worldwide deaths may not be so evenly distributed. The U.S. could end up with more casualties, per capita, than other parts of the world simply because it is going to be challenged more frequently than most other countries. The flip side is that the United States could institute provisions that may make it more difficult for weapons of mass destruction to be used. What strategies the country chooses to enact – for example, pre-emptive engagements such as Operation Iraqi Freedom, expanded national defense, and prevention with a strong reliance on women – will largely determine whether the U.S. death toll comes closer to 1.5 million or a staggering 10 million.

One last note: Even if the loss of life in the U.S. is limited to around 1.5 million people, that number is huge compared with Americans killed in previous conflicts. The U.S. lost 404,000 troops (on and off the battlefield) during all of World War II, and 116,000 during World War I.[32] In fact, the loss of life in *all* of the major wars fought by the U.S. has totaled less than 1 million.[33] Clearly, the killing of 1.5 million or more Americans on U.S. soil during a 30-year period will have a substantial impact on the nation – even though those deaths will represent only one-half of 1 percent of the population.

- Land, water and air resources in several parts of the world will become scarcer and more difficult to access because of nuclear and biological destruction or contamination.

Ironically, the problems of resource availability and distribution that are already triggering problems are only going to worsen as we struggle through the next few decades. The residual effects of nuclear and bioweapons incidents could possibly lead to – or surpass – the kind of resource shortfalls that Paul Ehrlich predicted in his much-maligned *The Population Bomb*.

We have plenty of evidence that confirms how human conflict has damaged the environment. Twenty years of war in Cambodia ruined 35 percent of that nation's forest cover. A 6-year civil war in Sri Lanka destroyed 5 million trees. Conventional hostilities in Angola wiped out nearly 90 percent of that country's wildlife.[34] The list is lengthy. However, what could happen to our land and water supplies may make our past transgressions look like minor infractions.

In the mid-1980s, Alexander Leaf, a clinical medicine professor at Harvard, wrote an article for the National Academy of Sciences that underscored the "lose-lose" outcome of a full-scale nuclear war. While we may be able to skirt an all-out nuclear holocaust, the probable use of many smaller nuclear and biological weapons could lead us to exactly the same place that Leaf described in his troubling article.

Soil would deteriorate in the wake of nuclear explosions, and water supplies would be reduced, Leaf warned.[35] He wrote that the "complex network of enterprises that involves not only farming, animal husbandry and fishing but also farm machinery, pesticides, fertilizers, petroleum products and commercial seeds" would unravel.[36] The result could lead to the starvation of millions of people.

- The disruption of economic, social and political systems will affect everyone.

It is doubtful that anyone will be able to dodge the bullet that is heading our way. Even if only a small percentage of the world's population is killed or injured by more lethal technologies that are to be unleashed during the next decades, survivors will also pay a price. Food shortages. Water restrictions. Security anxieties. Unemployment. Overall fear. Everyone's quality of life is going to be impaired to some degree.

Nevertheless, in spite of the problems ahead…

Humankind will survive.

Our species is not going to disappear on or before 2030. Far from it. However, it will be a vastly different world three decades from now. Just how different will depend on what steps we are willing to take today – steps such as engaging women to do more to alleviate poverty, curb hopelessness and slow down population growth in places already struggling to cope with an overload of people.

PART II
POVERTY

CHAPTER 4

OWNERSHIP

The U.N. says that more than a billion humans around the world live in unacceptable conditions of poverty – and that the majority of these people are women. The yardstick used to determine whether one is poor is usually linked to per-capita economics and other standardized benchmarks. However, poverty is a complex concept. Sometimes it can be found in the pit of the stomach, and at other times it is in the eye of the beholder. Only a fool would argue that men, women and children starving to death in Angola are not poor. On the other hand, a Bodnath monk living a Spartan life in Kathmandu may be poor according to U.N. definition, but he would likely see things differently.

How Women Can Beat Terrorism argues that the world needs to be more aggressive in attacking global poverty – and that women have to be on the forefront of that attack. However, before going after poverty with a vengeance, it makes sense to figure out what poverty is. Part II attempts to do that by breaking down poverty, which could be analyzed in numerous ways, into just two components: ownership and control, both of which are barriers to women.

Let's start with *ownership*.

# # #

I am the material girl, sang Madonna, the consummate consumerist who vocalized a fundamental human urge that is in all of us. That urge, the desire to own, is as prevalent in a primitive tribe as it is in a nation overflowing with worldly possessions.

Those who denounce materialism might claim that they do not need ownership. However, even anti-materialists struggle to acquire – to *own* – the basics. It's part of our survival mode. We do what's necessary to get food, drink and whatever other essentials are deemed crucial to our existence. Regardless of whether we buy, grow, beg, borrow or steal what we consider life's necessities, once we have the goods in our hands or on our backs or in our stomachs … then we are *owners*.

There is another dimension to ownership that goes beyond acquiring the tangible. We all own varying amounts of intellectual property. We have our *own* ideas, and we have our *own* beliefs. People may claim to be minimalists, but they are still owners of concepts, notions and thoughts. We all own. We all seek to own. It is *what* we own and *how much* we own that not only goes a long way in defining who we are, but also creates gargantuan chasms among those who have and those who don't.

In Chapter 6 ("Widened Societal Gap"), the point will be made that the inequities of material ownership (and its close relative, consumerism) become the raison d'être for what Part VI terms "negative envy" – and negative envy can be high-octane fuel for many fires that will be ignited between now and 2030. There is nothing new about ownership inequity, of course. What *is* new is far-reaching information technology that is able to inform most of the world about the imbalance of ownership and consumption levels. Ponder this statement from the United Nations Population Fund:

> *The world's richest countries, with 20 percent of global population, account for 86 percent of total private consumption, whereas the poorest 20 percent of the world's people account for just 1.3 percent.*[1]

If this statement doesn't irk the 20 percent of the world's population stuck in poverty (reminder: that 20 percent equates to more than a billion people), then maybe a U.N. footnote will: "A child born today in an industrialized country will add more to consumption and pollution over his or her lifetime than 30 to 50 children born in developing countries."[2]

So not only does the 20 percent of people living at the top of the population pecking order have extraordinary ownership and consumer benefits, but those same people also are leaving an ecological footprint that is not just deeper than that of the poor but "in many cases, exceeds the regenerative capacity of the earth."[3] This is the kind of information that could (and sometimes does) infuriate hundreds of millions who don't own much today and probably won't tomorrow.

Surprisingly, as lopsided as ownership tends to be throughout the world, not everyone who is short on material possessions gets exercised about what might be called an "ownership deficit." The religious and philosophical tenets of religions such as Buddhism, for instance, warn that obsessive craving can be a doorway into a world of suffering. Buddhists are advised to be wary of the negative side of the word "more." *Trishna* is a Sanskrit expression that describes the inclination to go overboard in stamping "it's mine" on as many things as possible. *Trishna* is the urge to own and consume as much as possible, and it can send people into such an ownership tizzy that their ability to appreciate what they already have becomes elusive, if not impossible.

Chart 4

Country	Percent
Thailand	95%
Cambodia	90%
Myanmar	88%
Bhutan	75%
Sri Lanka	70%
Tibet	65%
Laos	60%
Vietnam	55%
Japan	50%
Macau	45%
Taiwan	43%

Top Ten Countries with Highest Proportion of Buddhists
Source: Buddha Dharma Education Association & BuddhaNet, 2002

Buddhism happens to be the predominant religion in many countries where poverty is rampant (see Chart 4).[4] This combination of religious belief and economic circumstance may be one of the strokes of good luck for the world. Individuals who accept the notion that "less is more" are not as inclined to let feelings of negative envy and resentment provoke them into despising those who are awash with material excesses. Still, in an era where *trishna* and information technology are often joined at the hip (TV advertising, product placements in films, constant promotion of the rich and famous, and so forth), even Buddhists must feel the temptations of modern-day consumerism – and the disappointment of not having at least *some* of the trappings that seemingly come so easily to those in developed nations.

And that brings us to the other end of the ownership spectrum. *He who dies with the most toys wins* is the pennant for many people who live in a heavily capitalist-driven social system, where owning is a visible trophy of achievement. Whether rich or poor, there is an inclination not just to own but also to show off what you happen to possess. You *are* what you own – or at least what you *appear* to own. In the U.S., where the typical citizen has 6.5 credit cards and the average U.S. household carries around $8,500 in credit-card debt, "ownership" can be a debatable term.[5] In actuality, it is the lending institution that holds title to much of the "stuff" Americans drive, wear and consume. That, of course, is a mere technicality to those living in a country where leasing is as good as owning and where paying on installment is as American as instant gratification.

In his book *Lead Us Into Temptation*, James Twitchell reminds us that ownership and consumerism come easily to most people – "we are powerfully attracted to the world of goods," he states.[6] In places like the U.S., he says store-bought items have become the bonding agents for society – they are the common denominator for the masses. At the same time, our purchases give us identity. Tell me what you buy, and I will tell you what you are and who you want to be, Twitchell adds.

Cast in this light, ownership and consumerism are more than just niceties in highly developed social systems. They turn the wheels of commerce that move the gears of the economy. Ownership and consumerism are so powerful in the U.S. that they got the credit for keeping the country from slipping into an all-out recession after the September 11 terrorist attacks – at least that's what *Time.com* concluded and why it named the American consumer as its "Person of the Week" in March 2002.[7]

Shop. Buy. Own. Capitalism's three-legged throne.

Is it possible, though, that even in the richest of nations, the urge to own could actually turn on its citizens like a mad dog? One gets that feeling after reading *The Overspent American: Upscaling, Downshifting and the New Consumer*.[8] The book digs deep into the American populace and finds low-income people just as susceptible to the lure of consumerism and ownership. The obvious dilemma: People with low incomes don't have the cash to pay for the purchases they want to make. The book's author, Juliet Schor, says this unfulfilled urge to own results in a segment of society that is left with feelings of deprivation and failure. She notes that poor people surrounded by riches learn a hard lesson: In a culture where consuming (and owning) are so important, not having money becomes a "profound social disability."[9]

Thus, ownership (or lack of it) can be a force that can create cracks in even the most well-off nations. Ownership exerts the same kind of pressure within poorer countries as well. Why? Because that innate human desire is crawling around in everyone's cranium regardless of where people happen to live. Even in countries that are, on average, nowhere near as prosperous as most Western nations, ownership tells the story about who has made it and who is stuck in the economic muck that can be found at the bottom of any social system. Take China as an example:

"Home ownership is already changing Chinese society by fostering a growing sense of personal pride and individualism."[10]

It may be difficult to fathom, but in the People's Republic of China, where home ownership by individuals might seem contrary to the socialistic principles of the country, the nation's leaders are hyping real estate. And for good reason. Chinese economists see home ownership as the door opener to a broader economic rally driven by consumer purchases of furniture, TVs and all the other "things" people are inspired to acquire once they have their "own" roof over their heads.

Owning a home – could there be a more prized possession whether you live in an igloo, thatched hut or 25-room mansion?

Even in nations where repression is practically a commodity, owning a house is right up there with eating and drinking. The notorious Muammar al-Qaddafi wrote in his *Green Book* (the Libyan leader's version of Chairman Mao's *Little Red Book*) that a house is a "basic need" of an individual and his family. The book includes this passage:

> All attempts made by various countries to solve the
> problem of housing are not solutions at all. The reason
> is that those attempts do not aim at the radical and ulti-
> mate solution of man, which is the necessity of his own-
> ing his own house.[11]

It comes down to this: Everyone wants – needs – to own something. The statement is valid no matter where one lives, no matter what one's economic situation happens to be. Granted, maybe ownership is but a minor longing in some Buddhist cultures. However, in places such as Japan, where a large percentage of the nation's 120 million residents are Buddhists either by birth or choice, the desire to own is blatantly prevalent.[12]

Wanting to own is, of course, different from actually *owning*. That reality gets us back to the ownership disparity that exists (a) among nations and (b) among the different social segments within each country. Let's start with "among nations" and look more closely at ownership differences between what the United Nations labels "developing countries" and "more-developed countries."

On the international scene, there is a *lot* of distance between the bookends of those who own a lot and those who own practically nothing. If you have the misfortune of being one of the world's 18 million or so refugees or displaced people,[13] you probably own very little. However, until information technology gives you a peek at the material excesses of the developed world, you have no idea just how deprived you really happen to be. Then let's say that one day, via TV, the Internet or print media, you find out what ownership looks like in, for example, the U.S. You discover that:

- The average American kid lives in a household with three TVs, two VCRs, three radios, two tape players, two CD players, a video-gameplayer and a computer.[14]

- The typical older child in America gets an allowance of $50 a week, much of which is used to buy things – to increase the kid's ownership status.[15]

If you are one of the nearly three billion people around the world trying to live on less than $25 a week, this picture has to be nearly incomprehensible. Even if you happen to be a minimalist (Buddhist or otherwise), you're probably troubled by the ownership disparities that have become so evident throughout the world. If you're not a minimalist and you really *want* to own more but *can't* because you're caught in an economic snare, then the frustration can be overwhelming. You are, via information technology, constantly reminded that a mountain of material goods out there is completely out of your reach. Your pot begins to boil. Then you read an excerpt from another one of James Twitchell's books, *Living It Up*, and gag on the news that luxury spending in the U.S. has been growing four times faster than overall spending.[16] People in the more-developed world are acquiring things that are distant from the basic requirements of life –

basic requirements that you barely can afford. While you and three billion other people own so little that survival comes with a question mark, the more fortunate are annually scooping up 23,000 Porsche cars[17] and buying Patek Philippe wristwatches that can cost as much as $400,000 each.[18] To about half the people on earth whose discretionary income is nil, this is a disturbing state of affairs (see Chapter 2 – Charts 2A and 2B).

If you're one of the poorest of the poor and it appears as if your life has nothing to offer except more of the same, ownership is an in-your-face cue of life's unfairness. It is an irritating burr under your saddle that makes you intent on listening when someone begins shouting this message: *Do something about this unfairness! There are ways – thanks to accessible lethal technologies – to level the playing field!* Of course, if you do level the playing field, there are no guarantees that your ownership portfolio will get larger. Instead, you're being invited to join a team that wants to punch a hole in the over inflated ownership balloons that can be found floating around in those World Bank-designated places called "high-income nations" (see Chapter 2 – Chart 2E).[19]

Enough about poor folk standing on the outside who may be feeling increasingly resentful about the ownership excesses found inside the more-developed world. Now, let's turn to the people who live in countries of abundance but who are clinging to the bottom rung of the economic ladder.

Will ownership inequities give these people a dose of what Part VI calls negative envy? In some instances, the answer is: absolutely. However, being poor in a rich nation is not the same as being desperately impoverished in a developing country. The pain is not as severe. Most of Maslow's basic needs are being met if you're functioning (or trying to function) at or below the poverty line in a well-to-do country. As a result, there is less inclination to even the ownership score. This not to say, though, that all poor people will be able to keep their negative envy from triggering serious anti-social behavior. Being reminded repeatedly of how much there is to own when you have no capacity to become an owner is a good way to foster bitterness. And in countries like the United States, those constant reminders come in the form of 14.5 minutes of commercials, on average, for every hour of prime-time TV watched.[20] Reminder: Television is a *powerful* force in the U.S.:

- The average family turns the television on seven and a

half hours a day and is exposed to a constant stream of commercials.[21]

- Television taps into a human's need to own at an early stage – each year, the typical child sees more than 20,000 TV ads.[22]

- Television's influence spans a lifetime – by age 70, most people will have spent approximately 10 years watching television.[23]

Even if the TV gets switched off, the reminders are still there. Go to an Arizona State University football game and get blasted with 200 commercials while sitting for five hours in Sun Devil Stadium.[24] Drive America's highways and check out any of the more than 425,000 messages plastered on billboards lining interstate freeways and toll roads.[25] Radio, the Internet, direct mail, bus placards – even blimps. Information technology teases us all – rich or poor – with a cornucopia of material goods. That tease can be especially tormenting to those with little means who know that they have a slim chance of owning what's being hyped in the media.

Luckily, most people, regardless of how much money they have, are quite capable of balancing their wants with their means. Still, more than a few individuals surely will be angered not just because they have so little in a land of plenty, but also because they resent that a small segment of society owns so much. As the population expands in more-developed nations, so does the absolute number of people who are displeased about the lack of ability to own. For certain, some will try to balance the ownership scales by turning to theft, vandalism, embezzlement, carjacking, armed robbery or worse. They will rationalize their actions in two ways: by convincing themselves that first, they deserve to own more, and second, that some people own too much.

If the ideal of ownership becomes a factor in inciting a small fragment of a nation's populace to become a public threat, well, that's another one of those unfortunate facts of life, right? After all, history is filled with examples of violent acts that were triggered by motivations and disputes usually having something to do with ownership. We're not navigating into unchartered waters here.

Or are we?

The disquieting answer to the question is: no and yes. The waterways are well charted, but we are traveling with a new passenger called *more lethal technology.* If ownership-motivated violent acts end up hurting a lot more people than in the past (something that's already happening), then a new day has definitely dawned and the sunrise is far from beautiful.

One last observation about ownership. In many parts of the world, property ownership is too often a privilege extended to men but not to women. As the United Nations puts it: "legal and customary barriers to ownership or access to land, natural resources, capital, credit, technology and other means of production ... contribute to impeding the economic progress of women."[26] If women are to be instrumental in the assault on poverty, then we not only have to open the ownership doors wider, but we also need to post a sign that reads: *Females welcome.* If enacted, recommendations included in *How Women Can Beat Terrorism* are likely to make ownership easier for women in lesser-developed places around the world. At the same time, breaking down gender barriers may prove disruptive to certain societies where a woman's lack of property and other kinds of ownership bear a close resemblance to indentured servitude.

CHAPTER 5

CONTROL

The actor Tom Cruise has between 30,000 to 40,000 genes in his body. That makes him vastly superior to the nematode worm that has only 18,000 genes, or the fruit fly that, on its best day, has a mere 13,000 genes.[1] Logically, then, one might conclude that the difference between Tom Cruise and a worm or a fly is simply a numbers game. Not so. It is also about the *kind* of genes that are calling the shots in any living creature. The main difference between Cruise and a worm or a fly is that the actor has more *control* genes.[2]

Control is an enormously important function – and not just at the genetic level. Much of our life is determined by what or whom we control – and by what or who controls us. How content or happy we are is determined, at least in part, by the real, perceived or anticipated control we have as well as the externally applied controls that influence the way we live.

Whether a human or the environment has the upper hand when it comes to control is meat on the bone for a lot of social scientists. Behaviorists think the environment controls the behavior of an organism. In contrast, some believe in what is called the "perceptual control theory" – that the organism is in control of its environment.[3] This chapter examines each position, but in the end, the level of control we have over our immediate environment and the controls that are placed upon us in any societal setting are powerful forces that shape our lives.

• • •

To a certain degree, *everyone has a need to control*. It is a behavior that is crucial to our survival and well-being. "Control freaks" and people "out of control" are not the most beloved characters in any society. However, all of us are driven to control our immediate environment if for no other reason than to keep ourselves safe and to provide for other requirements of life. Even a monk who shuns every worldly possession still will act to influence his surroundings so as to ensure that his basic necessities are met.

While we may have a need to control, that doesn't mean the need is always satisfied; we're certainly not always happy. We may find ourselves in circumstances that, for all practical purposes, make it impossible for us to "take control" – something the estimated 8 million to 10 million people who are behind bars in different parts of the world would fully understand.[4]

You don't have to be incarcerated to feel the effects of external pressures so powerful (or at least perceived to be so powerful) that they suppress our range of personal control. Certain forms of government (socialism, for example) and the military create environments where personal controls may be limited but where, as an offset, organization members are assured that the system will meet their basic needs. This kind of excessive external control may not appeal to people living in a more-developed country who don't have to worry about satisfying their basic requirements and who cherish the "Live Free or Die" tattoo on their biceps. However, to the billions of people who have only a marginal level of control over their environment and who are locked in a day-to-day struggle for survival, there is great appeal to the notion of living in an externally controlled place where most of the "basics" are guaranteed.

On the bell curve of life, some of us have an abundance of control and others are heavily controlled. At one end of the curve are those in privileged positions with enormous power (that is, control). At the other end are those who either are – or feel they are – oppressed with little control over what they view as undesirable circumstances and events. Most of us go through life without experiencing either end of the curve. We go about our business exerting control in some instances and conceding to external controls on other occasions. This whole control balancing act, as one writer puts it, gives us "great survival and reproductive advantages" since humans are able to achieve goals "essential to their survival and reproduction despite an unpredictable, uncaring and often hostile environment."[5]

What happens when control gets out of whack? What are the consequences if external controls are absent, ineffective or excessive? Are there people living in generally acceptable controlled situations who still feel they have little or no control over their own lives – and, if so, is that a problem? And what does any of this have to with the risks we face between now and 2030?

To answer these questions, let's return to Abraham Maslow's

hierarchy of human needs (Chapter 3, Chart 3). That model sums up "the basics" we are all looking for in life: to be able to eat and drink; to have a sense of security; to feel like we belong; to have some level of self-esteem. Most of the time, we find that we need some semblance of control if we are to attain and nurture these basic components of life. If we have no control – or even if we *think* we lack control – we get distressed. Sometimes excessively distressed, as the following examples illustrate.

1. Control Void – Example A

Assume that you are a Muslim villager living in the mountainous Nuba region of central Sudan. Your country – the largest in Africa – has been locked in a civil war for 20 years. Sudan holds the record for the longest ongoing civil war in the world.[6] Nearly 2 million people have been killed as a result of the fighting or war-related problems such as food shortages and disease.[7]

The two sides of the civil war are largely defined by religion. In the south, Christians and animists have been fighting for autonomy from Sudan's Muslim-dominated government since 1983.[8] The Nuba mountains in the central part of the country have frequently been considered the dividing line for rebels and government forces. As a result, the hardships for people living in the region have been extreme. The area "faces the gravest humanitarian crisis in the war-ravaged country," says one Muslim publication.[9] Ordinance, human-rights violations and a water shortage make life miserable for most of the unfortunate people living in the mountains.

Life for you as a villager is a constant battle. Locating food and water is a challenge, as is finding shelter that protects you from bullets and missiles. It is virtually impossible to control your immediate environment in a way that allows your basic needs to be met in any predictable manner. Worse, you see nothing on the horizon that is going to change those circumstances. You're hungry, thirsty, frightened, worn out by war.

Along comes a Muslim cleric from Sudan's capital, Khartoum. He explains that Islam is the victim in this holy war. He explains that the real cause of the conflict is the Western world funneling money and ideology to the Christian-oriented Sudan People's Liberation Army in the south. After the cleric gives you his view of reality in Sudan, he makes a proposal. How would you like to help the Islamic cause and, at the same time, get your basic needs met (you will be fed, clothed and given decent housing)? In other words, you are being offered a chance to control your own destiny by moving to an externally controlled situation that will provide you with the "basics" of life. You ask for details. The cleric explains that you will be working in a factory that produces the nerve agent VX, a chemical weapon that will be used to bring pain to the nations in the West that are the root cause for all the suffering taking place in Sudan.[10]

2. Control Void – Example B

In 1978, Theodore Kaczynski mailed a relatively harmless explosive device to an engineering professor. It was the beginning of a letter-bomb crusade that initially targeted university personnel and airline officials – hence the moniker "Unabomber": "un" (for university), "a" (for airline) and "bomber."

Over the next few years, Kaczynski (who earned a Ph.D. in mathematics from the University of Michigan) became more proficient with explosives, and in 1985, he killed the owner of a computer store using a deadly nail and splinter device left in a California parking lot.

Before he was caught, Kaczynski murdered three people and wounded 29. Along the way, the Unabomber wrote *The New York Times* and declared that an anarchist group called "FC" (he later explained that the initials stood for "Freedom Club") was responsible for the attacks.

In 1995, Kaczynski again contacted *The Times*, along with *The Washington Post*, and said he would end his murder-by-mail campaign if the newspapers published a 35,000-word essay called "Industrial Society and the Future." The two newspapers ultimately agreed, and the Unabomber's "manifesto" went public.

In several sections of the manifesto, Kaczynski voiced concern over loss of control. "Our lives depend on decisions made by other people," he complained early on in his paper. "We have no control over these decisions and usually we do not even know the people who make them..."[11] Kaczynski's manifesto devoted an entire section to "Control of Human Behavior." One of the Unabomber's underlying concerns was that the ability of humans to control their environment in a way that meets their basic needs is being run over by technology.

•   •   •

How do these two examples relate to this book's warnings about what mankind is likely to experience between now and 2030?

Example A is a fabricated scenario intended to show that when our basic needs are not being met on an ongoing, predictable basis because we have little control of our immediate environment, then we become open to options that promise to improve our circumstances even if those options are detrimental to others. It's possible, of course, that we won't exercise those options because we think the downside outweighs the benefits – for example, our Nuba villager might fear being killed if the VX-weapons factory is attacked by pro-Christian forces; he might not want to risk being exposed to hazardous chemicals; he may feel that being part of a manufacturing operation that could contribute to the deaths of thousands or millions of people would weigh too heavily on his conscience. Regardless of whether he accepts the offer, the villager is tempted because it opens the door to a controlled environment that may greatly improve the quality of his life.

Apply this to the present state of humanity around the world:

- At least a billion people are having trouble meeting their basic needs – in some instances, they are falling so far short of satisfying those needs that they may not survive.

- In 1960, 70 percent of the world's population lived in less-developed regions where this "control void" is most often found.[12] By 1999, these less-developed regions were home to 80 percent of the world's population.[13]

- Growth projections for the next three decades tell us that more than 90 percent of the billions of new lives that will be added to the planet are going to be stuffed into the less-developed regions of the globe.[14]

If we could find the means of providing people in these less-developed places with the kind of control that permits them to meet their need for food, drink, security, socialization and esteem, they probably would not be as open to alternatives like the one presented to our villager. Now this is not to say that the offer made by the Sudanese cleric from Khartoum would be turned down even if the Nuba villager were well fed and safe – it is possible that the villager's "definition of death" (see Chapter 14) requires him to help manufacture weapons in defense of Islam. However, if the villager turns out not to be a religious fanatic, the cleric's chances for recruiting the man would vastly improve if the villager were short on control and lacking in ownership.

There is usually, although not always, a link between control and economics. How much one controls and how much one earns typically are closely related, which brings us to this prickly fact of life: In addition to our Nuba villager, *1.2 billion people live on less than $1 a day, and another 2 billion are only marginally better off.*[15] Finding ways to provide these people with more control—and with the means to make other improvements in the quality of their lives—is a staggering challenge today. Tomorrow, that challenge becomes even more mind-boggling. With billions more people about to enter these already population-stressed regions over the next 30 to 50 years, control is going to be in short supply.[16]

What the future has in store for us is more people with less control; more people born into circumstances that prevent them from controlling their immediate environment, which, as a result, makes it impossible for them to meet basic needs; more people susceptible to deals where they can get more control in exchange for performing acts that could prove deadly to a multitude of others.

What about those of us living in more-developed nations where most, if not all, of our basic needs are regularly met? Is control an issue in these locations?

Theodore Kaczynski gives us the answer. Developed nations have their share of the estimated 370 million people around the world who have been diagnosed with mental illness.[17] Most of these men and women are not even close to being a danger to humanity. However, some (along with other malcontents who have anti-social views) do represent a threat to what, in their eyes, are overly controlled social systems. Rules, directives and laws often trouble these individuals. And since every human social system operates with stated or implied regulations, these people are easily distressed by what most of us would consider rather unobtrusive controls.

Groups of people set standards and define boundaries. The local stamp-collecting club goes through this process. So does the Mafia. And most certainly, so do the governments of the 189 member countries of the United Nations.[18] In a broad sense, then, a "rule of law" essentially defines how little or how much control an organization has over its members. In the case of a family, the "laws" are probably verbal and largely parental. When it comes to government, the rules are more formal. While the following definition of the "rule of law" has been crafted for governmental bodies, it can be applied to virtually any organization regardless of size or purpose:

> The rule of law can be defined as a system in which the laws are public knowledge, are clear in meaning, and apply equally to everyone.[19]

The rule of law is an articulation of an organization's external controls. It is so important that, "without the rule of law, major economic institutions such as corporations, banks, and labor unions would not function, and the government's many involvements in the economy – regulatory mechanisms, tax systems, customs structures, monetary policy, and the like – would be unfair, inefficient and opaque."[20]

To the degree that they are understood and accepted by organization members, laws can be a cohesive force; when laws are not understood or are considered to be inequitable, they can become divisive. When a clear or perceived majority of people is willing to comply with the rule of law, an organization is likely to hold together. When a large enough number of people regard the rule of law as unsuitable or inequitable, the organization is vulnerable to change. An attempt to change the rule of law either peacefully or by force really comes down to an effort to adjust the external controls of an organization (government, corporation, union, religious institution, family) over its members.

On a smaller scale, people like Theodore Kaczynski wage their own battles against rules of law that, in their opinion, constitute an inappropriate level of control over mankind. Unlike our Nuba villager, Kaczynski had enough control of his immediate surroundings to ensure that his basic needs were met – food, water and shelter. Even so, the Unabomber still had a high enough level of discontent over external controls to react in a way that led to the death and injury of people. Here's what Kaczynski had to say about control in his manifesto:

> Since the beginning of civilization, organized societies have had to put pressures on human beings for the sake of the functioning of the social organism. The kinds of pressures vary greatly from one society to another. Some of the pressures are physical (poor diet, excessive labor, environmental pollution); some are psychological

(noise, crowding, forcing human behavior into the mold that society requires). In the past, human nature has been approximately constant, or at any rate has varied only within certain limits. When the limit of human endurance has been passed, things start going rong (sic): rebellion, or crime, or corruption, or evasion of work, or depression and other mental problems...[21]

All this adds up to the rather obvious conclusion that control can cause misfits and fanatics like Kaczynski to go haywire. It can also be the carrot on the stick to tempt people such as our Nuba villager into doing things that they might not otherwise consider. Still, there is nothing particularly new in all this, is there? There have been Kaczynskis and Nuba villagers throughout history. So what, if anything, has changed?

The answer comes in a word: technology. The Sudanese villager now has the capacity to cause a catastrophic ripple effect, one that will be felt thousands of miles away in what used to be the world's safe harbors. The next Unabombers may have lethal technology at their disposal that will give them the ability to move from letter bombs to mailbox biological weaponry. What's new? Between now and 2030, control-impaired men and women who can access destructive technology are going to give us the answer.

Control is an awesome force. All of us need some dimension of control to exist. However, when taken to excess, it can be destructive. One Northwestern University systems engineer found the darkest side of control when he wrote:

> Our whole society is a maze of contradictions that can be traced directly to attempts to run it by means of arbitrary control; no matter what else is good about our society, that one factor will destroy it. As long as each person feels a powerful need to control other people (even just some other people) in order to avoid being controlled himself, conflict is inevitable, and conflict between control systems is the worst thing that can happen to them short of physical destruction. Obviously, physical destruction is a highly likely outcome.[22]

Society may be "a maze of contradictions," but so is control. We have a minimum daily requirement for personal control. At the same time, mankind can apply external controls in such a way that social systems can be shattered. Control produces its own labyrinth of incongruities, and it is easy to get lost in the muddle. There is usually a price to pay if we can't get the balance of personal and external controls right. That price has occasionally been high (war, revolution, crusades), but thus far, mankind has always found a way to pay the tab. Today, things are different. Control imbalances come with a much higher price tag that could cost us dearly.

Tom Peters, the author and management guru best known for *In Search of Excellence,* uses this line when speaking to audiences: "Take control of the runaway train – or be flattened by it."[23] Although Peters' reference is to the locomotive speed and power of business, the comment is just as relevant to life in general. We all have a built-in penchant for at least trying to control factors that could harm or help us. At the same time, we all know there are forces beyond our influence that actually impose controls on us. One of those forces is technology, and if for some reason you haven't noticed, it is a train that is racing toward us with body-crushing velocity.

•   •   •

The negative attributes of control and ownership make them poverty's legs. They can carry people to places they don't want to be. And most of those who find themselves in these undesirable situations happen to be … women. Poor women make for a poor world, says the chief of the Inter-American Development Bank's Sustainable Development Department. She goes on to say:

> Because women are increasingly economic actors and
> heads of households as well as mothers, their poverty
> slows global economic growth. Moreover, in poor
> countries, their disadvantage feeds a destructive spiral of
> poverty, population growth, and environmental degra-
> dation. In a world of blurring borders, women's
> poverty creates enclaves of want in the midst of wealth
> and puts rising pressures on the developed world…[24]

Want to do something about global poverty? For starters, give women the freedom and tools to help themselves and their families. That means affording women a chance to read and write (for every 100 literate men in the world, there are only 74 literate women).[25] That means putting more girls in classrooms (in 1999, 77 million girls ages 6 to 11 were not in school compared with 52 million boys in the same age bracket).[26] That means extending to women the same rights and opportunities to own and control as are extended to men.

Part III

Hopelessness

CHAPTER 6

WIDENED SOCIETAL GAP

James Earl Carter Jr. got mixed reviews as America's 39th president, but as the nation's conscience, he has had far fewer critics. While in office, President Carter was hammered by an energy crisis, hostage takers in Iran, and runaway inflation. Campaigning for re-election, Carter painted a gloomy picture of what was going on in the world while his Republican opponent, Ronald Reagan, spoke of a new "morning in America." When the 1980 presidential ballots were counted, hope – not reality – won the day. Reagan collected 489 electoral votes while Carter's pessimistic platform was worth only 49. The embarrassing defeat sent the onetime fertilizer entrepreneur and peanut farmer back to Georgia, where most expected Carter would spend his involuntary retirement licking his wounds and fly-fishing. That didn't happen.

Unshackled from the presidency, Carter began stomping for human rights and the alleviation of human suffering. To this day, his message is candid and occasionally disquieting to those living in the world's lands of plenty. In a nutshell, Carter's headline is: "There's a growing disparity between rich and poor." That information is pretty much old news to most of the well-heeled people the ex-president bumps into on the lecture circuit. However, Carter's statistics, humility and passion have a way of getting under one's skin. He is still selling reality, and reality, it seems, is no prettier now than it was during the late '70s, when Carter lived in the White House. Here are a few of the statistics he tosses out to his audiences:

- Twenty percent of the world lives on a dollar a day or less.

- Three billion people live on $2 a day or less.

- While Norway spends 2.5 percent of its budget on foreign aid, the U.S. spends only about one-tenth of 1 percent on foreign aid.

"The United States is by far the stingiest nation on Earth."[1]
That statement, taken from Carter's standard speech, rarely fails to
hook the media. The ex-president complains that the nation's penny-
pinching attitude about foreign aid is "a problem the country has not
yet been willing to address." What's more, he adds from experience,
for anyone thinking about running for president in the U.S., tackling
the issue would be "political suicide."[2]

Jimmy Carter's platform is based on what his onetime speech-
writer Hendrick Hertzberg called a "moral ideology" rather than a
political philosophy.[3] However, even standing on what the former
president might think is the moral high ground, Carter has not been
immune from criticism. Some do not see the "wealth gap" as insidious – far from it. Take, for example, this comment from a speaker
taking part in a Cato Institute conference in Shanghai:

"Proposing to close the 'wealth gap' is worse than silly. It entails
a lie. The notion of economic equality is based on an ancient and ugly
falsehood central to bad economic thinking."[4]

While this is an interesting take on the wealth gap, the World Bank
views things differently. It is calling for global poverty to be cut in
half by 2015.[5] The bank says that 2.5 billion people lack access to
adequate energy supplies, and nearly a billion live in areas without
reliable roads.[6] The bank is worried that these infrastructure problems make it difficult for poor people to improve their economic condition. More discouraging is the bank's observation that private-sector
investments aimed at improving these infrastructure problems have
fallen off sharply in recent years.[7]

Even among economists who think the wealth gap should be
narrowed, there are differences of opinion as to what to do about the
problem. Could more foreign aid be the answer? Not everyone thinks
so. Peter Bauer, a professor emeritus at the London School of
Economics, contends that foreign aid "is demonstrably neither necessary nor sufficient to promote economic progress in the so-called
Third World and is indeed much more likely to inhibit economic
advance than it is to promote it."[8]

As the debate goes on about if and how developed countries
should address the wealth gap, that gap grows wider. While not often
mentioned as one of the causes, the human reproduction rate is part
of the problem. A surge of new births is projected for those countries
where a population overload only sustains or worsens poverty. The
Population Reference Bureau forecasts a 47 percent increase in the

world's population from 2001 to 2050 (see Chart 5).[9] If that projection holds, the population growth in less-developed nations will be *14 times greater*, on average, than growth in more-developed countries. What this will mean for certain already-impoverished countries is nothing short of disheartening: The population of Benin, in western Africa, is estimated to increase 174 percent over the next 50 years. Other projected increases in population are just as dramatic: Chad, 282 percent; Gambia, 195 percent; Liberia, 210 percent; Mali, 230 percent; Palestine Territory, 239 percent; Sierra Leone, 189 percent; Somalia, 240 percent; Yemen, 295 percent.

Chart 5

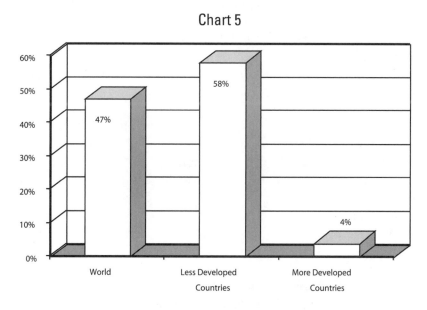

Projected Population Change, 2001-2050
Source: Population Reference Bureau

Population growth in these and other already-poor countries or regions is likely to create an even greater erosion of their fragile economic conditions. That fragility translates into serious issues for the multitudes of people who reside in these nations. Ownership and control tend to be elusive in a climate where personal income and spending power is so nominal that just surviving is a daily challenge. Along comes information technology with a salt-in-the-wound reminder that while these poor nations are going nowhere, the highly developed regions of the world are continuing to grow. This "rich get richer" sce-

nario results in an economic gap that is getting to look more and
more like a yawning fissure.

To grasp just how far apart poor nations are in comparison with
more-developed countries, do an analysis using per-capita gross national
incomes (GNI was formerly called gross national product). In 1999,
the GNI for the U.S. was $31,910. In Indonesia, it was $600; in
India, $440; in Nigeria, $260; in Ethiopia, $100. (All figures are in
U.S. dollars.)[10]

The economic spread between a poor country such as Ethiopia
and a wealthy nation like the U.S. is nearly impossible to comprehend. A child born in Ethiopia is destined to be 300 times worse off
economically than a child born and raised in North America. Could
things possibly get any worse for the Ethiopian infant? Probably. The
country is expected to increase its population by 164 percent over
the next 50 years. Unless an economic miracle occurs, by the time an
Ethiopian newborn of today reaches middle age, the gap could become
even wider.

Shortly after the September 11 terrorist incidents in America, the
International Herald Tribune polled opinion leaders in 24 countries
and found that the attacks were symptomatic of "an increasingly bitter polarization between the haves and have-nots."[11] Why should
those at the bottom of the world's economic heap be infected with
such an advanced case of negative envy, even as some Western economists see the economic disparity as normal? For people trapped in
developing nations, the answer can be delivered with a single word:
hopelessness.

In highly developed countries such as the U.S., there is a prevailing belief that with diligence and a little luck, typical workers can
inch their way up the economic ladder. In the land of opportunity,
that's not just dreaming – it's "doable." A U.S. Treasury Department
study tracked people in the bottom fifth of income earners and found
that 86 percent were actually able to improve their financial standings
over a nine-year period.[12] As one economist sees the results of the
study, income inequalities in America don't necessarily translate into
social inequities.[13] The same economist comes to this conclusion:

> The apostles of equality consider the rising inequality
> [a.k.a. the widening wealth gap in the U.S.] kindling for
> social unrest. But while that would be true if most
> workers on the bottom rungs were trapped there for
> generations, America isn't a caste society... Americans

have a remarkable ability to propel themselves upward.[14]

Some might argue that the significant wealth gap in the U.S. *is* firewood for at least a small percentage of America's "less fortunate" – after all, the pay gap between top executives and production workers grew from 42:1 in 1980 to 419:1 in 1998 – and that doesn't even include the value of stock options.[15] Nevertheless, even the country's poorest of the poor clearly have a higher "hope factor" than do most citizens of developing nations. Most low-income Americans can hope – even expect – to see their economic status get better over time. That is not the case in many developing nations. People clinging to the "bottom rungs" of economically depressed nations are likely to remain locked in place until the day they die. For most people trying to survive on $2 a day, there is little hope that things are going to change. Even more discouraging, the prospects for their offspring appear just as bleak and possibly even worse.

The societal gap gives us contrasts that border on the absurd. People who consistently go to bed hungry see or hear (compliments of information technology) reports about American gluttony. This is the information that gets passed along to individuals who have come to accept hunger as a way of life:

- One in four Americans is obese (30 or more pounds more than the norm), and 6 million Americans are clinically obese (100 or more pounds more than the norm).

- Some obesity can be blamed on genetics, but mostly people get fat because of too much food and too little exercise.

- Americans ingest 34 teaspoons of sugar a day, and eat three times as many starchy snacks as they did 10 years ago.

- People in the U.S. eat so much that their dinner plates have expanded in size from $10\frac{1}{2}$ inches to $12\frac{1}{2}$ inches.

- The daily caloric intake of an American has increased from 1,839 calories a decade ago to 2,200 calories today.[16]

To a near-starving villager in Asia, Africa or Latin America, this information can be maddening. Most of the more-developed countries have so much food that it boggles the mind. Example: the National Hot Dog and Sausage Council says that Americans eat *9 billion hot dogs a year*.[17] That is hard to believe if you are one of the 1.2 billion people in the world who have to make do with just 5 percent of all the meat and fish consumed on earth.[18]

Far-reaching information technology is giving the developing world the impression that on the lucky side of the widened societal gap are excesses galore. Those feelings explain why following the September 11 attacks, as Thomas Friedman of *The New York Times* put it, "millions of poor people gave passive support to those terrorists because they resented our greed."[19]

Given the width and depth of the worldwide societal gap, is there anything that can be done to either bridge the gap or at least narrow the distance from one side to the other? Billionaire George Soros has a few ideas that seem to be pointed in the right direction. In his book *On Globalization,* Soros thinks the traditional way of doling out foreign aid needs to be revamped.[20] Too many aid payments, he points out, are government-to-government exchanges fraught with all kinds of potential problems – not the least of which is a diversion of money into the wrong hands. Lack of coordination among the foreign aid payers and the bureaucracies that inevitably oversee these transactions are also problems that Soros thinks turn good intentions into poor investments.

When it comes to foreign aid, Soros knows something about what works and what doesn't. He is one of the world's most generous philanthropists, laying out about $500 million a year in support of programs and projects in 50 or more countries.[21] Soros recommends rich countries contribute to an International Monetary Fund-administered pool that will be used to underwrite development initiatives proposed by countries, nongovernmental organizations or both. What differentiates Soros' plan from traditional foreign aid schemes is that an eminent nonpartisan board would decide which proposals get the go-ahead. The Soros plan would allow funds to bypass the usual government channels that are, in his opinion, often plagued with problems. "The main cause of misery and poverty in the world is bad government," Soros told *The Wall Street Journal*.[22] For that reason, he excludes the World Bank from his plan since the bank's charter requires that it work through a country's government leaders.

The Soros proposal does something else: It gives "home grown" programs a better chance of getting financial support. Development ideas that bubble up from inside a country frequently will have a higher level of success than externally designed plans that are parachuted into a country.[23] This approach fits comfortably with recommendations that *How Women Can Beat Terrorism* spells out in Part VII ("The Solution").

The Soros strategy might also encourage an increase in international development funding. If that were to happen, the world would move a little closer to what the United Nations says is the amount of money needed to cut worldwide poverty in half – about $40 billion to $60 billion a year. Currently, the World Bank allocates about half that amount.[24]

A few public- and private-sector leaders also are pressing the more-developed world to deal differently with developing nations. One example: The French minister of economy, finance and industry has pushed hard for his country and other highly industrialized countries to transfer a larger share of their wealth to developing nations – and to come up with more-effective distribution strategies.[25]

Coming up with bold, new ways of helping developing nations is crucial. If the economic and societal gap continues to widen, a senior World Bank economist warns that 50 million reasonably well-to-do people at the top of the economic pile are going to have to protect themselves from 2.5 billion resentful poor people by taking refuge in well-guarded enclaves.[26]

Left unchanged, the "system" will continue to pump billions into old, often ineffective, development programs. While the intentions of organizations like the World Bank may be admirable (the World Bank president has urged wealthy nations to pledge that half of all new development aid go to Africa because of that continent's extraordinary needs[27]), the underlying strategies for narrowing the world's societal gaps may need some rethinking. Pouring more cash into sputtering economic-development programs isn't much different from pushing a car with a blown engine to a gas station and filling the tank with high-octane petrol.

Some experienced foreign-aid specialists think that all the major funding conduits to less-developed nations should be replaced. In addition to overhauling the International Monetary Fund and the World Trade Organization, this is what author David Korten says should happen to the World Bank:

> The World Bank should be closed. Its major function is
> to make loans to poor countries, which necessarily
> increases their international indebtedness. So long as
> the bank remains in business, southern economies will
> remain indebted to the international system. Creating
> indebtedness is not a useful function, and it is time to
> acknowledge that the World Bank was a bad idea.[28]

Even if the World Bank were to go away, every indicator tells us that solving the "gap predicament" is still going to require wealthy nations to supply more money. However, creative thinking and the boldness to try a few new ideas seem even more important than putting more hard currency on the table. The Soros plan (or some modification of the concept), for instance, may be worth a try, for it penetrates the top layers of poor countries and seeps into the ranks of the billions where hopelessness and negative envy are flourishing.

Whatever actions are taken, they should happen immediately. The chasm between the haves and have-nots is widening at an accelerated rate, thanks – at least in part – to information technology. A U.N. Human Development report concluded that the Internet is a factor in the growing separation of rich and poor, a division that the U.N. describes as "grotesque."[29]

Other technologies also are doing their part to put more distance between the well-off and the increasing numbers of poor people. The dizzying biotech field is a good example. The World Health Organization predicts that genetic research advances will only worsen the inequalities between rich and poor countries.[30] WHO notes that although there are likely to be major breakthroughs in the development of vaccines and drugs for malaria, AIDS, TB (and perhaps SARS), people who live in poor countries are going to have a hard time accessing these new treatments.[31] And that is yet another reason for more than half the people on earth to feel even more pangs of negative envy.

Six months before the September 11 attacks in America, *The Economist* ran an article by Robert Wade, a London School of Economics professor. Wade ended his piece with this warning:

> Growing inequality is analogous to global warming. Its
> effects are diffuse and long-term... The question is how
> much more unequal world income distribution can be
> before the resulting political instabilities and flows of
> migrants reach the point of directly harming the well-

being of the citizens of the rich world and the stability
of their states.[32]

A half year after Wade's words were published, terrorists added
a deadly exclamation point. True, they were not among the economically oppressed – none of them were struggling to make ends
meet on $2 a day. Nevertheless, their pent-up negative envy drove
them to carry out horrendous acts that exposed a vein of resentment
toward the U.S. and other more-developed nations. That vein runs
through much of the Muslim world as well as other economically or
socially repressed regions of the globe.

Like Jimmy Carter and Robert Wade, many politicians and economists have warned that the great societal gap is a fertile ground for
breeding bad feelings. The alarm had been largely unheeded – until
the morning of September 11. Today, more warning signals blare at
us. They remind us that seeds for catastrophe even more deadly than
the attacks on America are germinating in those deplorable conditions where more than half the world happens to live – conditions
that promise to get worse as populations expand.

Jimmy Carter is picking up allies as he pushes wealthy nations to
do more for the countries left behind. Even the "forget the rest of the
world" types appear worried that "disconnected capitalism" is putting
so much money into such few hands that we could be contributing
to a fragile house of cards. The media, like *The Christian Science
Monitor,* keep reminding the more-developed world that "trying to
root out terrorism without replowing the soil in which it grows –
which means rethinking the policies that breed anti-American senti-
ment – is unlikely to succeed."[33]

As politicians and thought-leaders continue to discuss what needs
to be done, the gap is still with us. Americans still eat their 25 pounds
of candy a year,[34] while hundreds of millions of people fall short of their
daily nutritional requirements. The 225 richest individuals on earth
continue to hold on to assets that are equal to the combined income
of 2.5 billion poor people.[35] And reproduction continues at a staggering rate on the side of the gap where life is the hardest. Remember:
Between now and 2030, more than 90 percent of the world's population growth will be in less-developed regions.[36]

The keepers of the "doomsday clock" state bluntly: "The growing disparities between rich and poor increase the potential for violence
and war."[37] If that isn't clear enough, they add these sobering thoughts:

Poverty and repression breed anger and desperation. Charismatic leaders with easy answers prey on the dispossessed and disaffected, channeling their anger into dangerous and destructive activities. The global community must recognize these facts and do much more to address them.[38]

Without a more effective economic intervention on the part of the developed world and a drastic reduction in the birth rates in poor countries, the have/have-not gap is going to get bigger, not smaller. Enlisting women to become more instrumental soldiers in the fight against poverty is one important way to turn things around.

CHAPTER 7

HOPELESSNESS AND HUMILIATION

Victims of hopelessness aren't just the billions of unfortunate people who have little or no hope. In today's world, with all its accessible and transportable lethal technologies, those of us living in prosperous countries can also get badly damaged by hopelessness. Why? Because hopelessness is an open wound inviting a kind of infection that can leap over oceans and national borders faster than SARS.

The classic Eric Hoffer book, *The True Believer,* includes this statement: "One of the most potent attractions of a mass movement is its offering of a substitute for individual hope."[1] If Hoffer is right, billions of people are susceptible to mass movements – especially religious or political movements – that use hope as a kind of societal flypaper. If those movements happen to jeopardize the safety and well-being of those endowed with hope, then hopelessness is the sharp side of the razor blade that, thanks to modern technology, can do us considerable harm.

This point is worth making again using different words. Just because we in the U.S., Western Europe and a few other highly developed nations are warm, comfortable and inundated with hope, that doesn't mean we should allow hopelessness in the rest of the world to go unattended. We do so at our own peril.

How Women Can Beat Terrorism contends that if poor people are given a greater ability to own and control, poverty is abated and hopelessness subsides. Turkey's best-selling novelist, Orhan Pamuk, sees it differently. To him, it's humiliation that is at the root of much upheaval in Third World countries and contributes mightily to hopelessness:

> Today, an ordinary citizen of a poor, undemocratic
> Muslim country, or a civil servant in a Third World
> country or in a former socialist republic struggling to
> make ends meet, is aware of how insubstantial is his
> share of the world's wealth... At the same time, how-
> ever, he senses in a corner of his mind that his poverty is
> to some considerable degree the fault of his own folly

and inadequacy, or those of his father and grandfather. The Western world is scarcely aware of this overwhelming feeling of humiliation that is experienced by most of the world's population.[2]

Islam or other organized movements may offer, as Hoffer argues, an alternative to humiliation, a substitute for hope. However, that humiliation would not be as pronounced, or perhaps it would not even be an issue, if poor people were on the road to greater ownership and more control of their lives.

Frankly, some poor nations *should* feel humiliated – not because of their worldwide economic ranking but because they have deliberately quashed a resource that could have lessened poverty and reduced hopelessness. The resource? Women.

A great story about how women can displace hopelessness with hope was folded into a speech that CARE President Peter Bell gave at Princeton University. Bell reflected on a visit he had made to Tanzania, where he toured a project called "Hujakwama," which in Swahili means, "You are not stuck."[3] The CARE initiative, which helped Tanzanian women gain access to better education and health care, gave these women more *control* of their lives. Hujakawama ultimately equipped women to take full advantage of income-generating opportunities. For more than 1,200 women, the project has yanked them free of the hopelessness that affects billions of people in hard-pressed parts of the world.

We need a lot more Hujakwama projects. We need to unstick women from those social systems that make them feel hopeless. By doing so, we move a step closer toward easing worldwide poverty and away from gender discrimination that is not only unproductive but also humiliating.

PART IV

POPULATION GROWTH

(IN POPULATION-STRESSED LOCATIONS)

CHAPTER 8

INTRODUCTION

Some experts say that population growth is a major concern. And other experts insist it is not.

Who's right?

Part IV of *How Women Can Beat Terrorism* attempts to find out by looking at the impact that population growth has on:

- Land and its capacity to produce food

- Water

- Air

- Homo sapiens

This analysis is important because it will help determine whether population growth is a serious problem in certain regions of the world and, in turn, whether there is a need to push for lower reproduction rates in those regions. *How Women Can Beat Terrorism* contends that lowering birth rates in economically-stressed countries is essential. Is such a step really that important? Or is population growth not that big a deal? Or is it possible that this a far more universal problem – one that goes way beyond making life more difficult just for those countries wallowing in poverty?

I decided that I could best scrutinize the population issue by slicing it in half. First, I would determine if population growth is destroying our land, water and air – and figure out whether it represents a threat to everyone on earth no matter how rich or poor they happen to be. Second, I would examine whether population growth in some parts of the world pits man against man in such a way that the odds for violence (including terrorism) are increased.

Ironically, I began part one of this exercise – examining what impact population growth has on the environment – while snarled in a traffic jam. Brought to a dead stop thanks to the usual 8 a.m. rush-hour madness, I tried to keep my road rage under control by thumbing through a printout of a U.S. Environmental Protection Agency report on urban sprawl.[1] The federal government confirmed my worst notions about how population expansion is ruining our quality of life and befouling our natural resources. Here is what the EPA says about the environmental consequences of sprawl:

- Air pollution – sprawl forces us to drive cars longer distances and, therefore, causes an increase in greenhouse gases.

- Water pollution – by converting agricultural or natural land to residential, industrial or commercial use, the quality of ground and surface water is threatened by a destruction of wetlands, urban runoff and soil erosion.

- Loss of natural areas – sprawl can destroy or degrade natural ecosystems and species.

Still gridlocked in traffic and sucking in car-exhaust pathogens like carbon monoxide, nitrogen dioxide and sulfur dioxide, I flipped to another clip in my *How Women Can Beat Terrorism* file. It was a 1998 article by Jerry Brown, the former governor of California and now mayor of Oakland, California. This is how it began:

"Human beings and the natural world are on a collision course." That was the apocalyptic warning uttered in 1992 by some 1,700 scientists from 69 countries, including 99 of the 196 living Nobel laureates. Tragically, no one with any power is listening. In the ensuing five years, corporate managers and political officials have only accelerated their massive tampering with the world's interdependent web of life.[2]

I glanced out my car window and thought that Mayor Moonbeam, as Brown has been called, could be right on. Aside from a sickly patch of grass and one spindly tree, the view was all tar, cement and an endless line of gas-guzzling conveyances.

By the time I arrived at my office, 10 minutes late, I came to understand why a book called *The Limits to Growth: A Report for the Club of Rome's Project on the Predicament of Mankind* had sold 12 million copies since it was released in 1972. The book, no longer in print, was translated into 37 languages and did a good job of scaring the world.[3] The publication didn't exactly predict that mankind was on the brink of extinction, but it did contend that if the world's consumption patterns and population growth continued at the rates recorded in the early '70s, the earth would be in deep trouble within a century.

While *Limits to Growth* was hailed in some quarters, it was also debunked in others. "Alarmist and pessimistic" were typical criticisms. The Club of Rome – a think tank of scientists, economists, businesspeople, civil servants and politicians from five continents – was accused of overlooking how new technology could be used to stave off starvation, environmental degradation and economic chaos.

Sure enough: Some of the projections in *Limits to Growth* have proved to be way off the mark. Still, one of the members of the club, Keith Suter, maintained in 1999 that the underlying warning in *Limits to Growth* remains valid.[4] He pointed out that the economic development of the Third World is exacting a huge toll on the environment. He also stated that First World countries haven't done much to make things better. Since 1972, industrialized nations have gotten richer, but they also have gotten meaner, he said. First World countries talk about "wealth creation" as the pathway to sustainable development in lesser-developed nations; however, the foreign aid that is often the stimulus to wealth creation has been cut back drastically by the United States and other rich countries.

I looked out my office window and felt certain that a dark cloud was, in fact, on the horizon.

Then I had a mood-altering experience as I looked at a book sitting on my desk. *The Skeptical Environmentalist* is the product of a self-proclaimed "old left-wing Greenpeace member" named Bjorn Lomborg.[5] A couple of clarifying notes. First, Lomborg, who is a statistics professor at the University of Aarhus, in Denmark, is not that old. Second, if he ever had a left wing, it certainly must have fallen off before this book was published in 2001.

The Skeptical Environmentalist attacks what it calls the "litany" of misconceptions about mankind's relationship with the environment. The book says we have been led to believe that:

- Our resources are running out.

- The population is ever growing, thereby straining food supplies.

- Air and water are becoming increasingly polluted.
- The planet's species are becoming extinct in vast numbers.
- Forests are disappearing.
- Fish stocks are collapsing.
- Coral reefs are dying.
- Fertile topsoil is disappearing.
- Nature is being paved over.
- Our wilderness is being ruined.
- The world's ecosystem is breaking down.

Things are worse than I thought, I told myself when thumbing through Lomborg's preface. Then the author turns things around with this staggering pronouncement: "We know the Litany and have heard it so often that yet another repetition is, well, almost reassuring. There is just one problem: It does not seem to be backed up by the available evidence."[6] Over some 500 pages (including 2,930 endnotes and a lengthy bibliography), Lomborg pokes holes in the Litany's contentions, which he maintains are not in step with reality. He says we're *not* running out of energy or natural resources. The percentage of people in the world who are starving is *less* than in the past. Global warming is *not* a big deal. Acid rain *isn't* decimating our forests. Water is becoming *less* polluted. These revelations bring him to this conclusion:

Mankind's lot has actually improved in terms of practically every measurable indicator.[7]

No wonder one book reviewer commented that there is no dirtier word ricocheting around the environmental world these days than "Lomborg."[8]

Curious about Lomborg's thinking, I clawed my way through piles of data and projections to see if there were others who shared his point of view. There are. Witness this editorial comment in the *Orange County* (California) *Register*:

OVERPOPULATION IS A CROCK
POPULATION EXPLOSION NOW A BIRTH DEARTH

The idea that unbridled population growth will lead to environmental and social disasters as the world meets its "carrying capacity" is a holy cannon of the environmental movement. Yet increasing evidence, including a new study released in Nature magazine this month, is painting a starkly different picture. Rather than continue to increase, world population is likely to stabilize at about nine billion in 2070 and begin declining from there, according to researchers in Austria.

In Europe, a "birth dearth" is threatening not only long-term population declines, but the viability of European economies. Without replacement levels of population, there are too few people to pay for the generous pension plans typical there. Sure, population rates are still high in poor countries, but as countries develop and become more prosperous, birthrates will fall dramatically in those countries as well.[9]

This editorial may appear hard-line, but it is tepid compared with the views of others who are quick to go after "dangerous environmentalists." Michael Berliner was the former head of the Ayn Rand Institute in Marina del Rey, California. These are his words:

Environmentalism is fundamentally anti-man... To save mankind requires the wholesale rejection of environmentalism as hatred of science, technology, progress and human life...[10]

Maybe these people are right, I thought, as I perused a publication from the National Center for Public Policy Analysis, which informed me that urban sprawl "poses no threat" to open spaces in the U.S.[11] We just *think* there's sprawl because 75 percent of the U.S. population lives on just 3.5 percent of the land. Actually, the center says, more than 95 percent of land in the U.S. remains undeveloped.[12]

All this new information started to convince me that a hefty percentage of the world's population is being deceived by a bunch of eco-kooks. I kicked myself for being among the deceived until I came across several articles that challenged *The Skeptical Environmentalist*. One of those critical of Bjorn Lomborg, for instance, is Tom Burke, a government and private-sector environmental adviser who wrote:

> [Lomborg] exaggerates for effect, substitutes forceful assertion for weight of argument, sometimes makes sweeping generalizations from particular instances, veers between the uncertain and the inconsistent in his use of logic, presents false choices and is highly selective in his use of evidence and quotation.[13]

Once again, I felt myself being pulled back to the "we're going to hell in a hand basket" crowd, especially when I read a statement from a nonprofit organization called the Overpopulation Group:

> Beyond a doubt, Man alone is responsible for … the greenhouse effect, oceanic breakdown and climatic changes on Earth – the larger the human population on Earth, the worse everything becomes…
> Unquestionably, the overpopulation problem on Earth is responsible for all the ills that now face humanity and the environment.[14]

I came to the uncomfortable realization that I was stymied. I didn't have a clue as to who was right and who was trying to deceive me.

Then, as if I weren't confused enough, I leafed through another file stuffed with statements and articles arguing that while population growth might create problems for the environment, it is a condition that is much more likely to set man against man in a deadly duel. In other words, even if mankind and the environment find ways to coexist, areas that are both heavily populated and economically depressed face even more hazardous situations if their populations were to increase.

Before mapping out a plan for engaging women in a campaign against poverty and hopelessness – my line of defense against terrorism – I needed to bring some clarity to these issues. Part IV is my attempt to do just that. I have tried to make each of the following chapters as fair and balanced as possible. Somehow, I suspect there will be those proselytizers and protesters who will think I have not tried hard enough. In any case, proceed with an open mind as best you can.

CHAPTER 9

PEOPLE AND LAND

Because each day we have thousands of more people to feed, and yet only 12 percent of the earth's landmass is suitable for agricultural and horticultural purposes, it wasn't a surprise when in early 2001 the U.N.'s Food and Agriculture Organization (FAO) said:

FOOD SHORTAGES IMPERIL 3 MILLION IN SOUTHERN SUDAN

Over 3 million people in southern Sudan are facing serious food shortages due to ongoing civil conflict and an emerging drought... Poor harvests have affected around 900,000 people, with 600,000 in need of urgent food assistance...[1]

Well, maybe it *would have been* a surprise if we had been reading *The Skeptical Environmentalist*, which reminds us that "globally, the proportion of people starving has fallen from 35 percent to 18 percent and is expected to fall further to 12 percent in 2010."[2] (The U.N. defines a "starving" person as someone who does not get sufficient food to perform light physical work.) Indeed, despite that U.N. announcement about Sudan, things are a whole lot better than they were in 1949, when a staggering 45 percent of people living in developing countries were not getting enough food.[3]

One reason starvation isn't as pervasive today is because the world has seen an impressive increase in crop yields, thanks largely to technology. It seems we have a lot of food in the world – so much food, in fact, that there have been occasions when we have amassed huge surpluses of grain in one location while people die from hunger in another. A writer in India put it this way:

The total quantity of food grains with the public sector (in India) has soared ... in June 2001... The output of food grains for 2001-2002 has set an all-time record... On the other hand, India continues to be home to the largest absolute number of underfed and undernourished people in the world. Thus, semi-starvation and undernourishment coexist with the mountain of the so-called "surplus" food grains. How does one explain the paradox?[4]

A California study found that food represented a high percentage of waste – especially in the restaurant and food store categories.[5] Approximately 840,000 tons of food ended up in the state's waste stream during just one year (1999).

Chart 6

Restaurants	56.0%
Food Stores	39.8%
Medical/Health	12.1%
Schools	20.0%
Hotels/Lodging	28.0%
Residential	20.0%

Food Waste
(Percentage by Sector in State of California)
Source: California Integrated Waste Management Board, 2001

It can be argued that we really don't have a food-shortage problem at all. Starvation and malnourishment are really the result of poverty (people can't afford to buy what's available), disruption of the food-distribution chain (war, corruption), waste (we throw out a *lot* of food that could be redirected to those who are hungry – see Chart 6) and a relief system that just can't connect hungry people with available food supplies. All we need to do is to design and implement a better system of getting existing food into the mouths of people who need it. However, we also need to give some thought to the consequences of just throwing free food at those who are starving or underfed. An article in an International Monetary Fund publication raised this red flag:

> Food production is not keeping pace with Africa's rapidly growing needs... At the start of this new century, Africa is even more dependent on food aid than it was 35 years ago... Not only have they [African countries] become dependent on foreign aid, but their increasing

food bill has become a serious budgetary and political obstacle to progress and growth.[6]

Putting together a system for dealing with the world's food crisis won't be easy, but at least we now have a handle on what the problem really is. Or do we? Is it true that there is and will be enough food to feed humanity, even taking into account that the world's population is expanding by 210,000 people each day? Here is what a biologist at University College in London (who is pushing for the genetic modification of certain crops to increase food supplies) has to say:

> There are those ... who think that there is no real food shortage in the world, and that famine and hunger are due to grossly unfair distribution of food, and to war. But the best estimates are that the world's population will increase from 6 billion to 9 billion in the next 25 years, which will require food production almost to double... One estimate from China is that by the year 2020, China will want to import the whole of the United States' grain production for its own use.[7]

Here we are back in that quagmire of mixed opinion. Do we actually have a current or potential food shortage? Is it essentially a matter of getting food that exists to people who are going hungry? Or are we faced with both problems?

The issues are confounding. We literally live off the land. We are dependent on the right kind of land for crop and livestock production. We dig in the land for natural resources, such as oil, coal, aluminum and iron, that are vital to our quality of life. The land plays host to nearly 90,000 species of vertebrates, 250,000 plant species and a million species of insects.[8] As important as land is, you might think there is – or at least should be – a consensus on where we stand, so to speak, on *terra firma*. Well, there isn't. Some people tell us we are callously stripping the land, exterminating species and over-consuming irreplaceable resources. Others refute these claims with data that show we are actually reasonable stewards of the land. What's the truth?

Perhaps the following scenario and analyses will help clarify things. Imagine, if you will, that Earth is a patient and is put through a routine exam by two land specialists, whom we call "A" and "B." Both specialists have respectable credentials, and both concur that the patient, Earth, is 71 percent water and 29 percent land.[9] From that point on, however, the opinions of the specialists diverge. Here are the status reports by those specialists on the health and well-being of Earth's water-free crust, along with notations by a case manager who reviewed the files:

Patient: Earth

Land Examination Results

Exam Category #1: Food Production

Specialist A:

Earth's land is producing more food for more people than ever before. Not only is the number of malnourished humans going down, but also food production is only going to improve over the next three decades.

I concur with the Skeptical Environmentalist, who says:

All the studies from FAO, IFPRI, USDA and the World Bank show that there is no imminent agricultural crisis or any approaching scarcity of food. Food will be cheaper and ever more people will be able to consume more and better food.[10]

Even though the world's population has steadily grown, the number of chronically malnourished people fell from 918 million in 1970 to 826 million in 1999.[11] We've got scientists developing vitamin-fortified rice that could prevent millions of premature childhood deaths each year.[12] Global meat production has been on the rise for more than 40 consecutive years.[13] The bottom line: The food supply per person is steadily increasing. Nothing to worry about.

Specialist B:

Specialist A is overlooking a critical point.

Granted, the "green revolution" in places like the United States has resulted in an extraordinary increase in food production. In the U.S., we use less than half the land for farming now than we did in the 1920s, and yet we produce far more food than we did 80 years ago.[14] And, yes, the Skeptical Environmentalist is right when he points out that the cost of food in 2000 is less than a third of the cost in 1957.[15] However, all of that good news means nothing to the hundreds of millions of people who, for a variety of reasons, can't get enough food to eat.

Let's not fool ourselves. There are regions of the world where food scarcity is a huge problem. In India, *53 percent* of all children are undernourished. In Bangladesh, the number is higher – 56 percent.[16] Ethiopia, Nigeria, the Indian subcontinent – these and many other regions of the world are all places where the right kind of food is difficult and sometimes impossible to obtain. These are locations where people not only get hungry, but they can also get angry and resentful. These are conditions that can cause serious problems on Earth.

I think the Worldwatch Institute is on the mark when it says "malnutrition is largely the result of rural poverty," and then reminds us that the world's poor live in places where "poverty and population growth are reinforcing each other."[17] Those places include the Indian subcontinent, whose annual number of births exceeds the total population of Australia.[18]   Just because some nations – especially more-developed countries – are producing greater quantities of food does not mean hunger and malnutrition are going to disappear. If worldwide population growth were stable, we would stand a better chance of figuring out how to produce and distribute food in a way that would guarantee adequate food supplies to most everyone on the globe. But with more and more people being added to countries already feeling the effects of hunger, that's going to be hard to do.

Case Manager Notes:

Science and technology seem to be in a position to increase plant yields sufficiently to meet human caloric requirements (at least for the near future). This is especially true if the world gets serious about genetically modified (GM) foods, or what critics refer to as "Frankenfoods." Assuming public perceptions about GM foods improve,[19] Earth could be producing a lot more of these products – including nutritionally rich products like golden rice, which is loaded with vitamin A.[20] This will only happen, of course, if GM foods don't prove to be either toxic or allergenic (the two major concerns).

Still, even if mankind gets more good food from each hectare planted than was possible in the past, that doesn't mean all people on Earth are going to be fed properly. In other words, as Specialist B points out, adequate food production doesn't equate to the elimination of hunger on Earth. It does seem that unless population growth is curbed in places where the human census already exceeds the "carrying capabilities" of the land, then there will be vast pockets of malnourished people – even the Skeptical Environmentalist admits that in the year 2010, according to his estimates, Earth will have 680 million starving people.[21] If Specialist B is right and we determine that these hunger pockets are breeding grounds for trouble (terrorism, for instance), then hunger may be only symptomatic of a much more serious ailment on Earth.

Thus, Specialist A is probably correct when she says that Earth can generate enough food for a much larger number of people. However, Specialist B is accurate when he says the issue is not food *production* – it's *hunger*. Both specialists agree that there are a lot of hungry people on Earth. And hunger, it seems, could be a precursor to other serious mankind-induced problems.

It could be that contraceptive use should be elevated to the same level of importance as food production and distribution if Earth is to have a decent chance of getting its arms around the worldwide hunger problem.

Exam Category #2: Erosion

Specialist A:

Those people who get exercised about how Earth is losing its topsoil and then claim that such a loss is going to cramp our ability to grow food are having an anxiety attack for no good reason. There is no denying that erosion exists. However, it has not been a significant problem. In the U.S., to cite just one example, erosion affects about 12 tons of topsoil per hectare.[22] However, the term "erosion" often conjures up an erroneous picture – the image of valuable land being washed away, never to be seen again. In reality, erosion is often just another word for soil transportation – dirt is moved from one location and deposited in another. In other words, "farmable" soil isn't lost at all. It just moves around on occasion.

Keep this in mind: The United Nations' Food and Agricultural Organization has pointed out that there is no clear tie-in between erosion and crop yields.[23] Thanks to irrigation, pesticides and fertilization, degraded soil can be revitalized for farming purposes. Once again, science and technology are ahead of the curve and, at least in more-developed nations, what little erosion occurs will be more than offset by mankind's ability to extract greater yields from the land.

Erosion is a non-issue for Earth.

Specialist B:

A non-issue? When it comes to erosion, Specialist A has her head in the sand – or, more to the point, nutrient-depleted topsoil.

The U.N.'s Food and Agricultural Organization (FAO) says it is a *big* problem. Soil fertility declined by about 13 percent between 1945 and 1990, the FAO says, and the situation is far worse in places like Central America and Africa.[24] Wind and water erosion are destroying vast expanses of land.

While industrialized countries may be in a position to protect or reclaim land threatened by erosion, that is not the case in less-developed locations. Two-thirds of Africans rely on agriculture for their existence. The International Food Policy Research Institute says, "Farmers are intensifying land use to meet food needs without proper management practices and external inputs."[25] The result is a soil-nutrient imbalance that is most serious in parts of the continent (notably the East African highlands) where there is significant erosion and where fertilizer doesn't get used properly or at all.

Even in parts of Europe, erosion is a serious concern. The European Conservation Agriculture Federation (ECAF) points out that crop yields in eroded soils are lower than those in protected soils. "In some locations, crop yields on severely eroded soils were 9 percent to 34 percent lower than those on slightly eroded soil," ECAF states.[26] The organization makes this damning comment about erosion:

> The use of large amounts of fertilizers, pesticides and irrigation help to offset the deleterious effects of erosion but in themselves have the potential to create pollution and health problems, destroy natural habitats, and contribute to high energy consumption and unsustainable agricultural systems. In fact, the effect of erosion is to increase agricultural production costs by 25 percent each year.[27]

Clearly, erosion *is* a problem for Earth.

Case Manager Notes:

This seems to be a case where both specialists are right. Because of the incredible food-producing power of places like the United States and a few other industrialized countries, crops are being grown in such abundance that they compensate for the poor yields (often caused at least in part by erosion) in other parts of the world.

Assuming the problem can't be solved in the short term by educating farmers in every developing nation about how to protect and increase the productivity of soil, then we have to circle back to *distribution* as the way to get food to the people who need it. The point has already been made: There seems to be enough food out there. And yet, large numbers of people still aren't eating enough or hardly at all.

Erosion does seem to be a problem in places where population growth is like a fertilizer to poverty. Logic says that if we expect poor developing regions to create food supplies sufficient to feed those who live in those locations (which most countries would agree is a desirable objective), then decent soil is a necessity. But protecting or revitalizing that soil is easier said than done when more and more people make such excessive demands on whatever arable land is still available. In some spots around the globe, the benefits that come from science and technology can't seem to catch up to the rapid human reproduction rate.

A postscript. Consider how women could be more instrumental in fixing the problem of erosion in poor localities. They are often the labor force for small-scale farming enterprises. If educated about soil problems and equipped with resources to do something about those problems, women could prove to be valuable land managers.

Exam Category #3: Forests

Specialist A:

Earth is under attack by misinformed extremists who try to paint certain corporations as tree-hating monsters intent on ripping up every sapling they can lay their profit-making paws on. Here is an Internet report from the Coastal Rainforest Coalition that goes after Staples, the office-products company, with a hatchet:

STAPLES DESTROYS FORESTS

Staples is the largest and fastest growing office super store in the world ... during 1999, Staples opened its 1,000th store and in a single day opened 22 retail stores. As the number of Staples stores increases, so does the number of forests destroyed ... Staples' sale of paper is driving the destruction of our endangered forests worldwide...[28]

Now let's take a dose of truth serum. The fact is, the entire worldwide consumption of wood *and* paper can be satisfied by just 5 percent of the current forest cover on Earth.[29] That may sound excessive, but remember that a lot of our paper and wood comes from reforested areas and tree plantations around the globe. About a third of the world's land mass is covered by forests, *and that figure has not changed a lot since World War II.*[30]

All this huffing and puffing about corporations denuding forests; the ranting and raving about rain forests being chopped to pieces; the nonsense about mankind cutting down Earth's "lungs" – this kind of hoopla is out-of-context gibberish that is needlessly getting people upset.

Specialist B:

My learned co-professional, Specialist A, throws a few isolated statistics at a problem and tries to make it go away. Well, no matter how she twists numbers, the problem is still with us. Focus on this:

> The combination of population growth and deforestation ... has cut the number of hectares of forest per person in half since 1960.[31]

What this has done is to put pressure on what remains of "old growth" forests. Tree farming only goes so far in limiting the destruction of these woodlands. Keep in mind that tree plantations account for only 0.5 percent of the world's forested lands.[32]

Old-growth forests are disappearing faster than they can be replaced with second-growth forests. That is particularly true in regions of Latin America, Africa and Asia. Deforestation diminishes biodiversity, increases the risks of erosion and reduces the uptake of carbon dioxide.[33] Population growth, excessive consumerism and unnecessary waste are causing our old forests to be chewed up. These are concerns for Earth.

To underscore these points, look at Indonesia. A report published by the World Resources Institute, Global Forest Watch and Forest Watch Indonesia confirms that corruption and lawlessness have resulted in an epidemic of illegal logging in the country.[34] The result? The country is losing nearly 2 million hectares of forest each year – double the annual deforestation rate in the 1980s. Indonesia is expected to add another 70 million people to its population between now and 2030.[35] What do you think that population growth is going to do to the world's third-largest contiguous area of tropical forest?

Case Manager Notes:

Like it or not, industrial tree plantations are a trend. As Specialist B points out, these plantations make up less than 1 percent of all forested land, but we get 22 percent of our timber and pulp from these places and 16 percent of the fiber used to make paper.[36]

The problem with plantations is that they are not the total answer to worldwide deforestation. Common sense says that animal species living in old-growth forests are not always replicated in plantations, especially when plantation trees are regularly harvested. Perhaps the greatest concern for Earth is that deforestation in those pockets of the world that are economically deprived often seems to make things worse for people living in those areas. The absence of trees sometimes exposes humans to greater danger from such natural disasters as erosion, which ruins the soil needed to raise crops.

The situation in Indonesia is not pretty. However, 98 million hectares of forest still cover parts of the country.[37] That's not to say something shouldn't be done to replant denuded areas or enforce sensible logging rules. Admittedly, these steps would be easier to accept if the country's population growth were to slow down. One of the solutions to the deforestation problem might be to find a way to curb human reproduction in the country.

Overall, deforestation does not seem to be quite as bad as some headlines make it out to be. But it is still an issue for Earth, and it needs monitoring as population growth continues.

Exam Category #4: Oil, Gas and Coal

Specialist A:

Until alternative energy sources are able to meet our needs, Earth is going to provide us with enough oil, gas and coal. More than enough.

There is a saying that goes, *The Stone Age did not end because there was a lack of stones, and the oil age will end, but it won't end because of a lack of oil.*[38] Earth has an ample supply of fossil fuels that will carry us through the day when other energy-producing systems will take over from oil, gas and coal. Once again, the hullabaloo over the alleged scarcity of fossil fuels is much ado about nearly nothing.

How can we be so sure that we can pump and dig enough fuel from the Earth to keep our worldwide economic engines humming? For at least two reasons:

First, vast amounts of oil and coal have yet to be extracted from the Earth. Places like China, India, the former Soviet Union and, yes, the United States have incredible amounts of coal at their disposal. Coal accounts for about 36 percent of all electric power generated worldwide, but we could produce much more low-cost coal-generated electricity if needed.[39] And even if we were to stop looking for new sources of oil, we have reserves for another 47 years.[40] In addition, the U.S. Geological Survey thinks there is another 530 billion barrels of oil yet to be found.[41]   Second, *technology* is enabling us to do a lot better job of tapping the full potential of coal, oil and gas. Here's just one of many examples: The typical car in the U.S. has improved its mileage by 60 percent since 1973.[42] So not only is there much more fossil fuel available to us than many environmentalists have led us to believe, but we are also squeezing out more and more energy from these fuels.

By 2030, we are going to see alternative energy systems come on line – fusion technology, for instance, which creates energy the same way the sun generates heat and light.[43] Between now and then, Earth has far more than enough fossil fuels to supply all of mankind's energy needs.

Specialist B:

The issue is not whether we have enough hydrocarbon fuels but rather what damage is being done to the environment as an ever-expanding human population uses these sources of energy. The American Petroleum Institute says that economically feasible ways of extracting and refining oil could extend the supply of that fuel for "hundreds of years."[44] Assume that statement is correct – what would that mean to Earth, whose atmosphere is already having trouble coping with greenhouse gases emitted primarily from hydrocarbon fuels?

The world is currently dependent on oil for nearly 38 percent of its energy needs.[45] Gas and coal each account for 21 percent of our energy needs.[46] While the future may bring us all sorts of new and renewable energy sources, those alternatives may not come on line as quickly as planned. In the meantime, the world's population increases, and every day the emissions from fossil fuels add to our environmental problems.

Humans use a phenomenal amount of oil and gas – about 40 *billion* barrels each year.[47] And because coal is a relatively cheap way to generate electricity, its use is expanding (not as a percentage of total energy production but in real volume).[48] In spite of improved methods of preventing hydrocarbon emissions from damaging the air, the increased use of oil, gas and coal is creating serious problems for Earth.

Just to be sure this point is clear, look at what comes out of a coal-fueled electric power plant smokestack: carbon dioxide, carbon monoxide, sulfur dioxide, nitrous oxides and other particulates.[49] Coal producers and users will argue that flue gas scrubbers can filter out most of these exhaust gases. Maybe that is true in industrialized nations where state-of-the-art equipment is available (and often mandated by government-imposed regulations or incentives). However, in less-developed countries, coal-burning furnaces are pumping a lot of harmful substances into the air.

Case Manager Notes:

All land specialists agree that oil, gas and coal reserves are finite – if civilization lasts long enough, mankind will eventually run out of these fuels. However, it doesn't seem that this is going to happen for a long time. Thus, given the human proclivity for paying attention to the "now" and not the "later," any campaign aimed at convincing people to "conserve oil, gas and coal" for the sake of saving those resources for later generations is probably pointless.

What about the arguments that we should move away from fossil fuels as quickly as possible because they are raising havoc with the atmosphere? Those warnings often get run over by the auto industry's claims that exhaust emissions are less problematic than ever and the electricity industry's reassurance that it has cleaned up its emissions act. People hear what they want to hear. When the U.S. Environmental Protection Agency says that vehicles produced in the United Sates have been spewing out fewer emissions since the country's Clean Air Act was passed in 1970, the public thinks, "Terrific!"[50] Drivers rarely stick around to listen to what else the EPA has to say about emissions: Since 1970, "the number of miles driven has more than doubled – the increase in travel has offset much of the emission-control progress."[51]

Because fuel is so plentiful (the U.S. Department of Energy notes that the world uses enough oil every year to fill a lake 10 miles long, 9 miles wide and 60 feet deep),[52] and because the harmful effects of using that fuel are largely ignored, shouting about the need to curtail fossil-fuel usage is futile.

Like other land concerns that Earth faces, it is fossil-fuel *distribution* that constitutes a problem. This is just not an issue for developing nations, many of which rely heavily on fuel imports to keep their economies going. It is also a huge concern for countries like the U.S. that depend on oil imports for much of their needs. In turn, the emphasis on every fuel-importing nation tends to be more on accessing fossil fuels than on reducing a dependency on the fuels.

One other point: Some experts predict that oil shortages will become a way of life in about six years. One of those people is Princeton University's Kenneth Deffeyes, who warns that new oil reserves are getting harder to find (for every 10 attempts to drill for oil, nine fail) and even those that are discovered are likely to be less productive than many think.[53] This may accelerate the push for alternate fuels, like using hydrogen as an energy source after extracting it from water.[54] Population expansion triggers added energy consumption. Clothes, food, transportation, housing – all of these things directly or indirectly devour energy, much of which comes from oil, gas or coal. With the greatest population expansion taking place in developing nations, will energy production be able to keep pace? Or will energy remain one of the commodities that is overly accessible to more-developed countries and economically out of reach for much of the developing world? It could be that Earth does indeed have enough oil, gas and coal for the short term. However, that doesn't mean these natural resources won't ultimately contribute to other problems on Earth. When energy doesn't flow to all energy-dependent parts of the globe – particularly those with growing populations – Earth might find itself in a great deal of discomfort.

Exam Category #5: Nonenergy Resources (Metals, Cement)
Specialist A:

Let's start with cement. We use a lot of it (around 1.5 *billion* tons a year).[55] Earth has such a huge supply of limestone and sand that we could go on making cement for another thousand years.[56]

As for other metals, we have ample supplies. Aluminum, iron, copper, zinc – not only can we easily produce enough of these metals to meet our consumption levels, but we also keep finding new sources. Sure, metals like gold and silver may not be as abundant, but demand for these metals has been waning, which means our needs can easily be met.[57]

Manufacturing technologies have also helped us produce more product with less metal. Take aluminum, for instance. To make 1,000 cans in 1963, it took 54.8 pounds of aluminum, whereas today we need just 33 pounds.[58]

This is another non-issue as far as Earth's condition is concerned. The Skeptical Environmentalist was right when he said that any significant scarcity of nonenergy resources is unlikely "because we continuously find new resources, use them more efficiently, and are able to recycle them and substitute them."[59]

Specialist B:

It is hard to get a feeling for what a forest looks like if you're only shown a few trees. When doing a checkup of the Earth's nonenergy resources, we can't just focus only on raw materials that can be, or have been, extracted. There are other issues that need to be examined in order for us to get a complete X-ray of Earth's condition.

Converting metals and cement into usable products takes energy. In some cases, a *lot* of energy. The production process also often creates water and air pollution. Even the Skeptical Environmentalist concedes that cement production accounts for about 3 percent of the global carbon-dioxide emissions.[60] And as for nonrecycled metals and materials, they have a hefty impact on waste streams around the world.

Since Specialist A has singled out aluminum, let's take a closer look at this metal. It takes about four pounds of bauxite to produce a pound of aluminum. Making a single aluminum can consumes the same amount of energy as a 100-watt bulb that stays lit for four hours. In 1998, 102 billion cans were manufactured in the U.S.,[61] where, according to the U.S. Department of Energy, only about half the aluminum-industry facilities conduct energy-management activities.[62] Do the math: Aluminum cans eat up a *lot* of energy.

In fairness, aluminum cans are the most recycled product in the United States – aluminum manufacturers reuse 63 percent of all cans, and less energy is needed to produce new products when recycled materials are available.[63] Still, more than 14,000 aluminum containers end up in U.S. landfills *every hour*.[64]

Consider what all this means as we increase the number of people living on Earth. The more humans, the more demand for nonenergy resources. The more nonenergy resources are produced, the more energy we use and the more pollution we create. Simply put, we have to look at all the consequences of using a resource – not just whether any particular resource is in short supply.

Case Manager Notes:
     Specialist A wins this round. There appears to be no immediate shortage of nonenergy raw materials. True, there are energy and pollution issues associated with the manufacture of end products using these materials. However, technology seems to be hammering away at those problems. In 1996, for example, aluminum companies saved the equivalent of more than 18.4 million barrels of oil by recycling – that's enough energy to meet the electrical needs of a city the size of Pittsburgh for six years.[65]
     Nearly a dozen or so elements (mercury, tin, arsenic and so forth) could be in short supply down the road, but mankind has a way of coming up with alternatives for these kinds of resources.[66] Of all the real and potential difficulties Earth has to be concerned about, nonenergy resources are far from the top of the list.

Exam Category #6: Waste

Specialist A:
     There is plenty of room on Earth for waste – and I mean *plenty* of room. The problem is a "not in my backyard" mentality; it's not an environmental concern. In the U.S., the most wasteful country on the planet, about 200 million tons of municipal waste get dumped each year.[67] That sounds like a lot, but half of it gets incinerated, recycled or used for compost.
     The Skeptical Environmentalist figured out that if the U.S. keeps tossing 110 million tons of waste into its landfills each year for 99 years, the entire amount could be shoveled into a hundred-foot-high dump 14 miles square.[68]
     We all understand the U.S. doesn't have just one national landfill – as far as I know, no country does. And that gets us to the nub. Waste gets discarded into a lot of different dumpsites, and that makes it appear to be a far greater environmental problem than it really is. Waste should be about location, location, location. Let's not distort it into a banner-headline environmental problem when it is really about something else.

Specialist B:
     Once again, Specialist A doesn't dig deep enough to unearth the real problem. Waste is not just about space. True, we have enough room to dispose of our solid waste. However, in more-industrialized

nations like the U.S., dumping waste wherever it is most convenient is no longer an option. There are stringent rules and regulations for landfill operations. That explains, in part, why more than 14,000 land-fills have been closed in the U.S. in the last 20 years.[69] That leaves 3,100 U.S. landfills still in operation.[70] Figuring out where to place a landfill in a more-developed country is not just a location concern – it is also a money concern. It's expensive to properly operate a land-fill, and keep the environmental inspectors at bay.

All of this doesn't get to the heart of the problem. There are many kinds of waste. Most attention is given to bulky trash that ends up in dumps that we can see and sometimes smell. For example, in the U.S., the nation's landfill waste stream (according to the U.S. Environmental Protection Agency) is made up of the following ...

Trash	Tonnage	% of Waste Stream[71]
Paper	71.6	40.4%
Yard trimmings	31.6	17.6
Metals	15.3	8.5
Plastics	14.4	8.0
Food scraps	13.2	7.4
Glass	12.5	7.0
Other *	20.8	11.0

* Rubber, leather, textiles, etc.

Other kinds of wastes are far more dangerous to Earth. In the U.S., for instance, 256 million tons of hazardous wastes are produced each year.[72] Those dangerous wastes prompted the U.S. to launch its "Superfund" initiative aimed at cleaning up the estimated 36,000 seriously contaminated dumps in America.[73] In nations where envi-ronmental standards are lower or virtually nonexistent, the hazardous-waste problem (along with all the health issues that go with it) is much more serious. Clearly, sometimes it is not *how much* waste is being discarded but what *kind* of waste.

Related to this point is the amount of human and animal waste that is excreted each year. This is not a pleasant subject, but it has to be considered when thinking about population expansion. The U.S. produces 134 billion pounds of human waste each year.[74] Even more astounding, livestock in the U.S. annually produce 2.7 *trillion* pounds of manure.[75]

Countries that have sewage-treatment facilities and effective waste-disposal regulations are in far better shape than developing nations where inadequately treated human and animal excretions contribute to the misery of millions. It is worth remembering that underdeveloped locations are where birthrates are highest – and where waste problems are only going to get worse.

Case Manager Notes:

Specialist B is correct – there is waste and there is *waste*. One of the most serious problems faced by countries that rely even in a minor way on nuclear energy is the disposal of generator waste. Although the U.S., for instance, is making an attempt to consolidate radioactive waste, it is difficult to find a state that doesn't have at least one nuclear waste site (see Chart 7).[76] It is obvious that, for public-safety reasons, this kind of waste *is* a problem in many parts of the world – and will become an even greater challenge as more and more nuclear-power plants come on line between now and 2030.

As for nonhazardous waste, a lot more of it is being dumped than Specialist A leads us to believe. True, American households generate 200 million tons of waste a year, but that pales in comparison with the 11 *billion* tons of waste that American businesses produce annually.[77]

It makes environmental and economic sense to focus on ways to reduce industrial waste since manufacturers churn out the lion's share of the world's waste. "Dematerialization" is a technical term the manufacturing industry uses to describe how it is reducing the amount of material consumed for each unit of output.[78] Since industrial production is going to have to expand in order to meet the needs of a larger population, dematerialization looms as increasingly important.

It is not just a matter of finding space to dump industrial waste – it is realizing that at least some of that waste creates other problems. Isn't it more logical to "dematerialize" as many manufacturing operations as possible in order to cut back waste production? We know this is feasible. In Japan, where landfill space is at a premium, companies such as Asahi Breweries, Sanyo, Canon and Toyota produce "zero waste" – they have found ways to eliminate waste or to sell their production byproducts to other industries.[79] Creating incentives or arm-twisting other manufacturers in other countries to follow Japan's example may prove useful.

Chart 7

State	# of Sites	State	# of Sites	State	# of Sites
AL	2	LA	2	NC	4
AR	2	ME	1	OH	3
AK	1	MD	5	OR	3
CA	9	MA	5	PA	6
CO	3	MI	6	RI	1
CT	2	MN	2	SC	5
FL	4	MS	1	TN	3
GA	2	MO	3	TX	5
ID	4	NE	3	UT	1
IL	10	NH	1	VT	1
IN	1	NJ	2	VA	4
IA	2	NM	4	WASH, DC	3
KS	2	NY	9	WI	4

Nuclear-waste sites in the U.S.

Source: Dept. of Energy

Overall, waste is the caboose on the train of problems criss-crossing Earth. Except for hazardous waste, which clearly is a health threat, much of the developing world directs too little attention to what it discards. As a result, waste becomes a bed for disease and a blemish that diminishes both the aesthetics and quality of life of a country. Waste is a problem for Earth. And it is likely to be much more so as the developing world expands.

Exam Category #7: Species

Specialist A:

The Sierra Club says that in the United States, 526 species listed in the Natural Heritage Central Database are extinct or missing.[80] Well, big deal! According to the World Resources Institute, there are somewhere between 2 million and 100 million species on Earth. And we're supposed to get upset about a handful of species that disappear every few years – most of which are bugs, fungi or arachnids?

Chart 8

Group	Identified	Estimated
Viruses	4,000	400,000
Bacteria	4,000	1 million +
Fungi	72,000	1.5 million
Protozoans	40,000	200,000
Algae	40,000	400,000
Plants	270,000	320,000
Nematodes	25,000	400,000
Crustaceans	40,000	150,000
Arachnids	75,000	750,000
Insects	950,000	8 million
Mollusks	70,000	200,000
Vertebrates & close relatives	45,000	50,000
Others	115,000	250,000

Species Spectrum

Source: Global Biodiversity Assessment, United Nations Environment Program

Most higher-order animal and plant species have been identified. However, a staggering number of fungi, bacteria, and insects have yet to be discovered.

The fear of losing species causes us to go to extremes to protect certain animals – the U.S. federal government, for example, prohibits logging within 70 acres of a nest of the northern spotted owl.[81] As a result, we cut the lumber industry off at the knees in places where the northern spotted owl lives – places like Sweet Home, Oregon, and other communities in and around the Willamette National Forest.[82] The endangered-species card gets played over and over again in America. It makes no sense at all.

Since the beginning of time, species have come and species have gone. That's life. Species are not being wiped out in droves. The few species that are disappearing have become a *cause celebre* for a bunch of overwrought environmentalists. This is not even close to being a problem for Earth.

Specialist B:

Specialist A doesn't get it. First, we are losing many more species each year than she tries to imply – the extinction rate is actually between 1,000 and 10,000 species per year.[83] Second, we need to understand *what* species are being snuffed out.

Since Specialist A gives an example of an endangered species in the U.S., let's take a broad look at all the species that have been destroyed in that country: 3 percent of the bird population, 1 percent of flowering plants, 11 percent of freshwater mussels.[84] Doesn't sound all that bad? Well, this devastation has occurred in just three human lifetimes.[85]

When the world loses a species of grass, it may not seem that serious. But if put in the context of an ecosystem, it can have a ripple effect that disrupts and possibly even eliminates many other life forms. Kill off one species and put many others at risk. It's all about biological diversity – something that is vital to Earth's health.

As the human population grows, other species get trounced. It happens every day. Hawaii is a good example since it has a limited land mass inhabited by more and more people. In that same three-generation timeframe noted earlier, the state has lost 269 species, including 10 percent of its native plants.[86] Consider Hawaii as a microcosm of the planet. Many species are being lost, and it's largely the result of human overpopulation.

Case Manager Notes:

Arguing that we can afford to eradicate a few hundred or a few thousand species because there are millions to go around is specious. True, Earth has a lot of species – 1.4 million at last count, and no one really knows how many others there might be.[87] However, quantity is not the only concern. As Specialist B notes, there should be concern over what species are dying off and what that means to the ecosystem.

Reports like the one issued by the North American Commission for Environmental Cooperation (the NAFTA-related organization created by Canada, Mexico and the U.S.) can't be ignored. "Half of North America's most biodiverse eco-regions are now severely degraded, and the region now has at least 235 threatened species of mammals, birds, reptiles and amphibians," the commission says.[88] "So what?" Specialist A might ask. The commission answers this way:

> North America's diminishing biological diversity has profound consequences. Because the loss is irreversible – species that are lost are lost forever – the potential impact on the human condition, on the fabric of the continent's living systems, and on the process of evolution is immense.[89]

Maybe some environmentalists do go overboard occasionally in an effort to save the spotted owls of the world. However, none of us should summarily hand out death sentences to any species without carefully pondering what the collateral damage might be.

Land Examination Report – Conclusion

So is Earth's land in good shape or not? It depends on which expert you believe. Here is what the case manager wrote as the conclusion to the land examination report:

> Earth seems to be experiencing a few land-related aches and pains, but its condition is not bad enough to warrant any radical (that is, expensive) intervention. Even more preventive health care isn't recommended at this time. Should Earth run into serious land trouble in the future, expect mankind to develop the technology to find the resources and make the necessary repairs – because there will be no alternative. As experience has taught us, this is the human way of dealing with problems.

CHAPTER 10

PEOPLE AND WATER

We surely got trouble
We surely got trouble
Right here in River City [1]

In *The Music Man*, fast-talking salesman Harold Hill shows up in a small Iowa town and warns citizens that they're face-to-face with trouble, spelled with a capital "T." There's ragtime, billiards, scarlet women, libertine men, dime novels, cigarettes, gambling and beer from the bottle. *"Oh, ya got lots and lots o' trouble,"* salesman Hill says, without ever mentioning that the town's tap water may be where the *real* trouble lies.

Assuming the city is downstream from a stretch of Iowa farm-land, the river running through the community probably is loaded with nitrates, thanks to livestock manure and fertilizer runoff. Of course, the water might also be laced with pesticides (in the mid-1990s, 60 percent of the well water used in agricultural areas through-out the U.S. contained pesticides).[2]

When Harold Hill fell in love with River City's librarian, Marian Paroo, the year was 1912. It is hard to speculate how healthy the town's river was in those days. What we do know is that as more and more people farmed, lived and manufactured along America's river-banks, the waterways got a larger and larger dose of fecal coliform bac-teria – those nasty little organisms that usually can be traced back to insufficiently treated sewage or runoff from pastures, feedlots and cities. As a result, people in River City probably long ago turned to well water for their needs – a reasonable assumption since 99 percent of the rural population in America relies on groundwater for drinking.[3]

Today, between 1.5 billion and 2 billion people around the world are dependent on groundwater.[4] The steadily increasing human demand for this type of water resource is causing more than a few scientists to get the chills. An International Water Management Institute paper opened with this unsettling statement:

Throughout the world, regions that have sustainable groundwater balances are shrinking by the day. Three problems dominate groundwater use: depletion due to overdraft; waterlogging and salinization due mostly to inadequate drainage; and pollution due to agricultural, industrial and other human activities. In regions of the world, especially with high population density ... many consequences of groundwater overdevelopment are becoming increasingly evident.[5]

The report goes on to cite water-related woes all over the globe – China, Yemen, Pakistan, Mexico, Jordan, and so on. Not only are groundwater supplies being depleted by the constantly growing water needs of man, but it seems that the world's aboveground reservoirs are also in trouble. The United Nations Environment Programme (known as Unep) reported in 2000 that the buildup of silt behind large dams is reducing reservoir capacity by an average of 1 percent a year. "On present trends, they [reservoirs] will lose about a fifth of their capacity within a few decades."[6]

All this bad news was bundled up in an article in *The New Yorker*. Here is an alarming excerpt:

The world is running out of fresh water... Lakes, rivers, marshes, aquifers, and atmospheric vapor make up less than 1 percent of the earth's total water, and people are already using more than half of the accessible runoff. Water demand, on the other hand, has been growing rap- idly –- it tripled worldwide between 1950 and 1990 – and water in many areas already exceeds nature's ability to recharge supplies. By 2025, the demand for water around the world is expected to exceed supply by 56 percent.[7]

Sounds grim, doesn't it? Well, the Skeptical Environmentalist sees the situation through a different pair of glasses. He points out that the problem is not so much a scarcity of water but the inability of certain people to access it. (Sound familiar?) He points out that in 1970, only 30 percent of the developing world could find clean drinking water. Today, the figure stands at 80 percent.[8] Of course, that still leaves more than a billion people struggling to find an acceptable water supply. And in spite of the Skeptical Environmentalist's optimism about the increasing accessibility of water, others think that the number of peo- ple living in "water-stressed countries" will grow dramatically.

In her book *Pillar of Sand: Can the Irrigation Miracle Last?* water expert Sandra Postel serves up a reminder that water and food production go hand in hand. She warns that future water shortages could cut the global food supply by more than 10 percent – a development that could lead to more hunger and battles over water.[9] Much of the problem, Postel contends, is linked to the inefficient way much of the world irrigates its farmland.

"Some 40 percent of the world's food comes from irrigated cropland – and we're betting on that share to increase to feed a growing population," Postel notes. She adds that irrigation sucks large amounts of water from rivers, streams, aquifers and lakes. Irrigation accounts for more than two-thirds of global water use, but less than half that water ever reaches the roots of plants, Postel observes.[10] "Without increasing water productivity in irrigation, major food-producing regions will not have enough water to sustain crop production," cautions Postel.[11]

There doesn't appear to be any major disagreement about agriculture's impact on the world's water supplies. Farming soaks up nearly 70 percent of the water used annually, while industry accounts for more than 20 percent of water usage. Households consume only about 8 percent of all water used each year.[12] While it still makes sense to turn off the tap while brushing your teeth and taking brief morning showers, these are not steps that will keep the world from drying up. Clearly, agriculture and industry are two key areas where big strides could be made in water consumption.

Some irrigation methods require far less water than traditional ways of watering crops. Drip or trickle irrigation, for example, sends moisture and nutrients more directly to a plant's roots and can increase the size and quantity of a crop without an excessive use of water. However, this method of irrigating crops is not widespread. Even in countries like the U.S., where the advantages are clearly understood, getting the capital to finance widespread drip irrigation is a major hurdle. "Although growers may be able to recover their costs in a few years with favorable yields and market conditions, many growers simply cannot put their hands on enough capital," concludes a report by three irrigation specialists.[13] If money is an impediment in highly developed nations, imagine how difficult it would be to implement these new irrigation techniques in countries that have limited financial resources.

If the United Nations Population Fund has it right, we need to do *something* about our fresh water supply. Since only about 2.5 percent of all water on the planet is drinkable, and one-half of 1 percent is accessible groundwater or surface water, there is little argument that fresh water is in short supply.[14] Just how short is the supply? Right now, 54 percent of fresh water is being used, but by 2025, population growth will result in a consumption rate of 70 percent. If less-developed countries start using water in the same quantities as developed nations, we would be at a 90 percent consumption rate.[15]

The extrapolations don't take into account the likely introduction of new technologies that will squeeze more agricultural production out of every liter of water. Nevertheless, easily accessible fresh water in the amount the U.N. says is required to meet our basic daily living needs (50 liters a day for drinking, sanitation, bathing and cooking) is not a "given" in many regions of the world.[16] And the situation could get a lot worse over the next three decades. The U.N. predicts that three billion people in 48 countries will be faced with water-scarcity problems by 2025.[17]

A shortage when 70 percent of the earth is covered with 326 trillion gallons water? It just doesn't seem to add up. Why not tap the ocean – where 98 percent of all our water can be found – for our drinking and agricultural needs? Answer: because removing salt and other minerals from seawater takes a lot of energy, and that equates to a lot of money.

Currently, there are two basic technologies used to extract potable water from seawater: (a) reverse osmosis, a process that filters out salt and other minerals, and (b) distillation, which requires boiling seawater and condensing the steam to capture a usable end product.[18] Reverse osmosis can produce 15 to 50 gallons of potable water for every 100 gallons of seawater treated, but doing so requires between 2,500 to 12,000 kilowatt hours per acre-foot.[19] Desalination can be a more efficient way of producing fresh water. Desalination plants coupled with power-generating facilities, for instance, can dramatically cut the costs of producing potable water. Improvements in filtration systems are also lowering desalination expenses. Still, the price tag for this kind of water production puts the option out of reach for many developing nations. Like so many other necessities and niceties of life, how much water you get equates to how much money you can lay on the table.

Consider an underdeveloped country where water is precious. Through information technology, you learn that per-capita consumption of water in Western Europe is about 566 liters per day (remember: average water use is 50 liters). Then you discover that in America, per-capita water consumption is *three times higher* per day than in Europe.[20] Such statistics can lead to what *How Women Can Beat Terrorism* labels "negative envy." And, as will be pointed out later, negative envy is the yeast that gives rise to confrontation and conflict.

Water is so vital and so unevenly accessible that, according to the United Nations, it could be the root cause of serious conflicts in the future. "Water wars" may spring up in regions where rivers or lakes are shared by more than one country.[21] The U.N. Development Programme singled out the Nile, Niger, Volta and Zambezi basins as places where water-related trouble may already be starting to boil.[22]

The Skeptical Environmentalist agrees that population growth may lead to "an increased tension and an increased political focus on water questions."[23] However, he doubts water scarcity will lead to warfare – partly because it would be cheaper to pay for desalinated water than it would be to finance a military operation. Even if the Skeptical Environmentalist proves to be right about water wars, that does not mean water won't inspire other kinds of hostile actions. Terrorist tactics used to arm-twist water-rich nations into sharing their liquid gold? If you don't *own* water rights, then the incentive is to find a way to *control* the flow of water so that you get what is perceived to be your fair share. As was pointed out in Part II of this book, this would be basic behavior that could prompt extreme action on the part of people who lack water – especially when they become more informed of just how deprived they are in comparison with other parts of the world and when they are given easier access to damaging technologies that could be used to force the water lords to be more generous with their resources.

Just how wide is the gap between the nations that have ample water and those that don't? The World Commission on Water for the 21st Century states that poor people in the developing world pay on average 12 times more per liter of water than those who are fortunate enough to be linked to a municipal water system.[24] As a percentage of household income, the cost of water can be significant in certain poor areas – in Onitsha, Nigeria, it's 20 percent; in Port-au-Prince, Haiti, it's 18 percent.[25] Furthermore, paying a premium for water doesn't necessarily mean the water is of good quality. Bad water incapacitates or kills millions every year.

"It is stunning that the poor pay more than 10 times as much for water as the rich do, and get poor quality water to boot," says Ismail

Serageldin, chairman of the World Commission on Water and a World Bank vice president. He adds: "A direct link exists between a lack of access [to decent water] and a host of diseases that attack the poor in developing countries."[26]

Even in more-developed countries, water pollution is an increasing problem. In the U.S. and the People's Republic of China, for instance, elevated nitrates have been found in drinking water tested near certain agricultural clusters. In both countries, nitrogen fertilizer appears to have been the culprit.[27]

Nitrate pollution is a huge concern worldwide and is getting more worrisome with every human birth. High concentrations of nitrates in water have been linked to digestive-tract and other cancers, plus a few other maladies (miscarriages and non-Hodgkin's lymphoma, for example). Fertilizer, farm animal waste and treated human sewage account for much of this particular pollution problem. Between a third and a half of the nitrogen fertilizer used on agricultural plants in the U.S. ends up in the soil and not in the crops, according to the U.S. National Research Council.[28] Unused nitrate dissolves in rain or irrigation water, and sometimes finds its way to aquifers.

If nitrate pollution is such a health hazard, then why not just stop using nitrogen fertilizer? The Skeptical Environmentalist has an answer. Nitrogen fertilizer gets a lot of the credit for the incredible increase in food production during the past 30 years. He cites sources that suggest if we were to limit the use of fertilizers to the amount used in 1960, we would need at least 50 percent more farmland to produce the quantity of food now grown around the world.[29]

Besides, the Skeptical Environmentalist adds, human consumption of nitrogen may not be that bad for us, after all. He discounts claims that high nitrate levels can be correlated with increased incidences of cancer. Nitrates are generally harmless because once they enter our digestive tract, they are neutralized by stomach acids. All of which leads him to conclude: "The concern over nitrogen health effects seems ill-founded."[30]

It could, indeed, be that the negative health effects of some pollutants have been exaggerated. Maybe we shouldn't get nervous over what the U.S. Geological Survey found when analyzing 140 waterways in America: trace amounts of reproductive hormones, prescription drugs and antibiotics.[31] However, perhaps there is reason to be uneasy since even the Skeptical Environmentalist agrees that for some people in some parts of the world, good water is hard to find.

Even using the most optimistic forecast about water improvements (for instance, new technologies to clean up impure water, better systems that can be used to transport potable water to locations where it is in short supply), a growing population is going to outstrip mankind's ability to sate everyone's thirst and will likely fall short of satisfying irrigation and water-dependent manufacturing needs.

Where does that leave us? Pretty much where we have always been: A percentage of our population is going to continue to suffer the consequences of too little water or water that is too polluted. The difference between today and yesterday, though, is that (thanks to information technology) those hundreds of millions of people who are water-poor are now far more likely to know that in many parts of the globe there is, indeed, "water, water everywhere" – and in other places, there's "not a drop to drink."

Water is another of those gaps between the haves and have-nots that fan the flames of negative envy. In the past, we looked on the water-deprived and remarked, "There but for the grace of God go we." Yesterday, those who were short on water were to be pitied – but not feared. Today, information technology and lethal technology have turned things around. Something to think about the next time you turn on the tap.

CHAPTER 11

PEOPLE AND AIR

Bing Crosby's dreams about a white Christmas are less likely to come true today than they were a few years ago. A study by the Oak Ridge National Laboratory reviewed weather statistics in 16 U.S. cities over the past four decades.[1] It confirmed what American old-timers have suspected all along – the number of Christmas Day snows of at least an inch have declined since the 1960s.

Is this proof positive that the earth is warming? Maybe. It seems many environmentalists are hedging their bets. Even the Oak Ridge Lab added a disclaimer to its report stating that global warming "might be" a cause of the changing conditions.

Still, there are some data that very few scientists dispute. Consider these points listed on the U.S. Environmental Protection Agency's Web site:

- Global temperatures are rising – the average land surface temperature has gone up by about 1 degree Fahrenheit during the last century.

- The sea level has risen worldwide by six to eight inches over the past 100 years.[2]

The logical conclusion one might reach after pondering the EPA's information is that (a) yes, we may have a global-warming problem, but (b) what's the big deal if high tide gets a few inches higher every century? It's not like Indianapolis, Brussels or Nagano will become oceanside cities within the next few years. So maybe there will be less snow to shovel 10 years from now – is that so bad? Answer: It depends on whom you ask.

Some scientists are *extremely* concerned about how population growth is messing up the atmosphere. Others contend that while mankind may have damaged the air on occasion, steps are being taken to repair those problems.

There is general agreement that earth is feeling the impact of the "greenhouse effect" – although just how serious that impact may be is open to debate. The greenhouse effect works this way: atmospheric gases (including water vapor and carbon dioxide) trap solar energy that is reflected off the earth's surface. The gases form a kind of cover similar to the glass panels of a greenhouse – hence the label given to the phenomenon. Without the greenhouse effect, scientists tell us that earth's temperatures would be so low that life as we know it could not exist.

Fossil-fuel burning has added a huge amount of carbon emissions to the atmosphere. The more people, the more carbon in the air. As a result, the planet's "energy balance" has been altered with a greater amount of solar radiation trapped by the greenhouse "cover." The result has been a warming of the earth's surface temperature. Just how toasty we could get without jeopardizing different life forms, including our own, is a question that regularly gets debated by experts. One Norwegian research report says the rise in temperatures is alarming. The report notes that the Arctic ice thickness has declined by 42 percent since 1950, and that by 2050, the Arctic may have no ice at all during summer.[3]

Don't be shocked: Other scientists disagree with that prediction. Consider the following:

> Carbon-dioxide emissions are supposed to be increasing temperatures on earth. But the research ... has never found a conclusive link between human activity and global warming. Satellite observations over the past quarter-century show no increase in heating just above the earth's surface, and observations going back thousands of years show natural cycles of warming and cooling long before the invention of SUV's and air-conditioning.[4]

The "don't regulate us" group cautions that if highly industrialized nations are forced to radically reduce carbon-dioxide emissions in industry, power plants, cars, trucks and the like, it will hobble economic expansion, which will lead to fewer Third World investments. Result? Less coughing but more poverty – particularly in countries that are already poor.

Poor, however, is better than dead, some scientists respond, pointing to the "Asian Brown Cloud," a mixture of pollutants hovering over the Indian Ocean and several Asian nations. The cloud, about the size of the United States, is the byproduct of vehicle and industrial emissions.[5] The mass is so dense that it blocks some of the sun's rays and cuts heat by up to 10 percent. As a result, the cloud reduces water evaporation, and that means less rainfall. Less rainfall means drought. For many parts of Asia, drought means famine, disease and death.

OK, so maybe there are some downsides to "bad" air. However, that should not lead us to the conclusion that bad air is totally ... well ... bad. An organization called the Joint Center for Regulatory Studies says ground-based ocluster (smog) actually could be a plus, not a minus, – for instance, it helps prevent skin cancer. "Great news for skin, but what about our lungs?" asks the U.S. National Park Service, as it equips its Yellowstone National Park rangers with respirators to protect them from snowmobile exhaust that frequently turns the winter mountain air into a haze.[6]

Habitat! implores WWF (the World Wildlife Fund). *Think habitat!* The organization is referring to a report that says many species could be destroyed because of the effect of climate changes on habitat in "one-fifth of the world's most vulnerable nature areas."[7]

Is there *any* global consensus about the current condition of earth's atmosphere, and is there an agreement on what steps that could or should be taken to clean it up? The squabbling over the Kyoto Protocol tells us the answer is "no." The protocol, which has been hotly debated, particularly in the U.S., calls for industrial nations to reduce their greenhouse gases by 5 percent below levels produced in 1990. Although the United States signed the protocol in late 1997, George W. Bush withdrew support, calling the document "fatally flawed." Withdrawal from the protocol has caused serious rifts within the environmental community.

Who's got it right? Is global warming that much of a problem? Is the cost of reducing greenhouse gasses so expensive that it would cripple economic growth and create more hardships for the billions of people already living in poverty?

Let's adjudicate the underlying assumption that many in the scientific community make about earth's air. In court, before a jury of our peers, the prosecution charges that mankind is corrupting the atmosphere and, therefore, subjecting the planet to significant and potentially dangerous climatic changes. The defense argues that the prosecution doesn't have a shred of credible evidence to support its claim.

The trial begins with the prosecution introducing a series of photos taken by NASA in 2002. The satellite shots show a mass of ice called "Larsen B" floating away from the Antarctic Peninsula.[8] If crushed, the iceberg, which is the size of Rhode Island, could be turned into 290 trillion five-pound bags of ice.[9]

With the Larsen B photos still on display, the prosecution presents a British Antarctic Survey report stating that a 4.5 degree Fahrenheit rise in temperature has occurred in the region during the past 50 years.[10] Then unveiled is a report from the National Snow and Ice Data Center (located at the University of Colorado at Boulder) that includes this statement: "This is the largest single event in a series of retreats by ice shelves in the peninsula over the last 30 years ... [and can be attributed to] ... a strong climate warming in the region."[11] The prosecution proceeds to bring to the stand a number of expert witnesses who finger greenhouse-gas emissions as the culprit in causing the ice to melt. "A harbinger of global warming," says Greenpeace, one of the prosecution's *amicus curiae* witnesses.[12]

The prosecution closes its case with a disturbing warning from the Snow and Ice Data Center. It seems other ice shelves in the Antarctic region may be close to collapse, and if the giant Ross Ice Shelf (which is 6,000 feet thick and the size of Mexico) should dissolve, global sea levels could rise by 15 feet.[13] The prosecution then rests.

Hold it, the defense fires back. This is another example of the mumbo jumbo that makes a relatively benign event sound like an apocalypse. In actuality, Antarctica has many "climates," and Larsen B is not an indicator of what is happening in other parts of the continent. As a point of fact, the West Antarctic Ice Sheet may be getting *thicker, not thinner.*[14] The defense then introduces a statement by a London University professor of biogeography:

> Over the last 50 years, the temperatures in the interior
> [of Antarctica] appear to have been falling. University
> of Illinois researchers have reported, in *Nature*, on tem-
> perature records covering a broad area of Antarctica.
> Their measurements show a net cooling on the
> Antarctic continent between 1996 and 2000.[15]

The South Pole isn't melting away, the defense claims. And the North Pole isn't, either, it adds. Then it turns once again to the London University professor, who makes this astounding counter-charge:

> The long-term temperature trend remains, over all, one
> of cooling. It may not be too long, therefore, before we
> see the ice spreading again. At worst, the emission of

greenhouse gases might help to speed the descent into the next glacial period. And what would you prefer, a warmer or a colder world?[16]

The defense rests. The jury disappears and deliberates for days. It returns hopelessly hung. The case is dismissed, with the public in the same place it was before the trial began: completely confused about whether earth's air is merely mildly compromised or gravely ill.

• • •

Like so many other environmental matters, the condition of our atmosphere is hotly debated in the scientific world. Some experts buy into the contention of the President's Council on Sustainable Development that climate change during the next hundred years is "one of the most important issues we will face as we work to achieve our sustainable development goals."[17] Others go along with a California congressman's complaint that global warming is nothing but a big "lie" that is being used to "justify a centralization of power in global government through the United Nations and other institutions that are run by unelected and unaccountable authorities."[18]

Should we worry about global warming at all? There are people with impressive titles who come forward with answers that are as opposite as push and pull:

* *I'm sure climate change is the biggest environmental threat that faces the world, and it's linked to many others. When some of the impacts begin to bite, they'll worsen the poverty in which so many people are already existing.*[19]
— Sir John Houghton
Intergovernmental Panel on Climate Change

* *As a scientist, I can find no substantive basis for the warming scenarios being popularly described. Moreover, according to many studies I have read by economists, agronomists, and hydrologists, there would be little difficulty adapting so such warming if it were to occur.*[20]

—Richard S. Lindzen
Massachusetts Institute of Technology

Amidst all the disagreement, scientists and environmentalists do see eye to eye on two points:

1. *Mankind is pumping a lot of carbon dioxide into the atmosphere.* Of all the stuff that we put into the air (sulfur dioxide; nitrogen oxide; methane; particulate matter of all kinds, ranging from jackhammer dust to paint-sprayer residue), scientists lose the most sleep over carbon emissions – especially carbon dioxide. CO2 is a colorless, odorless nonflammable gas that, when turned into a solid, becomes dry ice. It is the gas that makes carbonated soft drinks fizz and beer foam and somehow is used to decaffeinate coffee. As we were taught early in life, CO2 is what animals exhale and plants suck up in what is one of Mother Nature's most impressive balancing acts.

When carbon-based fuels are burned (via manufacturing plants, cars, trucks and the like) in the presence of oxygen, CO2 is produced. It whiffs into the atmosphere and joins the naturally occurring carbon dioxide in the sky. Here's the problem. Since the start of the Industrial Revolution in the mid-1700s, mankind has been burning fossil fuels with a vengeance, adding an estimated 271 billion tons of carbon to the atmosphere.[21] And each year, we load up the air with another 6.3 billion tons.[22] What's the result? Carbon-dioxide concentrations in the atmosphere have risen 17 percent over the last 30 years or so.[23]

The science crowd seems to be in general agreement (a rarity) that we have considerably more carbon dioxide in the atmosphere than once was the case. However, forget about trying to find a consensus about how dangerous or harmless all this added carbon is to earth's air.

The Intergovernmental Panel on Climate Change (IPCC), together with a number of other high-profile environmental groups, recommends cutting carbon emissions immediately if we want to avoid the unpleasant consequences of global warming. On the other hand, some experts have opinions that could not be more contrary:

> Bigger trees, increased resistance to bad weather, improved agricultural productivity ... are just some of the many benefits that carbon dioxide bestows on the environment. With little evidence that carbon dioxide triggers global warming but lots of evidence showing how carbon dioxide helps the environment, environmentalists should be extolling the virtues of this benign greenhouse gas.[24]

In fairness, most in the science community are not this blasé about CO2 emissions. If put to a vote, a majority of experts would probably agree that we should cut back on our production of carbon dioxides, which means curbing our use of fossil fuels, which means economic disruption, which all adds up to… *money*. That word brings more actors onto the stage: industrialists, economists and, of course, politicians. Once all these characters start sniffing the air, any hope of a unified position about carbon dioxide and global warming is asphyxiated.

2. The cost to reduce CO2 emissions would be astronomical. It's a pretty simple equation: The more we curtail fossil-fuel use as a way of reducing CO2 output, the more it's going to cost. Of course, there could be a huge expense (in both money and lives) if we completely ignore carbon emissions.
Let's look at both sides of the argument, beginning with: "do little or nothing about reducing carbon dioxide."

IPCC figures that global warming (largely the result of excessive amounts of CO2 entering the atmosphere) could cost the world around $480 billion to $640 billion a year.[25] The money would be needed to build dams to hold back rising water levels, develop more land for agriculture to offset the loss of farmlands made less productive by climatic changes, and so forth. Also factored into the estimate is the cost of land and resources that can't be salvaged – real estate and materials that would fall victim to the effects of global warming.

Now move to the "what will it cost to get CO2 emissions under control?" scenario. Since it was put on the table in 1997, the Kyoto Protocol has been the most-used calculator for guesstimating what the price tag for curbing carbon emissions would be between now and 2010 – and through the end of this century. There are different projections based on a slew of assumptions. However, the Skeptical Environmentalist concludes that Kyoto will "likely cost at least $150 billion a year, and possibly much more."[26] He adds that putting the brakes on global warming will take a lot of Kyotos, and that when all is said and done, cumulative payments could be as high as $107 trillion, whereas the cost of doing nothing about global warming through the close of this century would only be around $5 trillion.[27]

Regardless of whether we do nothing or go all out to reduce fossil-fuel usage, it's going to cost. A lot.

Who's right and who's wrong when it comes to Earth's air?

Scientists in Europe and the U.S. say there is a 9 out of 10 chance that global average temperatures will most likely go up 4 degrees to 7 degrees Fahrenheit by 2100.[28] Are we willing to run the economic and health risks associated with this warming of the atmosphere? Or should we listen to the Skeptical Environmentalist when he says, "if we want to leave a planet with the most possibilities for our descendants in both the developing and the developed world, it is imperative that we focus on the economy and solving our problems in a global context, rather than focusing – in the IPCC lingo – on the environment..."?[29]

Here's still another question to think about: could it be that we are already well on our way to solving our atmospheric trouble? Look at what industry is up to: BP Amoco's chief says that global warming *is* a problem and pledges that his company will play a "positive and responsive" role in identifying solutions[30]; DuPont has reduced its emissions 60 percent below 1990 levels, and United Technologies says it will cut its emissions by 25 percent within six years[31]; Alliant Energy Corporation has extracted an equivalent of 7.3 metric tons of CO_2 from its emissions over a nine-year period.[32]

Perhaps these industry vignettes are nothing more than slivers of light that are leaking through an ever-darkening cloud. Maybe Al Gore was on the mark when, as vice president of the U.S., he stated that the threat of global warming "is the most serious problem our civilization faces." Then again, perhaps the Hoover Institute's Thomas Gale Moore has got it right when he urges government to "stand fast against any steps to limit greenhouse-gas emissions" because an increase in carbon dioxide will actually benefit most people by boosting agricultural production, reducing heating costs and improving transportation.[33]

Pick your pony and place your bet. What will happen at the end of this horse race is anybody's guess.

CHAPTER 12

PEOPLE AND POVERTY

This chapter sums up our analysis of what population growth is (or isn't) doing to the environment, and concludes by connecting the dots between population growth, poverty, hopelessness – and women. First, some additional thoughts about human procreation and its impact on the planet's land, water and air.

Humans and Mother Nature

As the old adage goes, "All politics is local." Thomas P. "Tip" O'Neill, onetime speaker of the U.S. House of Representatives, gave legs to that phrase, even though it never did quite ring completely true. To the degree that the statement is *perceived* to be the case, let's add the following: "all environmental issues are local, too."

The Skeptical Environmentalist tells us "mankind's lot has actually improved in terms of practically every measurable indicator."[1] For the sake of making a point, assume that all the environmental experts were to agree with this declaration. Do you think people living in absolute squalor with limited access to food and clean water would care that the general state of human affairs has supposedly gotten better? Take, for example, a shepherd living in Copsa Mica, Romania, a place some call the "Black Village."

> So stubborn and insidious are the pollutants that had
> coated the Black Village that experts now believe the
> soil and the local food chain probably will remain con-
> taminated for at least another three decades.[2]

Copsa Mica is one of the dirtiest places in Europe. It was coated with soot and heavy-metal residue coming from factories that operated during the communist era. Conditions are so bad that sheep's milk used by villagers to make cheese comes loaded with toxic metals (lead, zinc and cadmium). Keep this mental picture in mind while reading the following:

Air pollution can be – and historically has been – combated in the developed world. There is also good reason to believe that the developing world, following our pattern, in the long run likewise will bring down its air pollution.[3]

Is such a statement supposed to comfort the Transylvanian shepherd who lives in a town labeled by one industrial risk-management expert as a "condemned place?"[4] Probably not.

Here's the point: If it turns out that, when viewed in worldwide terms, mankind actually has not seriously harmed the environment as many of us have been led to believe, we are still left with many pockets around the world where things are not rosy. Even if many people have enough to eat, can access drinkable water and inhale clean air, many others are not so fortunate. Consider:

- While it is encouraging to learn that the more-developed world has seen its food intake increase from 2,463 calories to 2,663 calories per person over the last 10 years,[5] that development isn't going to matter to the average citizens of Burundi, who lost more than 8 percent of their daily caloric intake between 1989 and 1999.[6]

- It is terrific that rivers and lakes in more-developed nations are less polluted than they were a few years ago, but tell that to the woman whose miscarriage has been linked to nitrate-laced drinking water.[7]

- Few will argue that the air quality in the U.S. is better than it was back in the 1960s and '70s. But to the citizens of Annistan, Alabama, who are suing Monsanto for discharging PCBs between the 1930s and 1970s (one-third of the residents examined in 1966 had elevated levels of the toxins), improved air quality isn't much consolation.[8]

Many of these "pocket problems" plague people who are short on control and ownership. They don't have the power, influence or economic wherewithal to bring about the kind of change that's needed to remedy the problems they face. The people who *do* have the power are not directly affected by what's going on in the troubled pockets scattered about the globe. And trying to get the authorities to muster the resources needed to fix problems that aren't theirs (or at least are not perceived to be theirs) is no easy task. There are a couple of reasons why:

1. Conflicting evidence. As earlier chapters in *How Women Can Beat Terrorism* have illustrated, it is virtually impossible to sort out the plethora of environmental data so that it becomes clear as to which expert is right and which is wrong. Is mankind committing a felonious assault on the environment? Difficult to say.

Trying to reach a judgment about what's correct and what isn't gets even more difficult when information and opinion keep shifting. "Plant a Tree and Save the Planet" was all the vogue for years, but now researchers are raising questions about the benefits of growing trees as a way to offset carbon-dioxide emissions.[9] It seems that leaving the land covered with grass could better keep carbon emissions under control.

Whenever controversial environmental issues are aired in public, we can be certain we will be overloaded with data from all sides of the issues. What's more, we will be told that the information being presented to us is the gospel truth even though some of it might be 100 percent false. A book called *Damned Lies and Statistics* explains how fake information can muddy the water:

> Once a number appears in one news report, that report is a potential source for everyone who becomes interested in the social problem: Officials, experts, activists and other reporters routinely repeat figures that appear in press reports. The number takes on a life of its own, and it goes through "number laundering." Its origins as someone's best guess are now forgotten and, through repetition, it comes to be treated as a straightforward fact – accurate and authoritative.[10]

One other related point: it isn't just bad data that make environmental controversies hard to analyze; it is also the way numbers are manipulated to mold public opinion. Here is an example:

The World Wildlife Foundation reported in 1997 that tree loss in the Amazon rain forest had increased by 34 percent since 1992.[11] However, the Skeptical Environmentalist cites figures showing that only 14 percent of the rain forest has been eradicated since mankind arrived on earth.[12] The first statement gives the impression that the rain forest is in serious trouble. The second implies that everything's fine in the Amazon. Actually, each percentage looks to be correct. However, you can see how the glass can be viewed as half empty or half full depending on one's point of view.

2. Pain-free power circles. With some exceptions, the most serious earth, water and air problems are not in the more-developed world. The poorer the region or nation, the more severe the environmental troubles. In fact, as has been pointed out in this section, environmental problems and poverty are often linked.

Where living standards are high, environmental matters creep into the headlines only infrequently, usually when Mother Nature is kicked in the shins. As a general rule, though, the more-developed world doesn't experience the daily inconveniences or out-and-out hardships that exist in regions where a degraded environment equates to little food, undrinkable water and dirty air. We get the message that environmental problems exist in places like South America, Africa or Asia, and we sort of understand that these issues might affect us in the future. However, until the more-developed world feels pain that is unequivocally linked to the environment, it becomes difficult to convince mankind to tackle problems that some experts say are not all that globally significant. Why?

Because if environment is local, it is also money.

To fix the environment means laying out cash. There are only so many francs, kronas and yen to go around, and every society has to set its priorities. National defense, economic development, education, human services and cultural programs all line up with long lists of needs. Environment is usually at the back of the pack, and by the time it gets to the table, it is lucky if it manages to walk off with a few scraps.

It isn't just government policy makers in developed nations who relegate the environment to a lower level of importance – it is also Mr. and Mrs. Average Citizen. That is easily validated in the U.S., where charitable donations are a good yardstick of social priorities and interests. There is no shortage of nonprofit environmental organizations in the U.S. (9,300 such agencies, institutions and programs are listed in GuideStar, a Web-based national directory of American nonprofit organizations).[13] And yet when it comes time for people to decide where to donate their money, the environment is low on the list. Historically, charitable environmental donations represent only about 3 percent of all charitable giving (see Chart 9).[14]

Chart 9

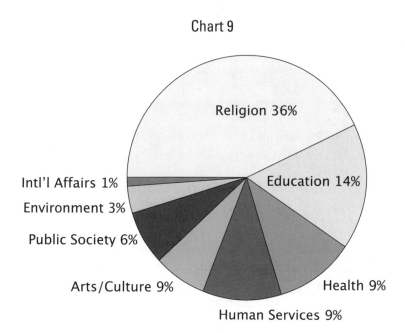

**U.S. Charitable Contributions (2000)
by Type of Recipient Organization**
Source: Giving USA 2001, AAFRC Trust for Philanthropy

Maybe the Skeptical Environmentalist is right. Maybe the earth is in better shape than some have made it out to be. Maybe, as Bjorn Lomborg says, we live "in a beautiful world."[15] Of course, Lomborg could be wrong. Maybe we are over-reproducing and over-consuming ourselves into extinction. Either way, not enough environmentally bad things are happening to people in power to convince them that population growth is a serious, potentially catastrophic dilemma.

However, when it comes to mankind's impact on mankind, the picture gets far less fuzzy.

The Human Pressure Cooker

There is a pile of evidence that supports the following statement: *High reproduction rates in poor, densely populated regions impede efforts to improve quality of life and contribute to increased poverty and hopelessness.*

Here's what high reproduction rates mean to a country struggling to stay afloat:

- As family size goes up, the investment in the education of each child goes down – with girls often the first to be squeezed out of the education system.[16]

- Civil and political rights are difficult to sustain.[17] The rule of law becomes fragile.

- The more dependents in a family, the less likely the family is to save and invest – cornerstones of a stable economy.[18]

The pressure of more and more people on a society too stressed to provide adequate services (housing, education, health care, safety) leads to increased or sustained poverty – and a loss of hope. Thus, while some may debate whether adding nearly 9,000 new lives to the planet every hour is causing significant harm to Mother Nature, there can be little disagreement over what high reproduction rates are doing to people living in some parts of the world.

Remember: Of the 78 million or so people who are expanding the human census every year, 96 percent end up in the world's poorest regions. Even scourges like HIV/AIDS are not a panacea for keeping the human population under control in these areas. Example: Even though 20 percent of Botswana's population is infected with the AIDS virus, high fertility rates will still cause that country's population to double by 2050.[19]

Population growth in those countries or regions already overtaxed by too many people leads to more poverty and more hopelessness. And, to repeat an earlier refrain, these human conditions not only inflict pain and suffering on billions of people living on the socioeconomic margins, but they also represent an increasing danger to people who are not poor.

If you come to the conclusion that population growth in certain parts of the world is detrimental to the environment, then heed this message from Nobel Laureate Amartya Sen:

> Advancing gender equality, through reversing the various social and economic handicaps that make women voiceless and powerless, may also be one of the best ways of saving the environment.[20]

Since women manage household resources such as water, cooking fuel, homegrown crops and so forth, it makes sense that their actions – when multiplied by billions – do have a tremendous impact on the world's ecosystems.

Let's assume you remain unconvinced that population growth in certain regions of the world is not a forerunner to an environmental crisis. You are still left with a problem much more difficult to shunt to the side: the negative impact population growth has on people living in places already saturated with too many people.

Whether population growth in some locations is viewed as an environmental challenge or a human dilemma, it is an issue that cannot be ignored. Those best positioned to do something about population growth?

Women.

PART V

THREE FORCES

CHAPTER 13

INTRODUCTION

We are who we are.

We have a built-in urge and need to *control* and *own*. These are the drivers that have pushed mankind to invent and explore, to produce and market. These same qualities have also been at the root of wars, inquisitions, insurrections, revolutions and terrorism.

For better and worse, the urge to control and own will persist.

So will an involuntary feeling that occasionally creeps into all of our heads: *envy*. In most instances, it is not what we will define in Part VI as *negative* envy. But the seeds are still there, and with a little outside encouragement, those seeds can germinate into truly negative actions that threaten the quality of life, if not the safety, of much of the world.

Each of us also harbors a view of what happens after expelling our last breath. There is absolutely no evidence that any specific *definition of death* is wrong. Of course, there is no definitive proof, either. It is a matter of faith. If you come to believe that infidels cannot be allowed to tarnish your religious convictions; if you think that certain sacred places cannot be occupied by anyone except those who share your views about the afterlife; if you feel that it is justifiable to kill in the name of your faith – then so be it. These are rules that fall under your definition of death. If your faith says those rules supercede whatever laws mortals may create, then you may chose to ignore those laws – even if that means risking persecution, prosecution or execution. Our views about death and its aftermath are a powerful motivator for how we act while we are alive.

We have survived as a species for a long time both because and in spite of our human characteristics. However, we have now arrived at a point on mankind's evolutionary continuum that is vastly different from any other.

Since the nuclear age exploded into existence more than a half century ago, humans have engaged in more than 150 wars that have taken the lives of 23 million people (civilians account for a majority of the lives lost in conflict).[1] Had nuclear, biological and chemical weapons been more widely used during this period, the number of fatalities would have been significantly higher.

Between now and 2030, we humans will take greater advantage of our mass-destruction arsenal. The loss of life is likely to exceed anything we have known, and, without doubt, the world will be vastly different from the way it is today.

Why?

Because we are who we are.

And because the planet's steadily expanding multitude of humans is going to feel the full effects of three powerful forces.

CHAPTER 14

DEFINITION OF DEATH

There is no greater equalizer than death. We stop breathing, our bodies disintegrate, and all the control and ownership issues that determined our respective stations in life completely disappear. Or do they?

Until our paths took us in different directions, the Reverend DeForest "Buster" Soaries and I would get together regularly for breakfast or lunch. Buster is one of those extraordinary people endowed with a multitude of talents. He is a spellbinding Baptist preacher and one of the most effective African-American community leaders in the U.S. He is as skillful at straightening out ex-cons as he was at handling his "side job" as New Jersey's secretary of state (1999-2001). One Midwestern newspaper writer once tagged him as "the next Martin Luther King."

A few years back, Pastor Soaries and I had a conversation about organized religion. The comment that Buster made that day left a lasting impression. He said that when some religious writings (parts of the Bible, Torah and Koran, for example) are taken too literally, they can become inspirationally dangerous.

Apply that observation to what powerful religions say about the "afterlife" and the curtain rises on a huge problem for mankind. Taken literally, religious views about what happens after we die are often in conflict with one another. Those who subscribe to the teachings of the Koran are told they are heading to "Eden Paradise," and all disbelievers will abide in the fire of hell (Al Bayyinah 6-8). The Bible says that Christ will be "dealing out retribution to those who do not know God and to those who do not obey the gospel of our Lord Jesus" (II Thessalonians 1:7-9). Retribution is likely to be (according to Revelation 21.8) an eternal swim in "the lake that burns with fire and sulfur," where, in addition to the faithless, you will find a large assembly of cowards, murderers, fornicators, sorcerers, idolaters and all liars.

Jews, Buddhists and Hindus have their own thoughts about life after death, just as do a countless number of smaller sects and cults. Most religious organizations describe what mankind needs to do while on earth in order to lay claim to a respectable seat in the celestial stadium. After September 11, 2001, we became all too familiar with the al Qaeda promise that if an Islamic warrior goes to his death while carrying out the will of Allah, then he is rewarded with 72 virgins. The notion that killing is acceptable on behalf of a religious cause is not just an Islamic fundamentalist belief. Ample examples in the Bible (for example, Numbers 31:7-18, Deuteronomy 2:34, Joshua 6:21, and Samuel 15:3-8) also are sometimes interpreted as being a justification for taking a life in defense of God. And, according to some rabbinical teachings, Torah restrictions are relaxed during any battle carried out against an enemy of the Jewish people.[1]

The definitions of death and the afterlife are at the core of virtually every organized religion: What goes on here on earth is largely a proving ground for what awaits you in the next life. That belief, when blended with other human traits, can, indeed, inspire people in such a way that they become dangerous, that they can be convinced to accept a definition of death that goes like this: end your life in a way that fosters your religion and you will reap immeasurable rewards later on.

Mosques, schools and religious institutions in places like Palestine, Lebanon and a host of other underdeveloped regions have an ample supply of young people who perceive their lives to be short on control and ownership. These same young people get a regular diet of information from TV, radio, print and the Internet that makes it clear just how shortchanged they are compared with Westerners, who, it seems, have all of their wants and desires satisfied. Infected with a serious case of negative envy, these young people are ripe for the rhetoric of a Hamas, Hezbollah or other organization that transmits "inspirationally dangerous" information.

Made vulnerable by poverty and hopelessness – and proselytized into accepting a radical definition of death – certain people are talked into becoming ambulatory ballistic missiles. They leave behind a marginal mortal existence in exchange for – so they are promised – a place of honor in the afterlife. Most susceptible to this alluring definition of death is the youthful unmarried male. If a little more incentive is needed to coax him into becoming a suicide bomber, he is guaranteed that any family members he leaves behind will be given more control of their lives – in fact, their basic needs will be met until the day they die. It is an attractive death benefit that is payable if people are willing to sacrifice themselves.[2]

Most religious groups do not emphasize inciting their congregants to kill themselves or others. However, those at the fringes of many religious institutions often border on the fanatical. A banner for many acts of violence has been: "In the name of (God, Allah, Brahma, Vishnu, Siva, Buddha or a slew of other gods)." Whether mobilizing massive numbers of followers (for any of the eight Crusades, for example) or motivating small faith-centered cells (Branch Davidians, for instance), religion can be a powerful force that can drive constituents to radicalism.

Chart 10

Religion	Members
Christianity	2,015 million
Islam	1,215 million
Hinduism	786 million
Buddhism	362 million
Atheists	211 million
Chinese folk religions	188 million
New Asian religions	106 million
Tribal religions	91 million
Other	19 million
Sikhism	16 million
Judaism	18 million
Shamanists	12 million
Spritism	7 million
Confucianism	5 million
Bahai Faith	4 million

Religions of the World

Source: World Christian Encyclopedia as referenced on website, Religious Tolerance.org (www.religioustolerance.org)

Just *how* powerful and influential religion can be becomes more obvious when you begin counting the eye-popping number of religious institutions around the world. Most humans migrate to a religious philosophy – 72 percent of the world is reportedly connected to one of the five most well-known religions (Christianity, Islam, Hinduism, Buddhism and Judaism).[3] Only 4 percent of the world admits to being in the atheist camp.[4]

It is astounding to consider how many definitions of afterlife mankind has been able to conjure up. *The World Christian Encyclopedia* tracks 10,000 distinct religions, with 150 of these having more than a million followers each. The number of subgroups within these religions is even more amazing. Would you believe there are *33,830 Christian denominations alone?*[5] Membership estimates for the 15 largest religious organizations in the world are shown in Chart 10.[6]

Although the world has 10,000 interpretations of what may happen after death, usually that does not cause problems – except in cases where a particular belief system imposes hardships on others. If a religion sticks mainly to its knitting and shows no intolerance for other points of view about the definition of death, life's waters are less prone to turbulence. When a belief system insists that it is the *only* avenue to eternal life and is hostile to other religious institutions, things can, and sometimes do, turn ugly.

The Pew Forum on Religion and Public Life tracks American attitudes about religion and its influence on life in the United States. Recently it found that while most Americans are fairly broad-minded when it comes to religion, 18 percent of 2,000 adults polled said that theirs is the "one true faith."[7] That percentage rises dramatically within certain religious groups (nearly half the Evangelical Christians who responded to the poll think there is only one road to heaven and they are on it).[8]

When tunnel vision alters people's views of the afterlife and when narrow-mindedness leads to a wholesale discrediting of other religions, conditions are ripe for conflict. Most people are well aware of how religion can be used to fan the flames of discontent and hatred. Indeed, it comes as no surprise that 65 percent of Americans (according to the Pew Forum) think religion plays a significant role in most wars and other conflicts in the world.[9]

One of those "other conflicts," ironically, deals with not the end of life but rather its beginning. No religious institution can escape confronting reproductive issues – namely contraception and abortion – that continue to confound and confuse people of every belief system in the world. These matters of the heart and mind are the source of many questions:

Is the prevention of conception comparable to aborting a fetus?

Does a blastula, embryo or fetus have equal human standing to a person?

Is the Ayn Rand Institute correct when it says that a mass of protoplasm in the womb is not an independently existing, biologically formed organism?[10]

These are timeless questions that continuously raise hackles and foster extremism.

Aside from the religious and moral issues dealing with these controversial issues, we can make this indisputable statement: Contraception and abortion have a mammoth impact on curbing population growth. If these two practices were removed from the population-control options, it would be *extremely* difficult to curtail reproductive rates in locations where population expansion is a serious problem.

Confronted with this reality, can religion, contraception and abortion peacefully coexist? A closer examination of how mainstream religious movements deal with these reproduction facts of life gets us closer to an answer.

Religion and Contraception [11]

Keep this point in mind: No major religion promotes childless marriages. A fundamental reason for holy matrimony is to produce children. Since contraception is about impeding such production, it isn't surprising that some religions have problems with devices, pharmaceuticals and methods that are designed for the express purpose of preventing conception.

Here is an overview of where five mainstream religions stand on birth control:

* *Christianity.* In 1930, the Church of England gave its flock the go-ahead to use "artificial" contraception (in addition to the "nonartificial" *coitus interruptus* and so-called "rhythm method"). Other Protestant denominations followed suit, and since then, most of the 317 million people around the world who are broadly labeled "Protestants"[12] have been declared sin-free if and when they use artificial contraception.

Such is not the case with the world's one billion Roman Catholics.[13] A 1930 encyclical issued from Rome (and reconfirmed in 1968) says that contraception interferes with natural law. As such, it is a sin. The Catholic Church endorses only abstinence and the "Natural Family Planning" method (which is, in essence, periodic abstinence).[14] However, just because Rome issues a mandate does not mean all Catholics adhere. For example, in Brazil (the world's largest Roman Catholic population), 88 percent of Catholics polled said they "don't follow" church teachings on birth control.[15] There are similar gaps between doctrine and practice throughout the world.

Other Christian groups such as the Eastern Orthodox Church neither support nor prohibit the use of artificial contraceptives. However, since these religious beliefs allow for sexual intercourse to be carried out as an expression of love and not just to procreate, there is an implied endorsement of contraception.

* *Judaism*. One of the Bible's most familiar phrases is "be fruit-ful and multiply" (Genesis 1:28). Orthodox Jewish leaders assign great importance to that passage; some even interpret it as *God's first commandment*. Because being fruitful and using contraceptives are at odds, it is understandable that the Orthodox opinion on birth con-trol (other than abstinence) is: don't use it except in circumstances where a woman's health might be compromised.

Conservative and Reform Jews are given far more latitude when it comes to contraception. Generally speaking, birth control is approved for married couples as a means of avoiding pregnancy for social and economic reasons.

* *Islam*. The Koran includes a few words (in both 17:31 and 6:151) that serve as a platform for the Islamic view of contraception. One statement reads: "You should not kill your children for fear of want." Those words get interpreted differently depending on the Muslim doing the analysis. Some think the passage makes reference only to infanticide and possibly abortion. Others think the words have to be applied more broadly, and that the use of contraceptives (par-ticularly certain kinds of contraceptives) should be banned.

As with other religions, dogma and practice don't always march together. However, although many Muslims use contraceptives, it a widely held that procreation is important – in fact, to many it is con-sidered a religious duty.

* *Hinduism*. Although Gandhi was a proponent of abstinence, the Hindu religion does not specifically rule out other forms of con-traception. Thanks to the lack of any clearly stated prohibition of dif-ferent types of birth control, the government in India (where the Hindu religion is dominant) has been able to put into place a popu-lation-control strategy that relies heavily on contraception use.

* *Buddhism and other religions*. Even though Buddhists may have different thoughts about contraception, the Dalai Lama supports birth control. The exiled spiritual leader of Tibet acknowledges that some

Buddhist factions have lined up against contraception. However, he says, the world has changed, and "it's time to break down those barriers."[16]

Other religious organizations are also struggling with defining the guidelines concerning artificial contraceptives. While most have approved of birth control, it is not uncommon to find dissidents who complain about any open or implied religious endorsement of contraception.

Overall, a "don't ask, don't tell" mentality about contraception seems to be prevalent within many religious camps. If that were not the case, it is doubtful that, according to the United Nations, 67 percent of all married women in the world would be using some type of contraceptive.[17] Still, religious leaders who preach against birth control can prove to be obstacles to population-growth campaigns.[18]

Chart 11

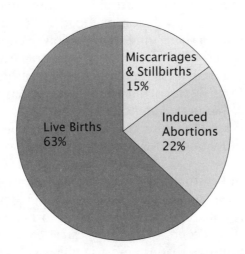

Worldwide Pregnancies
More than a third of pregnancies do not end in the birth of a baby
Source: The Alan Guttmacher Institute, 1999

Religion and Abortion

Few words tend to split people apart more than the term "abortion." Preventing the conception of life is one thing; deliberately taking action to expel a fertilized egg, embryo or fetus is quite another. This is where the definition of death (and life) becomes one of humanity's most controversial dividing lines.

Although this may be difficult, try to think about abortion without its moral and religious implications. How big of a role does this medical procedure play in keeping human population under control? The answer: a huge role.

Chart 11 shows that of the 210 million pregnancies in 1999, 22 percent, or 46 million, were terminated by induced abortion.[19]

Suppose the U.S. Supreme Court had rendered a different decision in *Roe v. Wade* in 1973. Suppose abortion had not only been outlawed in the United States but that all other countries had also made the procedure illegal. And suppose that in every year since *Roe v. Wade*, all of the pregnancies that were aborted had gone full term. If all of that had happened, the earth's population would not be 6.2 billion—it would be more than 8 billion.[20] And many of the issues that this book believes are ahead of us would have been confronted by now. What's more, even the Skeptical Environmentalist would probably concede that the population overload would have pushed the world's ecosystems to their limits and possibly even beyond.

Thus, regardless of one's moral compass regarding abortion, it is clear the procedure has had an enormous effect on limiting population growth. Are we sentencing 46 million women a year to eternal damnation in exchange for stunting the worldwide birth rate? Just how hard-nosed are the major religions when it comes to abortion? Surprisingly, there is more "wiggle room" than most people might think.

The written keystones of most religions are vague about abortion. This fuzziness has opened the door to much debate about if, or when, abortion constitutes a sin or some other breach of faith. Immediately after conception? First trimester? Examine the Christian and Hebrew Scriptures that are most familiar to Westerners and try to find indisputable answers to these questions. You won't find any specific reference to abortion. It is all a matter of interpretation. Do the following Biblical passages mean that embryos and fetuses are equivalent to fully formed humans who have made their way out of the womb?

"Lo, children [are] an heritage of the Lord: [and] the fruit of the womb [is his] reward..." *Psalms 127:3*

"Did not he that made me in the womb make him? And did not one fashion us in the womb?" *Job 31:15*

"Before I formed thee in the belly I knew thee; and before thou camest forth out of the womb, I sanctified thee, [and] I ordained thee a prophet unto the nations." *Jeremiah 1:5*

Since religious writings make no concrete reference to abortion, religious leaders lean heavily on the "thou shalt not kill" argument. Phrased differently in various religious texts, the notion of deliberately taking another life is generally frowned upon (however, there are numerous exclusions, exceptions and examples that suggest killing is acceptable under certain circumstances – for instance, God's commandment that the Israelites kill Midianite men and male children as described in the Bible's Book of Numbers).[21] Therefore, what the age-old wrestling match over abortion comes down to is a definition of if, or when, an unborn human becomes "another life." Here's how each religion addresses this issue:

* *Christianity.* The Catholic Church is singled out here because it is the largest Christian denomination and because the position it has taken against abortion is well known (other Christian denominations run the gamut on the "women's right to choose" debate). As with contraceptive use, there is not always a correlation between what the Catholic Church preaches and what many of its constituents actually do. According to the Guttmacher Institute, Catholic women in the U.S. are 29 percent more likely than Protestant women to get abortions.[22] And in many countries where Catholicism is the religion of choice (such as in Brazil, Colombia and Peru), abortion rates are relatively high.[23]

The Catholic Church has been inconsistent in its stand on the procedure over the centuries. Fifteen hundred years ago, St. Augustine voiced the opinion that abortion was not homicide but rather a kind of sexual sin. The price of absolution was not that severe. Eight centuries later, St. Thomas Aquinas agreed. The church's stand that abortion is a transgression serious enough to warrant excommunication only evolved in the last couple of centuries.[24]

While the Vatican denounces abortion today, the church's position on the procedure is not considered to be an "infallible" teaching. That gives church leaders an opening to adjust their stand on abortion should they be so moved by the spirit or more worldly developments.

* *Judaism.* Every so often, a comparison is made between abortion and the wholesale slaughter of Jews between 1933 and 1945. A recent example is a press release issued in 1999 by the World Life League. It linked RU486 (sometimes called the "abortion pill") with

the Holocaust and drew this response from the head of the Religious Action Center of Reform Judaism[25]:

> Comparing the difficult personal decision of a woman whether to terminate an individual pregnancy to the Nazi government's systematic extermination of 6 million Jews is an insult, both to the memory of those who perished and to the women who must wrestle with their conscience in making a deeply personal decision.[26]

As is the case with those who hold to different religious beliefs, Jews have widely varying opinions about abortion. Some interpret Jewish law to mean that a fetus is not a full human being. A passage in the Talmud ("*ubar yerech imo*" –" the fetus is as the thigh of its mother") is used to support this position.[27] Others, especially those adhering to Orthodox Jewish beliefs, are not favorably disposed to abortion.

As is the case in virtually every religious community, the views of the Jewish laity about abortion are far from harmonious. More than 10 years ago, a survey of B'nai B'rith members in the U.S. found 92 percent were pro-choice.[28] It is unlikely that a poll of Orthodox Jews would yield the same results. Abortion churns up different and often contrary opinions among Jews, whether Conservative, Reform, Reconstructionist or Orthodox. A side note: While there may be mixed views about abortion, there is a prevailing attitude within the Jewish community about government attempts to regulate abortion. The three non-Orthodox Jewish movements (Reform, Reconstructionist and Conservative) do not want the government involved in decisions they feel should be left to a woman, her husband and her rabbi. Even some Orthodox leaders agree with that stand.[29]

* *Islam*. One passage in the Koran is usually at the center of the debate over whether abortion is permissible: *Do not kill your children for fear of poverty for it is We who shall provide sustenance for you as well as them* (Surah 6: At-Talaqa 2-3). Some Islamic theologians claim the words apply only to the born (usually girls). Others say that the passage extends to the unborn, and that it is a prohibition against ending a pregnancy for economic reasons.[30]

Islamic leaders concur that the killing of a soul is prohibited. However, when does a soul exist – at the moment of conception? At some other point during gestation? After birth? These questions prompt a host of opinions and, consequently, Shiite Muslims often think differently about abortion than Sunni Muslims do. The result:

A range of attitudes about abortion is found in nearly every predominantly Muslim nation. In Tunisia and Turkey, for example, abortion laws are liberal. In other Islamic countries, more conservative thinking applies to abortion as well as other family-planning issues.[31]

Since Islam encompasses a large number of people, it is important to clearly understand the religion's position on abortion. For instance, there is some tolerance for abortion within 40 to 120 days after conception. However, to justify an abortion, a woman often has to make the case that pregnancy is endangering or compromising her health.[32] Electing to have an abortion for economic purposes pushes the envelope in most Muslim circles, although there are movements within the Islamic world that are making an attempt to liberalize abortion policies. One example:

Sisters in Islam, an organization in Malaysia, campaigns for Muslim women to attain "a high standard of sexual and reproductive health [and the right to] make their own decisions regarding marriage, motherhood, contraception, abortion and sexuality."[33] Whether these kinds of viewpoints will lead others to religiously justifying abortion remains to be seen.

* *Hinduism.* "Bad karma" is one way to sum up what many Hindus think about abortion. The procedure clashes with the reincarnation beliefs that are part and parcel of Hinduism. As Mohandas Gandhi wrote: "It seems to me clear as daylight that abortion would be a crime."[34]

Other more contemporary Hindu leaders are equally as strong pro-life advocates. One Indian swami writes, "They are killing the baby in the womb. How cruel! In this age of unwanted population, man is losing his compassion."[35]

Abortion is hardly a dull issue within the Hindu world. Hindu doctrine has been, and continues to be, interpreted differently by scholars and religious leaders. Hindu leaders endorsed the procedure, especially if a pregnancy endangered the life of a mother, as far back as the fifth century B.C.[36] With such a lack of clarity and concurrence on the subject, India (the largest predominantly Hindu nation) was able to pass a comparatively liberal abortion law in 1971. The law states that abortion is permitted when a woman's physical or mental health is negatively impacted by pregnancy.[37]

Today, an estimated 6.7 million abortions are performed annually in India.[38] That's 13 percent of worldwide abortions[39] in a country that has about 17 percent of the world's population.

* *Buddhism*. Like the other major religions, Buddhism has different ways of looking at abortion (see endnote about a concept called "personhood").[40] In Bhutan, Sri Lanka and Thailand, there are strict laws regulating abortion.[41] However, in Cambodia, a woman can request and usually get an abortion during the first 12 weeks of pregnancy.[42] The Japanese (many of whom are Buddhists) have a tolerant attitude about abortion.

Abortion tends to push Buddhists down one of three paths.[43] "Absolutist" Buddhists contend that abortion cannot be justified because it is an act of murder. "Utilitarian" Buddhists argue that abortion can be a compassionate act that takes into account a woman's health, the ability of a family to raise a child and even population growth. Finally, "virtue-oriented" Buddhists focus more on attitude and circumstances. If a woman became pregnant without thinking about the consequences of that action, then bad karma might result, whereas a woman who became pregnant because of a contraceptive failure would not be subject to the same misfortune.

* *Other religions*. Jainism, Confucianism, Taoism, Native American religions – whatever the belief system, there are many views about abortion.[44]

If this thumbnail summary of religion and abortion leaves you with the impression that there is a lack of religious clarity about "hominization," "ensoulment," and "personhood," you're right. Does an embryo or fetus come with a soul? Or is this converse opinion correct – "the embryo is clearly prehuman; only the mystical notions of religious dogma treat this clump of cells as constituting a person"?[45]

The Bible, Torah, Koran and other bedrocks of most major religions are so hazy about abortion and contraception that they provoke debate. Who knows? Maybe the authors were deliberately ambiguous so as to constantly force humanity to think about the parameters of life: when it should be prevented, when it begins and what happens when it ends. Whatever the reasons for the fuzziness, religion continues to be the arena where the definition of life and death get the most spirited discussion.

This all gets especially confused when an organized religion takes a hard stand against abortion and, at the same time, preaches that contraceptives shouldn't be used. Operating under these rules, a woman is far more likely to conceive. Therefore, it hardly comes as a surprise that large numbers of women ignore religious restrictions regarding the use of contraceptives. The logic seems to be that a contraception misdemeanor is a lot less serious than abortion, which some feel is a capital crime.

Another problem: If a woman wants to use a contraceptive even if in violation of religious doctrine, that desire doesn't mean much if she doesn't have access to birth-control products. In more-developed countries, accessibility is not as much of an issue as it is in developing nations. Hence, married women in developed nations use contraception 70 percent of the time, while artificial birth control is used only 55 percent of the time in poorer regions.[46]

Contraception and abortion go a long way toward preventing or ending a large number of unplanned pregnancies. However, millions of births resulting from unintentional pregnancies still occur each year. In more-developed countries, of all the pregnancies that end in birth each year, 13 percent are unplanned. In developing nations, the numbers are higher –16 percent of the 182 million pregnancies that go full term are unplanned.[47] This all adds up to 32 million children a year making an unexpected arrival on earth. Of course, not every unplanned pregnancy is unwelcome. Many are. Either way, these large numbers of unanticipated births put added pressure on social systems of developing nations that are already overburdened by too many humans.

Divinity's Divisiveness

Each of us tends to customize the definition of death (along with all of its religious ramifications). What is a prenatal atrocity to one person is simply a type of surgery or pharmacological intervention to another. A terrorist attack is mass murder to some, justifiable homicide to others. Inflicting death on someone to protect one's own religion can be seen as either defensible or a capital offense.

These beliefs are folded into a broader definition of death that is at the core of our faith (or lack of faith). Whatever we believe happens, or doesn't happen, after we die frequently has an influence on our behavior while we are alive. Do this and go to heaven; don't do that or you'll end up in hell. Few definitions of death lack this "cause and effect" component.

As has been noted, our beliefs and religious affiliations are not necessarily in alignment. An accident of birth, more than logic, brings many, if not most of us, into the ranks of organized religion. And our publicly declared faith is more often decided by heritage than our own analysis of what death means. However, how we behave does not necessarily conform to the religious tenets we ostensibly accept. We amend organized religion's rules to suit our own definition of death. Religious institutions become cafeterias that offer a variety of selections – some of which we put on our plates and others we simply disregard. So we convince ourselves that:

* Just because we're Catholic and use a condom doesn't mean we're lost souls.

* Just because we're Southern Baptist doesn't mean we can't have an abortion since, in our minds, we are doing nothing more than sloughing off tissue – not life.

* Just because we kill others while committing suicide doesn't mean we're acting contrary to the Koran because we're carrying out our own jihad in the name of Islam.

* Just because we take the life of an Arab doesn't put me in conflict with the Torah because we're removing a threat to Judaism.

Putting aside all the tweaking that goes on within the confines of a religion, the fact remains that vast numbers of people are connected to different religious institutions and their broad definitions of death. When the definitions inspire people to the point of hatred, violence can ensue. Add intolerance and extremism to the mix, and societies can be ripped apart.

Consider: As the world's population grows, so do incidents of intolerance – at least that is what the U.S. State Department found in its assessment of religious activities in 194 countries.[48] "Throughout the world, Buddhists, Christians, Hindus, Jews, Muslims and other believers continue to suffer for their faith," the State Department's report contends.[49]

Intolerance (along with its cousin, discrimination) is, regrettably, a fact of life. Fortunately, intolerance is often held in check by other social forces. However, there are times when extremism and fanaticism prod intolerance out of its cage, often using a definition of death as a poker. Look for the reasons why extremism succeeds in bringing intolerance into the open and you are likely to find *control* somewhere in the fray. If you apply too much control, people are inclined to resist; if you remove or even threaten to limit the control that individuals already have, anticipate a strong reaction that often comes in a package called intolerance.

As the world gets more crowded, tolerance is more frequently put to the test. Extremism catches fire easily in situations where control and ownership are uneven. The results can be found in too many places where antagonists can be distinguished by their religious creed:[50]

Conflict	Religious Combatants
Middle East	Jews, Muslims
Nigeria	Christians, Animists, Muslims
Philippines	Muslims, Christians
Sri Lanka	Buddhists, Hindus
Northern Ireland	Catholics, Protestants
India	Hindus, Muslims

There are 20-plus other international "hot spots" where religion and differing definitions of death help fuel ongoing violence.

A person's definition of death is rarely easy to sway – relatively few people can be proselytized away from their belief system. That means there likely will always be a bouillabaisse of beliefs that cannot be homogenized into a universal way of thinking about what happens after we die. A peaceful coexistence among these different philosophies requires tolerance. However, even with considerable effort, tolerance on a crowded planet is not easy to come by.

In 1999, representatives from all the major religions convened in Switzerland and signed what is known as the Geneva Spiritual Appeal. The short, pithy statement asks world leaders to *refuse* to do three things:

- Invoke a religious or spiritual power to justify violence of any kind.

- Invoke a religious or spiritual source to justify discrimination and exclusion.

- Exploit or dominate others by means of strength, intellectual capacity or spiritual persuasion, wealth or social status.[51]

As admirable as these goals may be, we continue to see spirituality and the differing definitions of death contributing to more than a few conflicts around the globe. Tolerance, it seems, is no match for the kind of frustration and desperation that are easily hatched in places unsuited to handle a dense compression of people. In such situations, conflicting definitions of death become divisive, sometimes even deadly. It's been that way since 2700 B.C., when the first religious ideological conflict occurred in Egypt. And the prospects for any change in the future are not bright.

Deeply entangled in all of religion's tentacles are women. They are the ones who have to decide whether to risk the wrath of God by swallowing a birth-control pill. They are the ones who must come to a decision about whether to endure the physical and religious pain of an abortion. They are the ones who are subjected to second-class treatment because their own faith defines them as not equal to men.

If women are to be soldiers against poverty and thwarters of terrorism, they can't be hindered by definitions of death (that is, religious views) that are so "inspirationally dangerous" they imperil mankind. Shaking off the religious shackles that repress women won't be easy. However, the alternative – which might lead to burying millions of people and rebuilding a civilization – could be a lot harder.

CHAPTER 15

ORGANIZATIONS

People are social animals. Except for a few hermits and isolationists, they are inclined to "get together" for a host of reasons, including education, recreation, safety, work and worship. The inclination to congregate is a powerful human characteristic that can move mankind to great heights – or tragic lows.

Cultural anthropologists tell us that "social bonding" – the cement that makes organizations possible – is what motivates people to assemble for different purposes. Anthropologist Mary Clark figured out that "early human species could not have survived without the expanded social bonding beyond parent and offspring... Social bonding to one's group was a biological necessity."[1]

Most of us have a built-in mechanism that pushes us toward the pack. As a result, our lives are defined largely by "gangs" (family, school, office/plant, social club, religious and so forth). Take, for example, the workplace, where people gather to be productive. In the United States alone, 6.7 million corporations and partnerships (this excludes the nation's 17 million sole proprietorships) *organize* people around a common business mission or set of objectives.[2]

We not only mobilize to produce but also to protect. After the great fire that swept through Chicago in 1871, the city's mayor issued a proclamation titled "Let Us Organize for Safety."[3] It was a call for citizens, the police, the military and health workers to band together to protect Chicago from looting and other post-fire problems that might beset the city. Armies, civil-defense groups, neighborhood watches all have a similar goal – they are organizations that function to ensure our safety.

Aside from organized activities that cater to our basic needs (earning a living, protecting ourselves from harm), people tend to congregate for other reasons as well. In the United States alone, there are approximately 1.3 million tax-exempt nonprofit organizations, most of which are religious, charitable, social-welfare and fraternal groups.[4] North America also has millions of other civic associations, athletic teams and social groups.

Of all the organizations that exist worldwide, none are quite as extraordinary as religious congregations. As noted in Chapter 14 ("Definition of Death"), a surprisingly large number of religious organizations have popped up in virtually every part of the planet. With some of these institutions having memberships in the millions, *organized* religion can have a powerful influence not only on one's spiritual views but also on virtually every other aspect of one's mortal life.

Given recent events, no organization is more front and center than Islam. While we've already examined some of the religious tenets that are at the core of Islam, this chapter digs deeper, looking at how those tenets are actually the glue that holds together a massive global organization. Islamic government bases a lot of its power on a concept called *umma* – a belief system that operates without geographic boundaries. The parameters are established by the religion itself, not by some man-made line in the sand, barbed-wire fence or border patrol. And it is the literal reading of the Koran that determines the rules – rules that supersede anything legislated by humans.

Although it is sometimes a rocky relationship, Islam (largely the 21 nations in the League of Arab States) and the secular world usually get along.[5] Many Muslim countries have ineffective or dysfunctional national governments, a predicament that led one career diplomat and now Yale professor to write: "The absence of credible political systems, and their inability to hold their own in a world of state powers, incites peoples to protest under the banner of Islam."[6]

Although institutions like Islam are powerful and internationally pervasive, they still are under pressure to comply with man-made rules of law – and most Arabs do just that. For extreme advocates of "pan-Arabism," however, putting the secular ahead of religion can be troublesome. For these people, cyberspace has opened up a universe of opportunity where political and geographic boundaries mean little. Computer downlinks connect the faithful regardless of where they may be.

This leap-frogging of secular governance worries a lot of people. One seasoned foreign-affairs expert puts it this way: "The past decade has been marked by a widening belief that the sovereign state is on the way out; that the information revolution, international 'civil society,' globalization, and other inexorable forces of change are rendering the state obsolete."[7] The concern is that by weakening the sovereign state, we risk destabilizing the core of modern-day civilization. The state, some say, has to remain dominant or we open the door to all sorts of problems, including terrorism. For better or worse, that door already seems to be ajar.

While Islam has been singled out as an example of a transnational organization that is using technology to its advantage, countless other institutions are being swept along by the same swift technological zephyrs. Some, like Islam, are based on well-established and largely well-respected religious principles. Others (commonly known as hate groups) are held together by that belief that they either are, or could be, under siege. We have entered an age where the anti-Jewish group Posse Comitatus can recruit and mobilize via the Internet. The white-supremacist organization World Church of the Creator can proselytize to a vast audience, thanks to the Web. It's a new era.

Sigmund Freud probed the inner workings of organizations in his unsettling book *Group Psychology and Analysis of the Ego*.[8] Freud dedicates a lot of space to Gustave Le Bon, a controversial French psychologist who pumped out numerous theories about nationalism and racial superiority. This is what Le Bon had to say about people who become part of an organization:

> By the mere fact that he forms part of an organized group, a man descends several rungs in the ladder of civilization. Isolated, he may be a cultivated individual; in a crowd, he is a barbarian – that is, a creature acting by instinct. He possesses the spontaneity, the violence, the ferocity and also the enthusiasm and heroism of primitive beings.[9]

Freud is a bit less negative about the fate of people once they join an organization. However, Freud characterizes organizations as a kind of "primal horde," and he goes on to state that members of an organization tend to regress "to a primitive mental activity."[10]

With the exception of a couple of notable motorcycle gangs, a handful of college fraternities and a smattering of European soccer clubs, people who become part of an organization don't all become the kind of primeval dolts as Freud might lead us to think. However, consider the dynamics of huge organizations like governments, large religious institutions, big businesses, and so on. Do individuals take on different characteristics once they get pulled into these large collective bodies? William McDougall, an Anglo-Scot physician-turned-psychologist, emphatically says yes. In his book *The Group Mind*, which Freud also refers to frequently in his analysis of human collectives, McDougall says an organization can stir up emotions to a level that people would find difficult to reach on their own.[11] Freud agrees and comes to this important conclusion:

> On the whole, therefore, it is not so remarkable that we should see an individual in a group doing or approving things that he would have avoided in normal conditions of life.[12]

Before applying all of this to the underlying themes in *How Women Can Beat Terrorism*, here is one more of Freud's observations about organizations: He believed that a "group still wishes to be governed by unrestricted force; it has an extreme passion for authority; in Le Bon's phrase, it has a thirst for obedience."[13]

These insights into how an organization influences behavior give us a better understanding of how groups like a little-known cell called the Al-Aqsa Martyrs Brigade can make headlines around the world. Al-Aqsa is a spinoff of Fatah, a secular nationalist movement within the Palestine Liberation Organization. It does not appear to be a huge organization, but it is big enough to tap into what William McDougall says is needed to turn a random crowd into an organized structure: "Individuals must have something in common with one another, a common interest in an object, a similar emotional bias in some situation."[14] Using Freud's terms, Al-Aqsa has strong "mental homogeneity," and as such, its members are psychologically in tune with one another, and that gives it an especially strong "group mind."[15]

Al-Aqsa is one of the organizations claiming responsibility for suicide bombings that have plagued Israel for years. On April 12, 2002, a 20-year-old seamstress and Al-Aqsa convert stood at a Jerusalem bus stop and detonated a belt of explosives strapped to her waist. The blast killed six Israelis and injured 104.[16]

What makes a young woman destroy herself and several other fellow humans? A perceived lack of control and ownership were part of the equation. Another female suicide-bomber recruit told *USA Today* that the dead woman came from one of the Palestinian refugee camps set up 50 years ago after Israel became a state. The recruit said those living in the camps "are suffering – we are dying while we are still alive."[17] This perception is a petri dish for cultivating negative envy that can lead to extreme and, oftentimes, destructive behavior.

Even with a sky-high level of dissatisfaction, the female suicide bomber would not have been able to achieve her deadly objective if the right kind of lethal technology had been inaccessible. Al-Aqsa presumably equipped her with the explosives and triggering device that have become all too common in the Middle East.

Add to all of this the bomber's own definition of death. She held the belief that the ultimate sacrifice – killing herself, in addition to others – is a way to honor God by carrying out the highest level of jihad.

While all of these components make for a potentially combustible mix, there is a strong probability that the woman would not have blown herself up had an organization not inspired her to do so. Al-Aqsa became the catalyst that, as Freud noted, induced the seamstress to do something she might otherwise have not done on her own. More than just equipping her with explosives and providing her with training, Al-Aqsa tapped into, as LeBon put it, the "violence, the ferocity and also the enthusiasm and heroism of primitive beings."[18]

Extremism does not always require the intervention of a well-defined organization. The Unabomber and Timothy McVeigh are examples of people who operated either on their own or in concert with a few others. In the future, however, the greatest risk to the developed world – for all the reasons noted in this chapter – will be extreme acts of violence orchestrated with the help of organizations. Not only is a group capable of motivating an individual to go beyond the normal boundaries of behavior, but it also is usually in a better position to access lethal technology than a person acting alone.

We know that more than a few organizations have problems with some elements of society. From the Invincible Empire Knights of the Ku Klux Klan to the Two Tone Skinheads (an actual organization in Arizona), there are a lot of societies, institutes, parties, sects, cults and assorted other groups that could provoke individuals to, as LeBon put it, "descend several rungs in the ladder of civilization."[19] Remember, though: Many of these organizations function in societies where people have reasonable levels of control and ownership. The kind of excessive negative envy that leads to mass murder and suicide bombings is less likely to take root in these environments than in places where control and ownership are perceived to be unacceptable – and hopelessly out of reach.

The majority of the groups in Chart 12 fall into the "have little control or ownership" category. The list is compiled by the U.S. State Department and includes groups broadly labeled as terrorist organizations. Some of these organizations are well known to the Western world – for example, al Qaeda and the Popular Front for the Liberation of Palestine. Others, such as Harakat ul-Mujahidin (usually referred to as "HUM," a Pakistani-based group that operates mainly in Kashmir and has called for attacks on the U.S. and other Western nations),[20] lack the media attention given to more high-profile organizations. Time will tell if the lesser-known groups ultimately emerge as the most dangerous to the more-developed world. Although these relatively small groups have, to date, lacked the technological wherewithal to do significant damage, that shortcoming is quickly becoming a thing of the past.

Freud says a group is "impulsive, changeable and irritable."[21] He picks up Le Bon's theory and provides us with these disconcerting words about what might be called group psyche:

> A group is extraordinarily credulous and open to influence... It goes directly to extremes... When individuals come together in a group, all their individual inhibitions fall away, and all the cruel, brutal and destructive instincts, which lie dormant in individuals as relics of a primitive epoch, are stirred up to find free gratification.[22]

A group made up of people who are short on control and ownership is especially "open to influence." Those on the poor side of the widened societal gap are prone to being organized, especially if the rallying cry taps into their negative envy. Mix in a definition of death that uses a promise of martyrdom to fire up "destructive instincts" and we end up with the collapse of the World Trade Center and a promise of much more to come.

Chart 12

Alex Boncayao Brigade (ABB)
Al-Ittihad al-Islami (AIAI)
Allied Democratic Forces (ADF)
Anti-Imperialist Territorial Nuclei (NTA)
Army for the Liberation of Rwanda (ALIR)
Cambodian Freedom Fighters (CFF)
Continuity Irish Republican Army (CIRA)
First of October Antifacist Resistance
    Group (GRAPO)
Harakat ul-Jihad-I-Islami (HUJI)
Harakat ul-Jihad-I-Islami/Bangladesh
    (HUJI-B)
Islamic Army of Aden (IAA)
Irish Republican Army (IRA)
Al Jama'a al-Islamiyyah al-Muqatilah bi-
    Libya
Japanese Red Army (JRA)
Jemaah Islamiya (JI)
Kumpulan Mujahidin Malaysia (KMM)
Lord's Resistance Army (LRA)
Loyalist Volunteer Force (LVF)
New People's Army (NPA)
Orange Volunteers (OV)
People Against Gangersterism and Drugs
    (PAGAD)
Red Hand Defenders (RHD)
Revolutionary Proletarian Initiative Nuclei
    (NIPR)
Revolutionary United Front (RUF)
The Tunisian Combatant Group (TCG)
Tupac Amaru Revolutionary Movement
    (MRTA)
Turkish Hizballah
Ulster Defense Association/Ulster
    Freedom Fighters (UDA/UVF)
Abu Nidal organization (ANO)
Abu Sayyaf Group (ASG)
Al-Aqsa Martyrs Brigade
Armed Islamic Group (GIA)
'Asbat al-Ansar

Aum Supreme Truth (Aum) Aum Shinrikyo,
    Aleph
Basque Fatherland and Liberty (ETA)
Al-Gama'a al-Islamiyya (Islamic Group, IG)
HAMAS (Islamic Resistance Movement)
Harakat ul-Mujahidin (HUM) (Movement of
    Holy Warriors)
Hizballah (Party of God)
Islamic Movement of Uzbekistan (IMU)
Jaish-e-Mohammed (JEM) (Army of
    Mohammed)
Al-Jihad (Egyptian Islamic Jihad)
Kahane Chai (Kach)
Kurdistan Workers' Party (PKK)
Lashkar-e-Tayyiba (LT) (Army of the
    Righteous)
Liberation Tigers of Tamil Eelam (LTTE)
Mujahedin-e Khalq Organization (MEK of
    MKO)
National Liberation Army (ELN)—Colombia
Palestine Islamic Jihad (PIJ)
Palestine Liberation Front (PLF)
Popular Front for the Liberation of
    Palestine (PFLP)
Popular Front for the Liberation of Palestine-
    General Command (PFLP-GC)
Al-Qaida
Real IRA (RIRA)
Revolutionary Armed Forces of Colombia
    (FARC)
Revolutionary Nuclei
Revolutionary Organization 17 November
    (17 November)
Revolutionary People's Liberation
    Party/Front (DHKP/C)
Salafist Group for Call and Combat (GSPC)
Sendero Luminoso (Shining Path, or SL)
United Self-Defense Forces/Group of
    Colombia (AUC)

Terrorist Organizations and Groups
Designated by U.S. Department of State

Source: Patterns of Global Terrorism – 2001
Office of the Coordinator for Counterterrorism, U.S. Department of State, May 21, 2002

Our planet is home to billions of seriously disenfranchised people. More lives are being added by the day to places where survival is elusive and hopelessness is constant. These are the regions of the world where *umma* is most appealing, locations where religious institutions debunk man-made laws. For organizations looking to release the "cruel, brutal and destructive instincts" of people, the poor and desperate are a ready-made audience since they are already inflamed with negative envy.

Organizations also can be formidable hurdles for women. Religious, cultural, political and educational organizations that prevent women from attaining the same rights and privileges as men are impediments to the changes the world needs to make. For women to break through a repressive organization will take determination and courage. Getting a hand from *organizations* in the developed world would help – a point that will be underscored in Part VII ("The Solution").

CHAPTER 16

TECHNOLOGY

"Technology is evolving at roughly 10 million times the speed of natural evolution. Hurricane speed. Warp speed."[1]

The Santa Fe (New Mexico) Institute professor who described technology's velocity as part of a *Scientific American* commentary added these words:

> For all its glitz and swagger, technology, and the whole interactive revved-up economy that goes with it, is merely an outer casing for our inner selves. And these inner selves, these primate souls of ours with their ancient social ways, change slowly. Or not at all.[2]

Thanks to technology, man's "inner self" has been powered up multifold and the results have been both positive and negative. On the upside, humans have been able to decode the mysteries of DNA and locate six new planets in a single year.[3] On the downside, mankind has figured out how to use technology to produce weapons-grade anthrax and to create a thermonuclear explosion by fusing hydrogen isotopes.

Our need to control or own makes for a heavy foot on technology's gas pedal. We've put ourselves in a racecar. The problem is, we don't always know where we are going.

This chapter closely inspects two types of technology: The kind that processes and transmits information; and the kind that more overtly can (and sometimes does) do us harm.

Information Technology - TV

If there is any country where television rules, it is the United States. That's because the number of TV sets in the nation nearly equals the number of inhabitants (805 TVs per 1,000 persons,[4] with 98.2 percent of the nation's 107 million households equipped with at least one set[5]). With so many households tuning in, it is little wonder that U.S. advertisers rely so heavily on the tube. Americans get fed a diet of around 3,000 TV commercials *each day.*[6]

The U.S. is a great laboratory for studying the influence of TV. Americans watch a lot of TV – 4 hours, 11 minutes a day, on average, in 2000.[7] Not only does television deliver ample amounts of entertainment in the U.S., but it also has become the major supplier of news and commentary. What's more, Americans have more trust in what they see on the tube than what they read in newspapers or hear on the radio (see Chart 13).

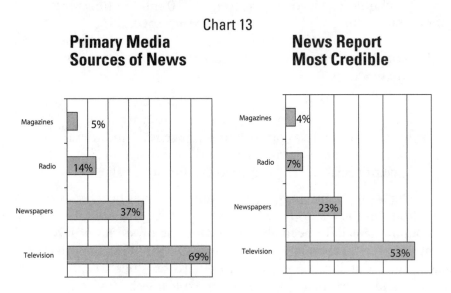

Chart 13

Primary Media Sources of News

Magazines 5%
Radio 14%
Newspapers 37%
Television 69%

News Report Most Credible

Magazines 4%
Radio 7%
Newspapers 23%
Television 53%

Source: Roper-Starch Worldwide, Inc., 1997
Adults 13+

Marketing strategists have known for a long time that TV can be used to (a) create a sense of need and (b) motivate viewers to respond to that need by persuading them to do something – buy a product, purchase a service or vote for a candidate. Beyond influencing these kinds of behaviors, there is growing evidence that TV can also shape our actions in other ways. Case in point:

Television programming and violence have an intimate relationship. By the time children finish high school, they will have been exposed to 18,000 TV deaths.[8] If the journal *Science* has it right, this barrage of blood and guts apparently is leaving a not-so-encouraging imprint on young people.[9] The journal cites a study that tracked more than 700 children for 17 years. Researchers found that, among other things, adolescents who watched more than an hour of television a day were roughly four times more likely to commit aggressive acts than others who were not as glued to the TV. The findings are in line with more than 1,000 other studies conducted over the past 30 years.[10]

True, some media experts question whether there is a cause-and-effect relationship between TV and violent acts (a spokesperson for the Independent Television Commission in the United Kingdom says there is ample research contradicting the link between TV and violent behavior[11]). However, six major pediatric, psychiatric and medical associations think such a connection does exist.[12]

TV isn't the media king just in the U.S. It also has a strong grip on most of the globe. Young men and women ages 15 to 30 in Singapore watch four hours of television a day (mostly sitcoms, sports and reality-TV shows).[13] The Japanese are in front of the TV more than four hours a day, and the Italians are just 10 minutes shy of four hours.[14] Since television has locked up most of the developed nations, the "growth market" for television is the developing world, and TV is wasting no time looking for audiences in low-income and lower-middle-income countries (see Chart 14). This is UNESCO's view of television around the world:

> Television is increasingly displacing radio as the primary means of receiving information and entertainment, even in developing countries... In 1980, there were over 16 times more TVs in industrial countries than in developing countries; in 1995, the ratio had fallen to little more than 5.5 times more.[15]

Chart 14 shows a large gap still exists between developing and more-developed nations when it comes to TVs per household. However, television is coming on strong in lower-income nations. Between 1980 and 1995, TVs per person in China grew *annually* by 145 percent; in Ghana, by 126 percent; in Senegal, by 200 percent.[16] As the International Telecommunication Union reminds us, there are nearly twice as many TVs as phone lines worldwide.[17] Television is on top when it comes to communications media, and its reach and influence continues to expand virtually every day.

Chart 14

Region	Radios (per thousand people)		Televisions (per thousand people)	
	1980	1995	1980	1995
World	294	362	126	204
Developing	97	185	26	115
Industrial	878	1005	424	527
Dev exc India/China	145	225	47	92
Ind exc USA/Russia	605	800	346	469
Sub-Saharan Africa	92	169	12	33
Arab States	164	251	55	109
South Central Asia	52	96	12	53
East Asia	127	277	61	249
Southeast Asia/Oc	143	201	38	91
Latin Am/Carib	260	387	99	192
North America	1869	1990	659	796
Europe	603	672	350	416

Source: "Culture, Creativity and Markets", World Culture Report 1998, Paris France: UNESCO

Television's ability to inform, establish a sense of need and motivate people to address that need is a formula that has worked wonders for businesses bent on selling anything from candy to cars. It also works for organizations marketing or dispensing a point of view. Western TV is replete with video ministries, political advertising, public-service announcements and telethons, all peddling a message that almost always cites a need followed by a call to action on the part of the viewer.

Even news and entertainment programs that don't look to be promoting any particular position can shape public opinion. What a TV broadcaster decides to put on the air – or what it chooses not to – can have an impact on societal attitudes. When the 6 o'clock news runs footage of atrocities inflicted by one side of a battle but edits out massacres committed by the opposition, television influences public opinion. When a sitcom portrays controversial human behavior in a way that implies endorsement (premarital sex, divorce, use of profanity), it affects the way people think and act.

TV's power is its visual effect (the age-old "a picture is worth a thousand words" notion). In little time, it can penetrate the mind with information that stirs up a need that, in turn, moves people to at least consider making a behavioral change. The power of television to move people to action is especially potent among developing nations, where the full effect of TV has yet to be seen. We can pick up signals as to just how influential television is going to be in the developing world during the next few decades by focusing on the rapid growth of a relatively new TV venture.

Thanks to the Iraqi Freedom campaign, most of us know that Al-Jazeera is the Arab satellite-TV channel with the highest viewer ratings in the Middle East. It claims an audience of around 35 million people.[19] The station got worldwide attention for its exclusive interviews with Osama bin Laden following the U.S.-led coalition's air strikes in Afghanistan in 2001. Al-Jazeera broadcasts from the Qatari emirate and is the TV outlet best known for reporting Middle East issues from "an Arab perspective."[20] According to some U.S. government leaders, that perspective includes too many anti-American views.[21]

Al-Jazeera has learned that information technology can be used as a type of satellite-transmitted flypaper to attract audiences that are defined by ethnicity, culture, religion or socioeconomic status. In today's satellite world, TV signals have no regard for national boundary lines. They cross borders and dispense information in both news and entertainment formats. In developing nations, broadcasters like Al-Jazeera do precisely what TV-network executives do in more-developed nations. They learn who their viewers are and then give the audiences what they want. For Al-Jazeera, an "Arab perspective" spells success. It also spells potential trouble for the rest of the world. Here's why:

We know that given enough time and exposure, TV rises to the top as the medium of choice for news and information. We know that viewers assign high credibility to what they see on television. We think that TV can lead to negative behavior (violence). Even if stations like Al-Jazeera are not guilty of deliberately slanting the news they choose to broadcast, these media outlets are passing along the kind of information that can foment dissatisfaction, create a need among viewers to do something about the enormous control and ownership gaps that exist among nations – and even incite an audience to take action (the ultimate behavioral modification).

Think about how a Muslim man or woman who has experienced nothing but lifelong poverty would react, if given a chance, to watch the following TV program:

> Using a "news magazine" format, a television station or
> network fishes for an Islamic audience. It produces a
> prime-time show that points out how half the world is
> struggling to get by but how 20 percent of the world is
> over-consuming and wasting resources. The production
> gives airtime to an outspoken Arab leader who hits all
> the predictable high notes: We need to level the playing
> field... Too few have too much... Too many have too
> little... Running behind the speaker are pictures of hun-
> gry Iranian children crosscut with footage of obese
> Americans.

This example is intended to emphasize the point that without fab-
ricating news, TV can attempt to sway public opinion by choosing
what facts are put on the air. The more TV is able to reach the socioeconomic needy, and the more television graphically conveys information about societal gaps in a way that stirs emotion, the more risky
the world may become.

Al-Jazeera isn't going to change its programming philosophy
any more than a successful Western TV network would. A large segment of the world is interested in TV with "an Arab perspective." Al-
Jazeera fills that void.

Television is one of the true wonders of the modern era. Like so
many other forces discussed in *How Women Can Beat Terrorism*, it
can move the world forward or be partly responsible for sending it into
a tailspin. As our population grows, so does TV's reach. Television
is becoming so ubiquitous that we sometimes take the technology
for granted as a benign dispenser of entertainment and general information. That's a huge mistake.

Information Technology — Internet

In 1962, an MIT scientist named J.C.R. Licklider wrote a series
of memos and spelled out his vision of a "Galactic Network."[22] If he
could give the idea legs, Licklider predicted the network could become
a globally interconnected set of computers that would enable users to
access data and programs from different sites. In his wildest dreams,
Licklider probably did not envision the revolutionary effects of his
Galactic Network. Thanks to a brain trust of government, industry and

academic experts, Licklider's concept was eventually transformed from a vision to a real-life technological wonder: the Internet.

Chart 15

World Total	544.2 million
Africa	4.15 million
Asia/Pacific	157.49 million
Europe	171.35 million
Middle East	4.65 million
Canada & USA	181.23 million
Latin America	25.33 million

The World Online
Figures as of February 2002, Compiled by: Nua Internet Surveys

Today, more than half a billion people are caught in the "Net" (see Chart 15).[23] The growth of this information technology has been astounding. The number of "host" computers (systems that contain data or are connected to a network that usually has access to the Internet) has expanded from fewer than 400,000 in 1990 to 72 million in 1999.488 In China, where personal computers were scarce only a decade ago, more than 15 million people are, or could be, plugged in to the Internet.[24] No technological information revolution has been more dramatic than the birth and rapid maturation of the Internet.

Today, hundreds of millions of people – including more than a few recalcitrant types – all around the world have instant access to mountains of information. And some of that information is perilous. If you think otherwise, find out for yourself. Hook up to the Internet and search for two words: "bomb making." On many of the 1.2 million sites[25] that will be found, you will be provided step-by-step instructions on how to design, assemble and detonate various kinds of explosives. Here is a Net recipe for a "small" bomb that can kill and maim only a few people:

> So you wanna make an inexpensive pressure bomb
> without messing with Drano and sulfuric acid and all

those other dangerous chemicals (you can burn the crap out of your skin if you are not careful). All you need is a battery, a 2-liter plastic bottle and hydrogen peroxide (3 percent by solution is fine), a hammer and a sharp nail.[26]

Interested in building something that goes boom instead of bang? Want a device that will leave behind a good-size bloodbath? Then here's what you need to do:

If you wanted to cause a big explosion in the workplace (with an absolute minimum of fuel and an absolute maximum effect), here's how you would go about it. First, you would need a bomb casing, something strong to confine the chemical reaction when the explosion starts... So let's start with a 45-gallon steel drum of the type used for a huge number of flammable liquids. It will do nicely...[27]

Suppose the goal is to create a blast that will create a catastrophe. A number of sites on the Internet will help steer you in the right direction:

Any 3-year-old can put one (nuclear bomb) together in his spare time. The main obstacle to assembling a nuclear bomb is the availability of the fissionable materials. A crude atomic bomb is really not as complex as is presumed.[28]

In today's technological wonder world, it isn't just the scientists working at the Los Alamos or Lawrence Livermore National Labs who are toying with mass-destruction weaponry – it might also be a group of disenchanted societal misfits.

Just as TV has its positive and negative attributes, so does the Internet. The World Wide Web embraces an awesome amount of valuable information that the private and public sectors of the world are increasingly using as fuel for their productivity. However, this same information technology has opened portals that are debasing and dangerous. The most evident example is pornography (a $3 billion Internet industry with one of four children now exposed to online porn).[29] Less obvious – although far more apparent today than prior to September 11, 2001 – is the important role the Internet plays in plotting and carrying out the kind of devastating attacks that this book predicts will take place over the next three decades.

The two faces of the Internet clearly revealed themselves in connection with the terrorist attacks on America. Within 24 hours of the calamitous events in New York, Washington and Pennsylvania, Web sites were set up to assist the families and friends of those killed or injured by the attacks. As CNN reported, "many who [used telephones] got busy signals ... and turned instead to e-mail and instant messaging, allowing people coast-to-coast to communicate with each other right away."[30]

The flip side of the story is the role the Internet may have played in aiding and abetting the terrorists who masterminded the events of September 11. As one "e-publisher" put it:

> A recent report from U.S. officials indicates that terror-
> ists' use of the Web for communication and coordina-
> tion through the use of encrypted messages is
> widespread, with numerous sites – many of which are
> unaware of the use to which they are being put –
> serving as conduits for terrorist conspiracies.[31]

Fast-moving Web technology combined with freedom-of-speech protection in many countries make it extremely difficult, if not impossible, to keep a leash on the Internet. Cyberspace is an unruly place, and it appears that in order to reap the benefits of the Web, we have to tolerate its downsides. Those downsides could become increasingly problematic, though, as more and more of the world – particularly the developing world – gets online. This forecast begs a few obvious questions:

Just how far will the Internet spread? Is the Web elastic enough to stretch to all parts of the globe – even to those economically forsaken boondocks that still don't have phone service? Is it realistic to think that poor people who are struggling to make ends meet on $2 or less a day will ever find themselves in a digital chat room?

The Internet Society, or ISOC, the principal professional organization for Internet engineers and architects, not only thinks that developing nations can and should be plugged into the Web, but it also is trying to expand the Net to these countries. The ISOC says it is conducting workshops "from Tunis to Hanoi, from Bamako to Bhubaneswar" as a way of helping regions of the world that are in the early stages of Internet-infrastructure development.[32] Why? Because the ISOC believes that "in order to achieve sustainable economic growth, developing countries must have access to technological progress."[33]

One of the modern-day gurus of the Internet world agrees. MIT's Nicholas Negroponte, who wrote a popular book about the Internet called *Being Digital*, is optimistic that the developing world will "rapidly become digital."[34] He reminds us that nearly half the people living in developing nations are under the age of 20, in contrast to less than a third of the residents of more-developed countries. Negroponte says this huge youth corps should be viewed as an asset because young people "when given a chance ... will jump into the digital world with passion, delight and abandon."[35] He proposes a new "United Nations for cyberspace ... to make the digital world immediately available to everyone."[36]

As Chart 15 makes clear, the Internet has a long way to go before it captures all or most of the world's 6 billion-plus souls. Regardless of how many people it eventually snares, however, the Internet's influence already has been established. Furthermore, as we learned from al Qaeda's use of laptops and Internet linkages, the Web's effect on the world can be profound.

Information Technology – Where Is It Taking Us?

More than any other media, television and radio are the dispensers of information that can make the greatest impact in the developing world. Literacy is not a roadblock to watching TV or listening to radio. People don't have to know how to read in order to be informed, entertained, inspired and incensed by graphic images and sounds.

Although the U.N. makes the point that "more than a third of the world's population does not have clean and affordable energy services,"[37] that does not mean that TV and radio are unknown to the 2 billion people around the globe who have no electricity. Watching and listening is a communal experience in certain developing nations where a TV or radio is a village resource and not a living-room staple. Even in those circumstances, electric media is still reaching its intended audiences.

Over the next few decades, television will become an even more instrumental medium for molding worldwide public attitudes than it is today. All of us in the Western world are swayed to one degree or another by TV's programming content, even if we think otherwise. We're beginning to comprehend how television can fan the flames of discontent in the Middle East. If there are any lingering doubts about the power of television, they will be swept away during the next decade or two.

The Internet likely is never going to match television's success as every person's information technology. It doesn't have to. The Net, along with its related computer technology, is a doorway into a vault filled with valuable as well as dangerous information. Over the next 10 to 20 years, maybe a billion to 2 billion more people will venture through that portal. A few of those individuals will pose a great risk to mankind, and they will make cyberspace the ultimate war room.

Information technology gets credit for many of mankind's recent advances. It has widened our base of knowledge and, simultaneously, it has given far more people greater access to that knowledge. The price the developed world is paying for all of these advantages is ...vulnerability. While we have been putting on technological muscle, we have been exposing our societal Achilles' heels.

TV is giving a larger percentage of the human race a look at who we are, warts and all. Depending on where you happen to be sitting when you do your channel surfing, the picture on the tube can be downright discouraging – so discouraging, in fact, that it can send twinges of negative envy racing through your economically deprived body. While TV may make you susceptible to messages from organizations that want the developed world to pay a price for the great social divides around the globe, it is the Internet that offers you an outlet to do something about the situation.

A London School of Economics professor captured the essence of what all this means when he wrote, "the result is a lot of unemployed and angry young people, to whom new information technologies have given the means to threaten the stability of the societies they live in and even to threaten the social stability in countries of the wealthy cluster."[38]

Welcome to the information age where knowledge is not just power but also potentially a powder keg.

Lethal Technology – Maximum-Power Nuclear Weapons

Technology gave us nuclear energy. En route, technology also gave us the capacity to extract plutonium from spent power-plant fuel. And eventually technology gave us the ability to use reactor-grade plutonium to produce effective nuclear weapons.

It is estimated that a dozen countries have extracted about 200,000 kilograms of plutonium from piles of nuclear waste. In his book *Lethal Arrogance,* Lloyd Dumas makes this alarming statement: "this is an enormous amount of plutonium, about the same amount used to produce *all* of the tens of thousands of devastating weapons in the world's nuclear arsenals today."[39]

And what about those weapons that have already been developed?

According to the *Bulletin of the Atomic Scientists,* more than 31,000 nuclear weapons are maintained by eight known nuclear powers.[40] For all the talk about nuclear disarmament, this represents a reduction of only 3,000 nuclear devices since 1998.[41] A side note: Many of the warheads in the United States that have been deactivated have not been dismantled – they have been placed in storage. Some estimates put the number of U.S.-warehoused nuclear warheads at around 5,000. That huge amount of nuclear weaponry in reserve is over and above the 16,000 operational warheads in the U.S. and Russia.[42]

This astounding amount of nuclear firepower means that huge piles of fissile material are still stockpiled all over the place. According to the *Bulletin of Atomic Scientists:*

> Russia has more than 1,000 metric tons of weapon-grade uranium and about 140 metric tons of weapon-grade plutonium, and the United States has nearly 750 metric tons of weapon-grade uranium and 85 metric tons of weapon-grade plutonium.[43]

The *Bulletin* reminds us that it takes just 55 pounds of weapons-grade uranium or 17.6 pounds of plutonium to construct a rudimentary nuclear weapon.[44] Does Russia – or any nuclear nation, for that matter – have such an airtight security system that it can prevent the theft of 55 pounds of uranium? According to a 2003 U.S. government report, Russia has weapons-grade nuclear materials stored in 133 buildings throughout the country, and only 14 have been upgraded with adequate security systems.[45]

While the United States openly worries (and complains) about Russia's porous nuclear-security provisions, it is less open about the holes in its own protective armor. "In the past five years, more than 50 reports by congressional investigators, the president's Foreign Intelligence Agency Board, the DOE inspector general and outside experts have detailed inadequate safeguards," wrote Massachusetts Congressman Edward Markey. He added: "I have interviewed numerous security officials who work at DOE nuclear weapons facilities who believe these problems to be extremely serious."[46]

These are the kinds of worries that prompted the Educational Foundation for Nuclear Science (the organization that publishes the *Bulletin*) to move its symbolic "Doomsday Clock" a couple of minutes closer to midnight in 2002.[47] We are now only seven minutes to doomsday and one reason, according to the foundation, is that there are "growing concerns about the security of nuclear-weapons materials worldwide."[48]

Maybe we are getting overly excited about the theft or "diversion" of uranium and plutonium. After all, even if the material were to fall into the wrong hands, using it to develop a nuclear-weapons program is no easy task. In fact, some people maintain that it takes a large amount of money and a lot of engineering brainpower to achieve a major-league nuclear-weapon capability – maybe $1 billion or more and as many as 1,300 scientists and technicians.[49] Considering that the U.S. spent an estimated *$5.5 trillion* (in 1996 dollars) to develop the first nuclear bomb, $1 billion may seem like a bargain.[50] However, assuming the goal might be to produce a less sophisticated nuclear device that could be delivered by suicidal terrorists instead of ballistic missiles, the cost would not be prohibitive.

Another gloomy point: There appear to be plenty of people who might be in the market to produce a nuclear device. A decade ago, the U.S. Central Intelligence Agency warned that thousands of Russian scientists working in the nuclear- and advanced-weapons fields were either jobless or at risk of being unemployed – a situation that hasn't gotten any better in recent years.[51]

In the mid-1980s, five former U.S. nuclear-weapons designers were asked if a workable nuclear bomb could be made from stolen plutonium or highly enriched uranium.[52] Back then, the answer was yes. They agreed it would be possible for a team of three or four knowledgeable specialists to put together a crude device probably weighing a ton or more. The explosive power of that kind of bomb would be around 10 kilotons. As a matter of comparison, the two bombs dropped on Japan in 1945 weighed around 20 kilotons.

Also in the 1980s, a particularly disconcerting scenario about A-bomb production appeared in the magazine *New Scientist*. The article claimed that if 30 to 40 pounds of nuclear material could be acquired, a two-story house could literally be turned into a devastating bomb. A couple of sticks of dynamite, 20 feet of pipe, a few sacks of cement, some gravel and a handful of odds and ends were the only other items needed to build a device powerful enough to kill at least a quarter of a million people.[53]

A decade and a half later, technology has given us the ability to more easily miniaturize nuclear weapons. Just so we have a clear understanding of what "miniature" means, experts say that now a nuclear bomb may only require between three and 25 kilograms of enriched uranium or between one and eight kilograms of plutonium. One kilogram of plutonium would be equal in volume to about 15 percent of the contents of a standard soft-drink can.[54]

Even with all the "advances" in nuclear-explosives technology, trying to jam a nuke into a suitcase is still not a simple task. One of the conclusions in a 1987 report produced by weapons designers apparently continues to hold true:

> Production of sophisticated devices should not be con-
> sidered to be a possible activity for a fly-by-night terror-
> ist group. It is, however, conceivable in the context of a
> nationally supported program able to provide the neces-
> sary resources and facilities.[55]

Let's imagine the unimaginable. What would happen if a fairly large nuclear device were to explode in a congested city or region?

A Princeton University physicist calculates that if a 15-kiloton bomb were detonated in Mumbai, India (population: 13 million), between 150,000 and 850,000 people would be killed in the short term.[56]

A clinical radiology professor in San Francisco says that a "suit-case-size bomb … would kill up to 50 percent of people a quarter-mile away."[57]

One of the most oft-quoted, worst-case projections about the nuclear "kill cluster" appeared in the *New England Journal of Medicine* in 1962. A group called Physicians for Social Responsibility published a forecast for what would happen if a 20-megaton thermonuclear bomb (a force equal to 1,000 kiloton bombs) exploded over Boston.[58] Here is the ominous prediction:

> Within minutes after the bomb exploded, one million
> people would die. Among the 1.8 million survivors,
> more than 1.1 million would be fatally injured. Another
> 500,000 would have major injuries from which they
> might recover if they received adequate medical care.[59]

People with burns, broken bones, ruptured eardrums, collapsed lungs (a condition caused by the bomb's concussion) and, of course, radiation poisoning probably would overwhelm whatever was left of the region's emergency health-care services. There would be no hope for those exposed to high doses of radiation (4,000 to 5,000 rads), for they would be afflicted with a condition known as central-nervous-system syndrome (swelling of the brain that would eventually cause the victim to convulse, pass into a coma and die). Even medium doses of radiation (400 to 600 rads) would be fatal to many victims, and the days before death would be excruciating since radiation would be eating away the lining of the stomach and intestines.

We have lived so long with the threat of an all-out nuclear battle that many of us have become numb to the consequences of such an attack, should it occur. For our own mental health, it is probably just as well that we don't dwell on facts like this one: A single U.S. Trident submarine that carries 192 nuclear warheads could inflict more than 50 million casualties if those missiles were aimed at Russian metropolitan areas.[60] In 1958, the U.S. government guessed that one in five Americans would die if the U.S.S.R. were to "nuke" the United States.[61] Today, a broadside nuclear attack on America would be far more devastating. Thanks to advances in lethal technology, we have greatly "improved" the kill power of atomic weaponry.

Until recently, it seemed remote that the world would experience the "shock and awe" of a 20-megaton bomb exploding over a major city. That remoteness disappeared when North Korean leader Kim Jong-Il let it be known that his country is not only willing to use nukes, but that it is now also has them. It's possible, as a result, that we may witness a full-scale nuclear shootout between now and 2030. The probability is even higher that smaller strategically placed nuclear devices will be detonated during the next few years.

Lethal Technology – Radiological Dispersion Devices ("Dirty" Bombs)

Since September 11, 2001, the media has hypothesized that radiological dispersion devices could emerge as the weapons of choice for terrorists. Speculation abounds that the U.S. or other more-developed nations will feel the sting of one or more of these so-called "dirty bombs" – and sooner rather than later, many experts warn. Those who once shrugged off such a prospect may have had second thoughts after learning of Jose Padilla (also known as Abdullah al Mujahir).

Padilla is an alleged terrorist wannabe who was arrested in Chicago in 2002 in connection with a plot to detonate a dirty bomb. Although the details of Padilla's involvement in the plot remain murky, his capture educated a lot of people about how conventional explosives (dynamite, for example) could be combined with radioactive materials such as cesium-137 or cobalt-60 (substances that are used in hospitals and a number of industries) to produce a radiological dispersion device.

Unlike maximum-power nuclear bombs, dirty bombs may be more bang than bite. The problem, however, is that they still scare people and can create economic fallout that can take a long time to fix. The president of the American Council on Science and Health offered her opinion of what impact a dirty bomb might have. Substantial physical damage would occur in the area where the device explodes, she predicted – the more conventional firepower used, the greater the damage. But the radiation release "would be minimal; it would not result in the type of 'plume' associated with a Chernobyl-style nuclear accident or the explosion of a nuclear bomb," the council president added.[62]

Some in the science community think the overall impact of a dirty bomb would be far more than "minimal." The science editor for a BBC news service says "a contaminated region could be rendered uninhabitable for years, and people exposed to radiation would have to be monitored for the rest of their lives."[63] As for buildings exposed to substances such as cesium-137, they might have to be torn down since cesium-137 can sometimes fuse with cement.

Any nuclear explosion, whether mammoth or minute, has a way of elevating the human fear factor. People are not going to be comfortable wandering back into an area contaminated by radioactive material, even if experts insist the level of radiation is relatively harmless. The media has made the public all too aware of the linkage between radiation exposure and leukemia, thyroid cancer and a host of other diseases. As a *Time* magazine correspondent noted, even though a dirty bomb might not kill thousands of people, "any bomb … that sets off Geiger counters would terrify a whole city."[64]

Consider what would happen if several dirty bombs exploded simultaneously in key centers of commerce within the borders of a single country. Getting back to business as usual would be no easy task. How likely is it that terrorists could get their hands on the "dirt" needed to make a bomb dirty? Answer: highly likely. Even in the United States, where radioactive materials are subject to relatively high levels of security, there is a long list of radioactive items that are "missing and unaccounted for." From 1996 to 2002, for instance, U.S. businesses and research facilities lost track of as many as 1,500 pieces of equipment containing radioactive parts.[65]

However, the primary supermarkets for radioactive materials can be found in Iran, Iraq, Libya, North Korea, Pakistan, and the former Soviet republics, all of which have ample amounts of such materials – and in some cases, apparently, the willingness to sell those materials. As the former director of Saddam Hussein's nuclear program in Iraq disclosed, "there are more sellers than buyers of nuclear materials" in the former Soviet republics.[66] Consider:

- In 2001, Moscow police seized a half-pound of radioactive cesium-137 that three suspects were apparently prepared to sell for $1.5 million to an unnamed Middle Eastern country.[67]

- In 2002, six Lithuanians were arrested for attempting to sell two pounds of cesium-137 on the black market.[68]

Accessible materials. Easy to build and use. Likely to create havoc. These are the characteristics of a weapon that would suit unhappy people overloaded with negative envy. Regrettably, radiological dispersion devices and people in the more-developed world may be about to meet. It isn't likely to be a pleasant encounter.

Lethal Technology – "BWs" and Chemicals

When it comes to killing large numbers of people, dirty bombs are small compared with maximum-power nuclear devices. If terrorists want a large body count, then a large-scale nuclear bomb would be ideal. However, we know that acquiring the necessary parts and engineering talent needed to make a maximum-power nuclear device is neither easy nor cheap. Suppose one could produce a weapon that had the same or greater lethal punch as a maximum-power bomb but would cost less than $100,000 to make and require just five biologists?[69] You're about to enter the world of biological weapons, or "BWs."

During the latter half of the 1700s, Lord Jeffrey Amherst was one of the true heroes of the British Empire. As commanding general of British forces in North America, Amherst had much to do with his nation's acquisition of Canada. He was also instrumental in Britain's victory over the French following a nine-year struggle popularly called the French and Indian War. By the time the Treaty of Paris was signed in 1763, when France gave up its North American possessions to England, Lord Amherst had become nothing less than an idol.[70]

"Amherst" still echoes in parts of Massachusetts – Amherst is the name of a town, a highly regarded college, and even a lovely inn that sits on the edge of a postcard-perfect New England common. All of this for a man some regard as the chief importer of germ warfare to North America.[71]

Historians who have studied letters written by Amherst to one of his colonels conclude that the British commander probably sanctioned distributing smallpox-infected blankets and handkerchiefs as a means of decimating the Indian population that had sided with the French. Some dispute this charge, but Amherst's own correspondence contains more than a few hints as to his genocidal leanings: "bring about the total extirpation of those Indian Nations... put a most effectual stop to their very being..."[72]

Regardless how it came about, a smallpox epidemic raced through the Ottawa tribe in 1763 and demonstrated how gruesomely effective a BW could be.

Amherst is not the father of germ warfare. Primitive warriors learned centuries earlier that excrement on the tip of an arrow enhanced the potency of the weapon. There are records of biological attacks dating back to 1346, when Tatar soldiers hurled people killed by the plague into enemy camps. The tactic worked. Opposition forces became infected with "the black death" and, soon after, were driven from their strongholds by Tatar warriors.[73] In 1650, a Polish general filled hollow tubes with saliva from rabid dogs to produce harmful ordnance.[74]

Although biological weapons have been around a long time, they have been used sparingly. The obvious problem with BWs is that, in many cases, they can just as easily wipe out the user as the enemy. Of course, attempts have been made to tame BWs and turn them into a more practical military resource. Perhaps the most notable and notorious example of BW experimentation took place in 1932. The Japanese infected at least 11 Chinese cities with anthrax, cholera, shigellosis, salmonella and the plague, and an estimated 10,000 people were killed.[75]

During World War II, the U.S. and other countries got serious about building offensive BW programs. Twenty-five years later, huge stockpiles of BW agents had been produced. In the U.S. alone, the military successfully created weapons out of anthrax, botulism, tularemia, brucellosis, Venezuelan equine encephalitis and Q fever. Most of this lethal stew was largely destroyed in 1972 after the U.S. signed the Biological Weapons Convention, which prohibits the developing, producing, stockpiling, acquiring and retaining of BW agents or the means to deliver them.[76]

Chart 16

AGENT	Downwind Reach (km)	Dead	Incapacitated
Rift Valley Fever	1	400	35,000
Tick-borne encephalitis	1	9500	35,000
Typhus	5	19,000	85,000
Brucellosis	10	500	100,000
Q-fever	>20	150	125,000
Tularemia	>20	30,000	125,000
Anthrax	>20	95,000	125,000

Health Aspects of Chemical and Biological Weapons
Source: World Health Organization, 1970

Treaties, accords and conventions may have curtailed the use of BW agents, but they have not put an end to the development and "improvement" of these weapons. The alleged undercover production of anthrax, botulinum toxin and aflatoxin in Iraq was one of the reasons that the "coalition of the willing" recently invaded that country. However, Iraq is (or was) only one of an estimated 17 countries that are either known to have an offensive BW program or are suspected of having such a program.[77]

It's not just nation states that represent a BW threat. Dangerous biological materials are increasingly accessible to small groups and individuals. What's more, BW delivery systems also are becoming more available, thanks to *technology*. Hence, we may be close to finding out if the World Health Organization was right when, in 1970, it projected what would happen if 50 kilograms of a biological substance were effectively dispersed in a city of 500,000.[78] Chart 16 provides an overview of the WHO forecast.

Let's assume that three cities of 2 million people each were attacked simultaneously with anthrax (revisit Chapter 3 about why this concurrent multi-city attack strategy may be a likely scenario between now and 2030). If the WHO projections are right, nearly 400,000 people would die in each city (a total of 1.1 million deaths) and 1.5 million would be disabled.

Governments may say the possibilities of such a coordinated attack are remote. *Technology*, however, is increasing the odds.

In the book *Germs*, three *New York Times* reporters describe how the U.S. Defense Department was able to construct an anthrax factory using off-the-shelf materials. "With precious little money…," the authors note, "a state, or even a group of terrorists, could build and operate a small-scale germ-weapons plant, probably without the intelligence agencies' knowledge."[79]

The awesome power of BWs is nearly beyond comprehension. Botulinum toxin, for instance, is the world's most toxic compound. One theory states that a single pound of the compound could kill a billion people if it could be dispersed effectively (no easy trick).[80] Now consider this: prior to the Operation Desert Storm conflict, in 1991, Iraq reportedly produced 5,000 gallons of this same toxin.[81]

The list of potential bioweapons is painfully long (more than 50 different viruses, rickettsiae and other bacteria are on the menu). The U.S. Centers for Disease Control has nominated a few substances as the most significant threats. Here is a snapshot of the "big six"[82]:

- Anthrax. The U.S. had good reason to be concerned about the anthrax-by-mail incident in 2001. If contracted and untreated, anthrax kills nearly every person it infects – a kill rate far exceeding other pathogens such as the plague. A cough and fatigue (flu-like symptoms) usually signal the onset of the disease. Patients may experience a brief recovery (called the "anthrax honeymoon"), but then relapse when their respiratory systems collapse. If fully "weaponized" – that is, if it were made more virulent and stable and processed into a fine powder – anthrax could be dispersed by aerosol spray. Such an attack could prove devastating. In 1970, the World Health Organization concluded that an aerosol release of anthrax that floated over a population of 5 million could kill 100,000 people and sicken another 150,000. Later, the U.S. Office of Technology Assessment estimated that if 100 kilograms of anthrax were dispersed via aerosol spray over Washington, D.C., between 130,000 and 3 million people would die.[83]

- Smallpox. During an incubation period of less than two weeks, victims would be virtually incapacitated by high fever and fatigue, coupled with severe headaches and backaches. A rash would develop over the body, along with sores. The good news is that most people infected by smallpox would survive an attack. The bad news: They would be left with pockmarks to remind them of the experience.

- Botulism. If exposed to this toxin, victims exhibit such problems as blurred vision, nausea, lethargy, slurred speech and muscle aches. Unless treatment (an anti-toxin) is administered fast, a victim becomes paralyzed and most likely dies. Even if treated immediately, there is no guarantee of full recovery, and recuperation usually takes weeks or months. The toxin is relatively easy to produce and carry, according to some specialists, but dispersion is tricky.

- Plague. The "Black Death" was responsible for wiping out millions of people in the 1300s. Antibiotics, hygiene and improved living standards make the plague less of a threat today – unless, of course, the bacteria are introduced in the form of a BW. The effects of the disease generally appear within six days. The first signs: fever, fatigue and blood-tainted coughing. If not treated, victims experience kidney or respiratory failure, or both. A form of pneumonia would eventually set in – 50 percent of pneumonic-plague victims die.

- Tularemia. Although not as well known to the public, this bacterium has been studied as a BW since World War II. Although tularemia is treatable with antibiotics, it can spread rapidly. The symptoms are similar to the flu – chills, headaches, fatigue and so on. The Center for Civilian Biodefense Studies at Johns Hopkins University says that, depending on the strain and the speed of treatment, tularemia could kill between 5 percent and 60 percent of its victims.[84]

- Hemorrhagic fevers. People intent on using these viral infections as weapons are at high risk of infecting themselves as well as others. Still, fevers like Ebola, Marburg, Lassa and dengue assault the body so gruesomely that they might be selected because of their terrorizing potential. Someone infected with Ebola, for instance, would experience a high fever, vomiting and chest pains, and shortly after exposure would bleed both internally and externally (as a few Hollywood movies have demonstrated). Hemorrhagic fevers are the most graphically powerful of all BW options.

Many other potentially deadly viruses and bacteria could be added to a BW arsenal, including Q fever, typhus, viral encephalitis and hantaviruses. Most of these viruses and bacteria cannot be blamed on technology, per se. They are naturally occurring and have been around for eons. What technology has managed to do is to draft these bugs into military service, a process that no longer (thanks to information technology) takes a lot of money or expertise. *Time* included this unnerving paragraph in a 1997 story about germ warfare:

> One truth about bioweapons, says a Pentagon official, is that they can be produced using a recipe found on the Internet, a beer fermenter, a culture and a gas mask, with a total investment of about $10,000. "If you buy commercial equipment," he says, "and put it in a very small room, you can be producing kilogram quantities of anthrax within a month." And each kilo "has millions and millions of potential deaths in it."' A study by the U.S. Office of Technology Assessment estimated that 100 kilos of anthrax spread by crop duster over Washington could cause 2 million deaths.[85]

If making a BW is relatively easy and inexpensive, dispersing it is difficult, for the dispersal process often destroys a bug's lethality. Still, aerosol and other delivery technologies have come a long way over the past decade or two. Even before the first Gulf War, Iraq was trying to develop an effective BW dispersal system (in 1990, in fact, it flight-tested a remote-controlled plane equipped with a 2,200-liter tank and sprayer[86]). It seems inconceivable that there will not be effective BW dispersal systems well before 2030.

Another potential BW threat is something called "ethnic weapons." The fungus *Coccidioides* immitis, for example, causes fever, coughs and chills, and it can be life threatening. The kicker: It kills black people far more effectively than whites.

One of the great paradoxes of our time is how mankind's almost incomprehensible understanding of gene sequencing may be catapulting us toward the development of even more sophisticated and terrifying BWs. Could we be facing a future that resembles the following?

> Bioterrorists could equip a relatively harmless vector
> (for example, adenovirus, a common respiratory virus)
> to deliver a payload of deadly genes – one that could,
> for example, prevent blood from clotting. They could
> concoct a genetically engineered stealth virus – one
> that, like many naturally occurring viruses, including
> herpes simplex, would infect a person but remain harm-
> less unless triggered by a specific stimulus... Scientists
> might engineer pathogens that would direct the body's
> immune-system cells to commit mass suicide, or would
> cause pancreatic cells suddenly to secrete enormous
> amounts of insulin.[87]

All of these biological developments may sound unbelievable. Unfortunately, they are real, and scientists continue to experiment with and develop new pathogens.

If we are on the brink of being assaulted with dirty bombs, then we may be just as likely to undergo a major BW attack. There simply are too many pathogens tucked away in germ labs around the world – and too many people who are willing to use them as armaments. At one time, an estimated 60,000 biowarfare scientists, technicians and support staff were working on BW projects in the old Soviet Union alone.[88] Most of these people have been forced out of their jobs, as have BW experts in other countries – all casualties of downsized or abandoned germ-warfare programs. This crop of potentially discontented and, in some instances, financially strapped scientific experts, worries groups like the Center for Nonproliferation Studies, which sent out this warning to the U.S. Senate:

Some [of these displaced BW experts] may be enticed by high salaries and other inducements to work for foreign governments, sub-national groups and criminals to develop biological weapons.[89]

The 1972 Biological Weapons Convention was supposed to block the research, development and production of offensive biological weapons. That agreement, however, contains loopholes that permit countries to conduct BW "defensive" work. As worrisome as those loopholes may be, they run a distant second to the BW threat posed by rogue states, nongovernmental organizations and shadowy confederations bent on developing and using biological agents as weapons.

"We conclude that the threat of germ weapons is real and rising, driven by scientific discoveries and political upheavals around the world," notes *Germs*.[90] This conclusion may be foreboding, but it certainly comes as no surprise – not in a world where information technology is providing BW blueprints for converting pathogens into a "poor man's A-bomb."

Lethal Technology – Conclusion

The following quote, widely attributed to Albert Einstein, sums up mankind's relationship with technology:

"It has become appallingly obvious that our technology has exceeded our humanity."

PART VI

NEGATIVE ENVY

CHAPTER 17

PULLING DOWN

VERSUS PUSHING UP

Let's start with a dictionary definition of "envy": "1. a sense of discontent or jealousy with regard to another's advantages, success, possessions, etc. To *envy* is to feel resentful because someone else possesses or has achieved what you wish to possess or to have achieved: *to envy the wealth, a girl's beauty.*

With all due respect to the Random House dictionary, Aristotle gave the concept of envy a different spin. To him, jealousy and envy were not synonymous. This is the distinction he made between the two terms:

> *Jealousy* is both reasonable and belongs to reasonable
> men, while *envy* is base and belongs to the base, for the
> one makes himself get good things by jealousy, while
> the other does not allow his neighbor to have them
> through envy.[1]

According to the Greek philosopher, then, jealously is fine since it motivates, inspires or drives you to acquire or achieve what someone higher up the ladder already has. Envy, on the other hand, is *not* something that pushes you higher. It is a force that you apply to bring others to a lower level, where you yourself happen to be. It is the old "if I can't have it, I'm going to make sure you don't have it, either" way of thinking.

Like Aristotle, the world's major religions also disparage envy. The Bible says, "Love does not envy" (I Corinthians 13:4). The Torah warns that "envy and anger cause the death of one driven by sensuality" (Part 27, Chapter 5, Verse 2). The Koran bemoans the "evils of the envious when they envy" (Sura: 113:5). Is it any wonder that envy was named to the list of "The Seven Deadly Sins" that Dante Alighieri and others immortalized? In "Purgatorio," one of three epic poems included in *The Divine Comedy,* Dante lays out all seven of the major vices of life: pride, wrath/anger, sloth, avarice/greed, gluttony, lust and envy.[2] Centuries later, the controversial Ayn Rand agreed, but added this qualifier: Envy can be divided into two parts. She said "bad" envy is repugnant, but that a more acceptable kind of envy equated to what Aristotle termed jealousy – "a feeling [that] may mean nothing more than a momentary concretization of a desire for wealth." There's nothing wrong with a man envying someone's house, car or overcoat, for instance, because it actually "may be an added incentive for the man to improve his financial condition," Rand wrote.[3]

At its worst, though, envy does not inspire someone to climb to a higher level or to acquire things that another individual has. Instead, it is a feeling that seeks to devalue, diminish or destroy – something Rand calls *negative envy*. It is especially troublesome when directed at personal virtues, she says. Rand points out that negative envy can lead to a "hatred" of people who are "beautiful or intelligent or successful or honest or happy."[4] Rather than trying to improve one's appearance, to develop or use one's intelligence or to achieve happiness, the envious person wants to destroy the value within the person being envied.

Human forces can attempt to contain negative envy. Probably the most notable can be seen in Buddhism. Two of Buddha's four "noble truths," the cornerstones of one of the world's great religions, diffuse some of the potentially dangerous effects of negative envy:

- Much suffering in societies and individuals arises from excessive and unrealistic desires.

- When attachment to such desires ceases, suffering abates.[5]

If you don't "desire" what's probably unattainable, then you won't suffer the pain of unfulfilled expectations. Ergo, you will be more at peace, and when at peace, "negative" envy struggles to survive.

How does all of this apply to what we see happening to the world between now and 2030?

Circle back to Buddhism's noble truths. In the 21st century, "excessive and unrealistic desires" are enhanced by information technology. A lot of carrots constantly are being dangled in front of six billion noses. This is a world where exported goods and services exceed $6.3 *trillion* a year,[6] with many of those exports being hyped even in the remotest corners of the globe. While Buddha's two noble truths

may still have validity, they get sorely tested in an era when temptation is at the heart of so much programming, editorial content and
advertising that come at us so consistently via different information
channels.

That brings us back to Aristotle and Rand, who made the distinction between "good" envy (jealousy) and negative envy. If, as
Aristotle put it, good envy inspires people to get good things or if, as
Rand put it, good envy is an added incentive for getting ahead, what
happens if people perceive that "getting ahead" is impossible? Suppose
existence comes down to a day-to-day struggle to survive? Would
the spirit of good envy turn sour and become something different? And
what happens when information technology consistently informs individuals who are stuck in the world's basement that millions of other
humans are living the good life in more-developed nations?

What we are witnessing in the world is a growing number of
people who have little chance of climbing to a higher societal or economic level, no matter how hard they try. They are *hopeless*. There is
little point in wasting good envy on the unattainable. Instead, good
envy turns ugly and, in some cases, putrefies into actions that are
intended to do harm to those being envied.

In its worst state, negative envy means aspiring to dispossess,
humiliate and do damage to those who have what is being envied.
Negative envy is not about absconding with something of value from
the envied – rather it is more about making the envied pay a price.

And that is where we are in some parts of the world today. Of
the literally billions of people who feel "disenfranchised," some have
been tainted with negative envy. They don't just want to elbow their
way to the edge of the world's materialistic trough – they also want
to sting those who have more of just about everything there is to
have; they want to punish those whose perceived avarice, greed and
overall unfairness are thought to be the causes of much of the world's
misery.

Throwing money or other resources at the root causes of negative envy is not likely to have an effect. People riddled with negative
envy want more than just a small adjustment to the balance beam of
life. In their minds, they have a score to settle. The objective is to pull
you down, not necessarily to lift themselves up.

Apply all of this to the most obvious international problem we
face today, what many writers and commentators are labeling "the
clash of cultures" or the "prelude to civilizational war." It is the West

in the near corner, Islam in the far. And, at least according to some observers, it is negative envy that is shoving the Muslim world into the center of the ring. Harvard's Samuel Huntington (who warned a few years ago that Western intervention in the affairs of other civilizations is the "single most dangerous source of instability and potential conflict in a multicivilizational world")[7] included this statement in a *Newsweek* article:

> Throughout the Muslim world, and particularly among Arabs, there exists a great sense of grievance, resentment, envy and hostility toward the West and its wealth, power and culture.[8]

Why the hostility, resentment and envy? According to Iran's spiritual leader, Ayatollah Ali Khamenei, the West is a greedy society that is destroying the world. In 1997, he told 50-plus Islamic leaders: "Western materialistic civilization is directing everyone toward materialism, while money, gluttony and carnal desires are made the greatest aspirations."[9]

Ponder what the ayatollah is saying. Western materialism is such a seductive force that it is pulling the world, including Islam, toward its corrupt core. In the ayatollah's mind, there is no room for "good" envy (how could he endorse a kind of envy that would motivate Muslims to move toward a Western lifestyle that he denounces?). From where the ayatollah is standing, there is only one way to fix the problem: Change the West. Reduce the West's ability to become the envy of the rest of the world. The ayatollah does not want more of what the West has; he wants the world to have less of what he believes the West so flagrantly flaunts.

This is a *colossal* dilemma for the world. Islam blames the West for substituting, as Khamenei says, "sincerity, truthfulness, altruism and self-sacrifice" with a long list of "indecent features."[10] In direct contrast, the West thinks, as one writer put it, that "the central source of animus from the Arab world is, quite simply, envy."[11]

How do we protect ourselves from individuals, nations or cultures that have an oversupply of negative envy? On the international front, one conservative American columnist, Jonah Goldberg of the *National Review*, says countries like the U.S. are going to be resented for their success "no matter what."[12] He recommends that the U.S. (and presumably other Western countries) hunker down and protect its own interests, then wait for nations critical of America "to grow up."[13]

Time does have a way of resolving many of life's difficulties.

However, waiting around for cultures, countries or individuals to "grow up" is a risky strategy in an era when lethal technology has practically become a commodity. Given the ultimate objective of a campaign fueled by negative envy – to take the envied down a notch or two – it matters little which tools are selected to get the job done. The more lethal a weapon is, the more desirable it becomes. If the goal is to create societal wreckage, then go for the most damaging technology available. Negative envy gives rise to a bleak forecast for the next three decades.

If "waiting it out" is not the best way to deal with negative envy, what is? Part VII ("The Solution") in *How Women Can Beat Terrorism* suggests ways to minimize negative envy and its dangerous fallout. One proposal is to get much more serious about slowing down population growth in the world's depressed regions. The more people born into hopeless circumstances, the more we are going to have to deal with negative envy's extended family: bitterness, resentment, anger and so on. Consider the Population Reference Bureau's projections for population growth in developing regions. The less-developed countries are now home to 4.9 billion people, and *that number could swell to 7.7 billion by midcentury.*[14]

Remember: Of the billions of people who will be added to the planet in the next 30 to 50 years, more than 90 percent will end up in developing nations. That means more pressure will be applied to social systems that, in many cases, are already stressed by too many people. For sure, control and ownership issues that are major concerns in developing nations today are only going to worsen tomorrow. Brace yourself for more frustration, more disillusionment – and more negative envy.

One of the most noted and quoted authorities on envy is the German sociologist Helmut Schoeck. In his aptly titled book *Envy: A Theory of Social Behavior*, Schoeck credits Friedrich Nietzsche with this comment: "When some men fail to accomplish what they desire to do, they exclaim angrily, 'May the whole world perish!'"[15] In Nietzsche's era, the late 1800s, that kind of wish was largely claptrap. Negative envy might drive someone to inflict minor damage to a community, but likely no one thought that negative envy could actually lead to mankind's demise. Today, "perish" has possibilities. Lethal technology has given us – a *lot* of us – the ability to do great harm.

Envy is ubiquitous. It is a characteristic built into every person. It crops up in every social setting. Envy doesn't have to turn negative, but when it does, it can be dangerous and destructive. Negative envy tends to flourish in places where control and ownership are limited, where hopelessness abounds, where too many people overtax available resources. If those of us living in the "envied" part of the world think these "least envied" places are too remote, too far removed to be of much concern, we're wrong.

In the 21st century, negative envy is mobile. It can travel great distances. In fact, it is already on our doorstep.

CHAPTER 18

WHAT IT ALL MEANS

Following the Taliban's collapse in Afghanistan, journalists came across a publication called the *Manual of Afghan Jihad*.[1] The 11-volume "how-to" instruction book was produced by al Qaeda before the September 11 attack on America.

The manual illustrates the power of an *organized* movement that is propelled by an access to dangerous *technology*. The book gives step-by-step instructions on ways to cripple a country (for example, "four targets must be simultaneously hit" and "the strikes must be strong and have a wide impact on the population").[2] While the tactical information included in the book may weaken the knees, the *negative envy* that infests the manual is far more ominous.

Extremist organizations that have religious (or "definition of death") underpinnings represent a significant threat to mankind because their belief systems often wander outside sectarian rules of law. To these groups, the Nuclear Non-Proliferation Treaty, the 1972 Biological Weapons Convention and the 1973 Chemical Weapons Convention mean little or nothing. At least some of these organizations may be willing and able to access and use the most lethal technology available. As one comparative-religion ethics scholar puts it:

> What will be the story of religion and war for the next quarter century? From all indications, it will be less the story of enhanced diplomatic initiatives ... and more the story of increasingly bloody conflict, fostered by a resurgence of group identities. In such conflict, religion will serve less as a force for peace, more as one of several factors establishing differences between groups, and legitimizing their irreconcilable claims.[3]

Against this perturbing backdrop, let's review the status quo:

We're at a juncture where half the world's 6 billion-plus people are poor (lacking in ownership and control); where the gap between the rich and the downtrodden is getting wider; and where hopelessness is too easy to find in too many corners of the globe. We're living in a world where many have the perception that population growth is under control, even though it is playing havoc with lesser-developed nations. We're overrun with differing and sometimes conflicting definitions of death. And we're being tugged into the future by technologies that are evolving at breakneck speed.

Then there's negative envy. It doesn't exist everywhere. But where it has materialized, it is a time bomb. Those of us living in the United States, Europe and other developed nations have a decision to make about this kind of envy. We can ignore it at our own peril. Or, preferably, we can devote the energy and resources to do something about the conditions and circumstances that give rise to negative envy.

Part VII, "The Solution" to negative envy, lifts the curtain on a corrective strategy that relies heavily on the will and problem-solving capabilities of women.

PART VII

THE SOLUTION

CHAPTER 19

LIBERATE, EDUCATE, MOTIVATE, CELEBRATE AND ELEVATE WOMEN

During the 16th century, Michel de Nostredame (a.k.a. Nostradamus, the royal physician to King Charles IX) emerged as the world's most influential soothsayer. For some, he remains king of the prophets. Nostradamus wrote 942 poems that, although obscure and subject to wide interpretation, have scared people silly for centuries. According to one writer, the final predictions of Nostradamus warn that an Islamic dictator – the anti-Christ – will spin the world into war and that by 2030, only one-third of the earth's human population will be left standing.[1]

Although *How Women Can Beat Terrorism* also views 2030 as a watershed year, this book bases none of its forecasting on Nostradamus's prognostications or, for that matter, any other prophecies rooted in religion, metaphysics or the occult. Instead, this book's projections are drawn from the convergence of three powerful forces destined to shape our future: (a) the spread of poverty and hopelessness; (b) population growth in places that are already overcrowded and where the addition of people would further degrade the quality of life; and (c) technology that is traveling at an almost incomprehensible speed and becoming accessible to a wider body of people. Any conclusions that are similar to the ambiguous "predictions" made by Nostradamus are sheer coincidence.

There may, indeed, be a significant loss of human life between now and 2030. Will two-thirds of all humans be wiped out, as Michel de Nostredame suggested? Not likely. Just how much death and destruction mankind will suffer hinges on what steps we are willing to take *now*. We have the ability to positively affect the future. While terrorism and warfare will take their toll in the years ahead, casualty estimates can be greatly reduced if we implement a few changes. The plan is relatively simple because:

We know *what* to do.
We just don't know *how* to do it.

• • •

One of the conclusions reached by participants at the 2002 World Economic Forum was that global terrorism cannot be eliminated without dealing with the poverty and disheartenment that helps create terrorists.[2] At a meeting of the Third United Nations Conference on the Least Developed Countries, participating nations issued what has been called the *Brussels Declaration*. In effect, it says that the "eradication of poverty" is intertwined with "the peaceful resolution of armed conflicts."[3]

As pointed out earlier, cause-and-effect theories about poverty and terrorism are not accepted by everyone. Still, most would agree that far-reaching global poverty and hopelessness make it more difficult to root out terrorism. At the very least, poverty and hopelessness are used by terrorists to help justify their actions. Whittling away at poverty will not eliminate all terrorism, but it is likely to put a dent in the frequency and severity of terrorist attacks. For that reason:

We need to improve the control and ownership status of half the world's people and thereby begin to close the chasm between the world's haves and have-nots. And if it's not possible to make that happen in the near term, then we at least need to give impoverished people *hope* that the quality of life for them and their offspring is going to improve.

A few Western nations claim they are committed to doing something about poverty and hopelessness. The U.S., for instance, has publicly declared that it will help countries solve problems that make them hotbeds for terrorism – that America will take steps to "put hope back in the hearts of people."[4] Other Western countries have sent out similar messages. Of course, talking the talk is easy; walking the walk is much more difficult.

Assuming that most prosperous nations really want to do something about global poverty, *how* should they go about it? *How* does a wealthy country instill hope in people who live in places where hopelessness is endemic? Will throwing more money at the problem make it go away? Former U.S. Treasury Secretary Paul O'Neill doesn't think so, and many economists would agree with him:

> Over the last 50 years, hundreds of billions have been
> spent in the name of economic development, with so

many of the countries that have been major recipients still not showing strong evidence of positive change.[5]

If cash can't close the societal gap, what's the solution?

How to Solve the Problem

Extreme poverty and hopelessness are a kind of potting soil in which negative envy can take root. Leaders galore in the Western world say they want to lick poverty, but they usually offer few specifics on how to get the job done. Does the world even agree on what poverty is? At what point do poor people become *un*poor? When every human on earth owns a DVD player and a dishwasher? Or is it more realistic to hope that we can create a climate where people have (or perceive a chance of having) adequate control of their lives, *plus* have a level of ownership that will allow them to meet their basic needs?

How Women Can Beat Terrorism maintains the latter objective should be our polestar. Given that there are so many poor people in the world, such a goal is going to be tough to reach – and made all the more challenging if reproduction rates in some population-stressed countries continue at their current pace.

To have any chance of pushing back poverty and hopelessness, we need to do two things at once. We need to stem the flood of new life into regions that are more and more destabilized by population overload. And we need to do the kind of systemic repair work that will restore the muscle and bone of social systems that should be giving people the control and ownership opportunities they deserve. These are monumental problems that, at first blush, may seem beyond solving. Yet, one resource, if used effectively, could give us a chance at succeeding. That resource is one of the world's most powerful and often stifled resources:

<u>WOMEN</u>

U.N. Secretary General Kofi Annan told a recent International Women's Day event that women's unrestricted participation in preventing and solving conflict should be the "credo for a more peaceful millennium."[6]

Well said. However, for many women around the world, unrestricted participation is nothing more than a distant dream.

Nonetheless, women *could* play a more significant role in preventing conflict if they could go head-to-head with two formidable forces: poverty and hopelessness. However, we won't see that happen unless women are:

- Liberated
- Educated
- Motivated
- Celebrated
- Elevated

A decade ago, the United Nations High Commissioner for Human Rights issued a fact sheet loaded with statistics showing alarming economic and social gaps between men and women. Women still make up the majority of the world's poor. Between 1975 and the early 1990s, the number of women living in rural poverty increased 50 percent.[7]

The plight of women in many regions of the world has actually gotten worse. When Afghanistan became an international focal point in 2001 and 2002, we learned about the ruling Taliban's ugly repression of women. Gender discrimination is common in other nations as well. Women and second-class citizenship seem to be one and the same in places like:

- Nepal, where as Time magazine put it, "Thousands of Nepali women … endure social injustice and discrimination, most of it sanctified by religion – and ignored by law."[8]

- Zimbabwe, where women make up 51 percent of the population but account for 75 percent of the country's poor.[9]

- Kuwait, where the parliament recently voted down a bill that would have given women the right to vote and run for office.[10]

In parts of the globe where women are most needed to bring about reproductive, economic and social stability, they are too often shoved to the sidelines with few rights and little or no influence. The result? We have a lengthy list of places where women are virtually powerless, places where females are denied privileges long extended to men. No right to own land. No right to inherit property. No right to access credit.[11] By design, women are put in a position where they have little control and not much hope that their circumstances can or will improve.

"We must strive to integrate women more effectively in peace processes worldwide," Kofi Anan said.[12] It's a fine objective, but it likely will be accomplished only if women have their shackles removed.

A global plan is already on the table that, if fully enacted, could go a long way toward the *liberation* of women. It is called the Convention on the Elimination of All Forms of Discrimination Against Women (CEDAW). The U.N. General Assembly adopted the convention in 1979 and, as of 2002, it has been ratified by 169 countries (including 11 Arab nations).[13] By signing the convention, a country commits itself to ending discrimination against women by:

- Incorporating the principle of equality of men and women in its legal system, abolishing all discriminatory laws and adopting appropriate ones prohibiting discrimination against women.

- Establishing tribunals and other public institutions to ensure the effective protection of women against discrimination.

- Ensuring elimination of all acts of discrimination against women by persons, organizations or enterprises.

Like so many statements of intent, the convention doesn't mean much unless its provisions are turned into actions and not just words. CEDAW, for instance, is supposedly supported by several nations where gender equality is virtually nonexistent. This sorry state of affairs prompted columnist George Will to write a blistering attack against CEDAW, which he called nothing more than an "exhortation to be nice" and a "gesture ...[that] ... encourages the bad habit of moral preening."[14] Will's sentiments may help explain why the U.S. is one of the few countries that have not ratified CEDAW.

The main complaint about CEDAW is that the 23-member committee set up to assess how countries are doing in their efforts to improve women's rights is largely ineffective. However, individual countries themselves could enforce CEDAW on their own terms, especially if pressured to do so by nations handing out foreign aid payments. More-developed nations could say to lesser-developed nations, for instance: *Don't come to us looking for a grant or loan unless you can give us verifiable proof that you are living up to CEDAW's requirements – hard evidence that women are not only free from discrimination but are actually being brought on board as players in economic-development plans for your nation.* One convincing way for lesser-developed countries to offer such proof is to create a network of women who are responsible for the allocation and accounting of foreign assistance provided to those nations.

If women are to be liberated at least to the point where they can make critical decisions for themselves and their families, then *education* has to be provided. According to UNESCO, women continue to account for around 64 percent of the world's illiterate adults.[15] Just as troubling is that girls constitute 60 percent of the 132 million school-age children in developing countries who are not in the classroom.[16]

Clearly, females do not choose to be illiterate. In some parts of the world, women continue to be victims of a deep-rooted cultural belief that if you are not a man, then your place is in the field or the kitchen – not the schoolhouse. At the top of a lengthy list of reasons why that attitude is backward are points made by UNICEF's executive director:

> Education for girls is the key to health and nutrition of populations; to overall improvements in the standard of living; to better agricultural and environmental practices; to higher gross national product; and to greater involvement and gender balance in decision making at all levels of society.[17]

Case study after case study shows that when women are given access to education, birthrates decline and the overall economic conditions of a region improve. That's a double-barreled win. Reproduction rates go down in places where overpopulation is a curse. Quality of life improves, and negative envy can begin to subside. The U.N. Development Fund for Women sums it up nicely:

> Economic empowerment gives women control over money and assets, and access to the opportunities they need for success. When women control their livelihoods, the whole family benefits.[18]

Being liberated and educated won't get women to where this book proposes they need to be unless they are *motivated* to take action. Enlisting women to inspire women is one of the best ways to get and keep the ball rolling. Showcasing women who have achieved higher levels of control and ownership can be a force for other women to do the same. The results can prove beneficial to an entire community, not just to women. For example:

Fandane Wolof is a village in Senegal where a women's group manages a mill that grinds millet into flour. The organization charges a small fee for using the mill. The income funds a credit system open to women who want loans for cottage-industry ventures such as producing peanut butter.[19] In this village, control and ownership are up; negative envy is down.

When women make progress in locations like Fandane Wolof, where gender issues have historically been a problem, or in thousands of villages where female education has been elusive, their successes need to be *celebrated*. We should be giving a standing ovation to countries that are making progress on this front – like some parts of Chad where enrollment in girls' schools quadrupled between 1997 and 1998, or a number of villages in Egypt where 70 percent of girls are now in school compared with 30 percent only a few years ago.[20] When developed countries get the news that microlending in El Salvador and Honduras has increased the productivity and wealth of women farmers, a round of applause is in order.[21]

Finally, enough women should be *elevated* to positions of authority at all levels of government in nations around the world. We need more gender balance if women-focused initiatives that combat poverty and hopelessness are to be managed and evaluated properly.

These may all come across as rather small and relatively insignificant steps forward. Maybe so, but tiny strides add up. Put enough of them together and perhaps pent-up negative envy in certain parts of the world can be vented and, in turn, we might be able to modify the gloomy forecast presented in Part I ("The Problem").

Attempts to empower more women means hurdling over a high barrier: men. To many males, each step a woman is allowed to move forward is tantamount to a step back on the part of a man. This is a way of thinking that either needs to be changed or circumvented.

The executive director of the United Nations Populations Fund summed up just how critical it is for women to become more influential in developing countries. There is a lot riding on her words:

Everything we have learned shows that when women are empowered – through laws that ensure their rights, health care that ensures their well-being and education that ensures their active participation – the benefits go far beyond the individual; they help the family, the community and the nation… When women engage in development, families, societies and nations gain substantially – economically, socially and culturally. Women are key to development and, therefore, we must invest in their participation in development.[22]

CHAPTER 20

THE TEST

Now comes the hard part.

I hope *How Women Can Beat Terrorism* has made a convincing case as to *why* women should be more fully engaged in combating the conditions that are proving increasingly dangerous to people everywhere – regardless of how rich or poor they might be. We have also looked at *what* women could do to lessen poverty and hopelessness, if given a chance, and *what* consequences might await us if we continue to ignore women as a problem-solving resource. Now I want to address the *how*. How can we give women the latitude and resources they need to improve the standard of living in the poorest regions of the world, to curb population growth where it is detrimental, to help overcome hopelessness, and to create a global climate that is inhospitable to terrorism?

This chapter offers steps that women – and men – can take to push the U.S., Western Europe and other more-developed nations to:

1. Use foreign aid primarily to attack poverty and hope-lessness at the grass-roots level.

2. Give women and women's programs the highest priority when deciding how to allocate foreign aid.

3. Put the brakes on population growth in places where the addition of more people increases the probability of global problems.

We need to reach these three goals long before 2030. Here is why each objective is so important:

1. Use foreign aid primarily to attack poverty and hopelessness at the grass-roots level.

Initially, Goal #1 may seem to have little to do with women. Actually, it is a linchpin to every other recommendation in this chapter. Foreign aid is the heavy-duty armament that women in developing countries are going to need to make significant inroads when battling poverty and hopelessness. Yes, other kinds of fiscal weapons can be used, such as charitable gifts, private loans and so on, but these "small arms," on their own, just can't get the job done. What's required is the bunker-busting force that comes from large sums of foreign assistance.

Goal #1 says Western countries should use foreign aid to beef up the control and ownership of people living in the "have-not" regions of the world. This goal doesn't advocate using foreign aid as an extension of a nation's military budget. It doesn't call for the dumping of foreign-aid payments into the outstretched mitts of high-level government leaders and then watching that money get filtered away by layer upon layer of intermediaries. It says foreign assistance should chiefly be used as an injection into the grass-roots segment of a country's social system.

Goal #1 is not an alms-for-the-poor proposal. It is an investment opportunity. Wealthy nations should be using most of their foreign aid to support initiatives that create and sustain conditions in poor parts of the world that nurture personal control and ownership. In many locations, this won't require reinventing the wheel. Successful prototypes are bountiful. It means picking and choosing models that have a strong probability of succeeding. And while this book pushes hard for women to be at the core of grass-roots programs in developing countries (see Goal #2), many "gender neutral" models deserve support – programs that are beneficial to women *and* men. A good example is a project that made its way to the front page of *The Wall Street Journal*:[1]

The Journal story detailed different ways the government of Egypt is attempting to cope with the annual surge of 630,000 young people into the employment ranks (as of 2002, the country had a 15 percent unemployment rate). With 60 percent of Egyptians living in or near poverty, the country knows that being poor often equates to being vulnerable to the rhetoric of Islamic fundamentalists. Egypt, in turn, has singled out jobs as its best defense against social unrest – especially in rural areas where desperation and hopelessness create a fertile ground for terrorism. As one businessman put it:

Keep people busy, treat them as human beings, show them some success stories – then you don't have a terrorist problem.[2]

If the economic status of the people at the very bottom of the societal barrel is improved in a way that gives them a semblance of control and ownership (something that doesn't always happen when people accept unadulterated charity), then extremism is less likely to ferment into harmful negative envy. Of course, certain fringe elements aren't necessarily going to reject fanatical views even if they find steady employment. There will always be people whose hate will make them a threat to the mainstream. The trick is to minimize the number of these outliers.

How does Egypt – the Arab world's most populated country, with 67 million people – muster the resources to create a job base that provides people with a suitable level of control and ownership? The answer is twofold: (1) a national determination to make jobs the top priority, and (2) using *strategically placed foreign aid* to develop those employment opportunities. Many nations that troll for foreign aid give lip service to this same two-point plan. However, as foreign-aid critics have rightfully acknowledged, what a country proposes to do does not always equate to what actually happens once foreign aid arrives.

Inefficiency, diversion of funds and corruption are on the recipient side of the foreign-aid equation. But there are other problems. Too many well-to-do nations are overly tightfisted when it comes to foreign assistance – and too many others use foreign aid in a way that has little impact on curtailing poverty and hopelessness. Is it any wonder, then, that we end up with a world where the chasm between the wealthy and poor countries gets wider by the year? In spite of foreign-aid allocations, few poor countries are showing any meaningful improvement, and, in fact, just the opposite is happening in many regions of the world. Let's use Chad as an example. In 1965, the gross domestic product per capita in the U.S. was 15 times higher than in Chad. In 1990, it was *50 times higher.*[3]

Goal #1 says foreign aid should be used "primarily" to fund initiatives that create jobs, open up cottage-industry opportunities (especially those that benefit women), launch literacy programs for girls, and so on. However, the first goal also leaves room for more-developed nations to use foreign aid to help feed, clothe and meet other basic necessities of needy people living in developing countries. In the wake of a horrific natural or man-made disaster, for instance, out-and-out charity is certainly appropriate. Help should be given with no strings attached. But when it comes to sustained humanitarian relief – the ongoing assistance that is needed to stave off starvation and illness that have become constants in some lesser-developed countries – foreign-aid spending should be based on a different set of rules.

Baby boomers will remember George McGovern and his unsuccessful bid for the White House in 1972. The former senator from South Dakota got almost as much media attention for his work as U.S. ambassador to the United Nations agencies on food and agriculture as he did on the campaign trail. McGovern has been passionate about finding a way to end hunger wherever it exists on the planet. "I can think of no investment that would profit the international community more than erasing hunger from the face of the earth," he said.[4]

McGovern contends that for $5 billion a year, we could cut world hunger in half over the next 15 years. If that same annual investment were to be made through 2030, he says, it would be hard to find a malnourished person anywhere on the planet.

Assume that McGovern's estimates are correct and that the United Nations managed to convince the U.S. and other developed nations to pick up the tab for such an initiative. And assume that the money actually did eradicate hunger. Would all the world's control, ownership, hopelessness and negative-envy problems disappear? Probably not.

A better plan would be to distribute food and water as something other than handouts. To paraphrase an adage, everyone benefits from *teaching* people to fish instead of *giving* them fish. That approach requires transforming charity into a barter system – we give you something to eat; you give us something in exchange. Example: provide food to a village in exchange for a pledge from local leaders to let women manage a village microlending program.[5]

On top of the billions of dollars needed to curb world hunger, how much more money would be needed to underwrite Goal #1 – to successfully attack poverty and hopelessness?

In 1992, the 20-plus members of the Organization of Economic Cooperation and Development (OECD) agreed that each country should put 0.7 percent of its gross domestic product toward what is called "Official Development Assistance" programs. As Chart 17 shows, targets are sometimes missed. Only five countries reached the 0.7 goal: Denmark, Luxemborg, the Netherlands, Norway and Sweden. Although the U.S. is the world's second-largest foreign-aid donor in actual dollars ($9.9 billion in 2002), that amount as a percentage of gross national income is so low that the U.S. has become the poster child for chintzyness.[6] An article titled "America's Shame: Foreign Aid Should Be a U.S. Priority" in *The Guardian* serves up three reasons why America gets such low marks:

> First, the U.S. spends far too little on aid... Second, Washington sees aid as a tool of foreign policy. Large sums of U.S. development money prop up client states ... or the cash is 'tied' so that the poor are forced to buy American goods. Third, only 17 percent of American aid goes to the 48 least-developed nations."[7]

Chart 17

COUNTRY	ODA/GNI %
Australia	0.25
Austria	0.25
Belgium	0.37
Canada	0.23
Denmark	1.01
Finland	0.33
France	0.34
Germany	0.27
Greece	0.19
Ireland	0.33
Italy	0.14
Japan	0.23
Luxembourg	0.80
Netherlands	0.82
New Zealand	0.25
Norway	0.83
Portugal	0.25
Spain	0.30
Sweden	0.76
Switzerland	0.34
United Kingdom	0.32
United States	0.11

Source: Organisation for Economic Cooperation and Development - 2002

Development Assistance
As a % of Gross National Income (2001)
Source: Organisation for Economic Cooperation and Development - 2002

Europe loves to criticize the U.S. for its parsimonious foreign-aid policies, but the foreign-aid payments of many European countries (as a percent of their respective GNI's) are nothing to brag about, either.

The Center for Global Development (CGD) and *Foreign Policy* magazine pointed out that of the $50 billion that rich countries provided in grants and low-interest loans to poor nations in 2002, two-fifths was paid out as "tied aid."[8] "Tied aid" refers to financial assistance mandating that a recipient country spend some or most of the aid on goods and services provided by the donor nation. Furthermore, CGD and *Foreign Policy* say that based on a USAID statement, a whopping *80 percent* of the United States' foreign assistance is used to purchase U.S. goods and services.[9]

The hard reality is that the majority of developed nations are cheap when it comes to offering the "untied" foreign assistance that is often vital in combating grass-roots poverty. Even though we know the wealth gap is growing wider by the year, and even though we know that poverty is the incubator of negative envy, hostility and possibly even terrorism, more-developed nations are disinclined to both increase their foreign-aid payments and view those expenditures as a kind of "insurance" that could help fend off *big* problems that are growing by the day. Goal #1, then, is about the need for economically advanced countries to commit reasonable amounts of foreign aid – preferably in line with OECD guidelines – and to put that aid toward programs and activities that will alleviate poverty by increasing control and ownership in hard-pressed regions of the world. Next: How women can leverage those resources to deliver the greatest good.

2. Give women and women's programs the highest priority when making foreign-aid decisions.

How Women Can Beat Poverty is heavy with statistics. More numbers could be used to make the point that women have the capacity to overcome poverty even if they are given relatively small amounts of money. One brief story, however, will probably make more impact than another mountain of data[10]:

In 1972, an economics professor named Muhammad Yunus returned to his homeland, Bangladesh, after studying in the U.S. for three years. He was frustrated by how difficult it was to apply the economic theories he had learned in the classroom to the poverty-ridden reality of his own country. Then Yunus met Sophia, a woman who made woven bamboo furniture by hand. Although she had worked hard for years, she was nearly destitute. He soon found out why.

Sophia could not afford to pay for the raw materials needed to make her furniture. Like many others in villages throughout Bangladesh, she was forced to buy bamboo on credit from a local trader. When she finished her work, Sophia sold her furniture to the trader who pocketed most of the money as debt repayment. The interest on her loan? Ten percent a *day*.

Yunus decided to lend Sophia 50 taka (about U.S.$3). Now able to buy raw materials up front, the woman quickly developed her own business, repaid Yunus and increased her income sevenfold.

That lending exercise led to the launch in 1976 of what has become the best-known "credit delivery system" for the poor. Called the Grameen Bank (*grameen* means rural or village in Bengali), this extraordinary program offers credit, without any collateral, to the poorest of the poor in Bangladesh. Borrowers are provided loans based on their ideas for simple income-producing concepts. Literally thousands of cottage industries have cropped up in Bangladesh as a result of this program – transportation services, pottery manufacturing, garment making, and so on.

Grameen Bank now has more than 1,100 branches that service 41,000 villages throughout Bangladesh. Each branch makes small loans that almost always deliver big results. There are few defaults.

The bank is not focused exclusively on women. However, the impact on women throughout the country has been nothing short of phenomenal. In 2002, of the 2.4 million Grameen Bank borrowers, *95 percent were women*. Those receiving funds from the bank have household incomes typically 50 percent higher than others in the same village.

The notion of using microcredit to empower women is not limited to Bangladesh. In Cameroon, a small organization called the Rural Women Development Council has helped 200 women become income-producing farmers and develop trades.[11] In Zambia, the People's Participation Program has opened hundreds of village banking systems that mainly serve female clients.[12] In Tanzania, CARE sponsors a program called Hujakwama (which means "you are not stuck" in Swahili) that has trained more than 1,200 women in entrepreneurial skills.[13] The list of such successful programs is long and impressive.

What about predominantly Islamic countries where women face particularly high barriers? Is it realistic to think women in these nations can take on central roles in improving the socioeconomic complexion of their communities? It may come as a surprise that women can, and do, hold leadership roles in grass-roots activities (including running small businesses that produce goods and provide services). This is happening, at a slow pace, in post-Taliban Afghanistan and other Muslim countries. In Saudi Arabia a generation ago, few, if any, women were managing companies, but today about 10 percent of private businesses are now run by women.[14] And when women are given an opportunity to make an impact on a local or even national economy, they don't take long to prove their effectiveness.

Foreign aid injected into women-focused programs can produce remarkable results. However, those who make foreign-aid decisions first have to find the right projects to fund, and second, to make sure the proposals are promising. How do more-developed countries locate funding opportunities for women that have a strong probability of success? By taking three steps: (1) Use nongovernmental organizations (referred to as NGO's) that have a credible track record. (2) Put out a call to NGOs (and other public or private groups) for what the grant-making world dubs "requests for proposals" (RFP's). (3) Use independent, expert panels to sort through the proposals and recommend which ones to fund and how much to allocate.

This goal begs an obvious question: just how many NGOs are there that have a proven capability of implanting and replicating successful women's programs in underdeveloped countries? Answer: a lot. Not only is the list of organizations long, but the menu of initiatives that these NGOs carry out or sponsor continues to expand. because information about these organizations and their programs is so constantly changing, *How Women Can beat Terrorism* has instituted http://www.womenbeatterrorism.com, a companion internet link. The site carries an updated overview of these NGOs and the impressive work they are doing in some of the most challenging locations on earth.

Goal #2 does not mean that all foreign aid should be used for women's programs. There are many community-based projects open to men and women that deserve support. But especially in locations where past attempts to beat back poverty and hopelessness have failed, women's initiatives should be sought out, evaluated and, if judged to be viable, funded.

3. Put the brakes on population growth in places where the addition of more people increases the probability of global problems.

Let's not be lulled into apathy by a recent U.N. projection suggesting birthrates are now declining in places like India, Mexico, Egypt and Brazil.[15] Yes, new data do confirm that women in some less-developed nations are giving birth to fewer children than was predicted only a couple of years ago. That's terrific news. However, don't forget what else the U.N. has told us: There could be a *50 percent increase* in the overall number of people on earth by the middle of this century. Let's also remember: *Nearly all that growth will occur in less-developed nations that are ill equipped to handle large numbers of new people.*

In this book, the principal argument for curbing birthrates is not based on the premise that, in general, human overpopulation is a significant problem (as Part IV tried to convey, there is no clear-cut evidence as to whether the earth can or cannot tolerate a few more billion people). Instead, the argument is based on a selfish premise that says: Excessive population growth in impoverished countries already overtaxed by too many people is not just a quality-of-life issue for those nations but it also is downright *dangerous* for those of us living in more-developed parts of the world.

Remember: In a world where information technology is pervasive, the poorest of the poor are able to size up the gap between the haves and have-nots like never before. They get a clear view of a bleak picture: a constantly expanding mass of poverty-stricken human beings who are not likely to experience any significant improvement in quality of life – *ever*. Negative envy breeds quickly among those who are hopeless, deprived and resentful. It is in these locations where organizers – some of whom use their religion's definition of death as a rallying banner – have a good chance of recruiting the new self-sacrificing "warriors" of the 21st century.

We know that an attempt to slow population growth means dabbling with some bristly issues: abortion, contraception, eugenics and so forth. We know moving women to the front line in the campaign to cut birthrates, particularly in the developing world, means forcing women to deal with these controversial issues. That won't always be easy, but it is necessary if we have any chance of improving the outlook for people locked in poverty-plagued regions of the world.

We also know something else. We know that the phrases "curb population growth" and "foreign-aid policies" often make for strange, and sometimes conflicting, bedfellows. Nevertheless, for those more-developed countries that are sincerely interested in doing something about global poverty, population growth cannot be avoided.

Goal #3 says there should be "tough love" strings attached to foreign aid offered to developing nations where population expansion is a problem. Assistance should be provided in a way that discourages population growth – or, put another way, constantly *encourages* national polices and programs that are designed to lower birthrates.

Will this lead to a world of China-like nations that impose the one-child/one-family requirement that has been so maligned in recent years? That question begs a closer look at population-control activities in the Peoples Republic of China.

During the days of Chairman Mao, the Chinese were encouraged to bear as many children as possible. A *lot* of people pitched in. The population nearly doubled from 1949 to 1979. With a landmass about the same size as the U.S., China found itself with a national census nearly four times that of North America. Even more problematic, China also found itself short on water, forests, oil and arable land. People were drawn to those parts of the country with ample resources, and as a result, 94 percent of those living in China are jammed together in the southeastern section of the nation.[16]

In 1979, the government concluded that, with all due apologies to Chairman Mao, its runaway population was a ticket to disaster. The country instituted a controversial policy of one child per family that included rewards for those who complied with the regulation and penalties for those who did not. Couples with just a single offspring received one-child "certificates" that could be redeemed for better housing, upgraded child care, longer maternity leave, and so on. The policy also inspired a long list of horror stories, including women sterilized against their will, forced abortions and infanticide.

While many have criticized China's methods to try to achieve its goal (to keep its population below 1.4 billion until 2010),[17] the actions it has taken have, indeed, reduced the birthrate – from six children per woman 30 years ago to around two children per woman today. As one U.N. Population Fund official put it: "For all the bad press, China has achieved the impossible – the country has solved its population problem."[18]

"Partially solved" might be more accurate. China's population-control policy has brought about these results: 117 boys born for every

100 girls (men are now having a hard time finding brides)[19]; a huge aging population that is dependent on a smaller work force for meeting its needs; and an urban state of mind that is steering young people away from raising a family (one poll revealed that nearly 30 percent of city-dwelling young people have little or no interest in marriage, children, or both).[20] The nation's State Family Planning Commission admits the country does face new problems, but these problems appear far less onerous than if China had not dealt with an oversupply of people.[21]

The "China experiment" offers important insight for how other countries might tackle their own overpopulation issues. Gradually, China has moved away from using what detractors have called "womb police" to enforce the nation's one-child policies. Instead, the country is moving toward a women's health and outreach campaign that, through education and easy access to contraceptives, discourages large families. There is one other disincentive for having large families – an additional tax is imposed on couples electing to conceive more than one child.[22]

Here is the lesson learned: Where China is ending up with its population-control campaign is where other nations may want to start.

In many countries that claim to have a handle on their population-growth problems, birthrates continue to be high – or are climbing higher. Obviously, there is a difference between going through the motions and actually conducting a campaign. This is where the foreign-aid spigot could become important. If aid-allocating governments would agree that the spigot only gets turned on when recipient countries agree to carry out appropriate and *verifiable* programs to control population growth, then we would be making one giant leap forward – not just for poor countries but for all of humankind.

What exactly needs to be done to achieve Goal #3? There are two controversial – and necessary – parts of virtually any plan to slow down population growth: (1) allow for the use of contraceptives, and, if appropriate, help make them accessible; (2) allow for voluntary abortions and impose no foreign-aid penalties on countries that permit such voluntary abortions.

Let's look at contraceptives first. This is where religious and moral convictions start slamming into what some will call social engineering. Fortunately, most of the world buys into the use of contraceptives. The problem is that not enough women and men use birth control, at least in regions where such use is most needed.

The U.N. Population Division says that two-thirds of the world's women who are in their reproductive years (usually considered from 15 to 49) and who are "married or in union" use some method of contraception.[23] However, when contraceptive use is broken down country by country, it is easy to see a correlation between relatively low contraceptive use and relatively high birthrates. The following regional data from a U.N. report show "contraceptive prevalence" based on how rich or poor a country happens to be:[24]

Region	% Women Using Contraception
Industrialized countries	78%
Developing countries	65%
Least-developed countries	32%

Now scan the list of countries where less than a third of women in their reproductive years use contraceptives:[25]

Country	% Women Using Contraception
Cameroon	19%
Cambodia	21%
Burkina Faso	11%
Cote d'Ivoire	15%
Ethiopia	8%
Ghana	22%
Guinea	6%
Haiti	28%
Iraq	14%
Lethoso	23%
Malawi	22%
Mali	7%
Mauritania	4%
Nepal	28%
Nigeria	7%
Pakistan	24%
Rwanda	21%
Senegal	13%
Sudan	8%
Uganda	15%
Tanzania	24%

If you think these percentages are low, only a few years ago (1990) contraception use in the least-developed nations was only *half* of what it is today.[26]

Contraceptives – when and where they are readily available – have had a phenomenal impact on reproduction rates. The fertility statistics below make that point clear:

Fertility Rate - 2000[27]
(Lifetime births per woman at current fertility rates)

Region	Number of Births - Lifetime
Industrialized countries	1.6
Developing countries	3.0
Least-developed countries	5.4

Many observers will fixate on the 1.6 births per woman in the industrialized world and complain that *too many* contraceptives are being used since 2.1 births per lifetime per woman is generally regarded as the world's population-replacement level. However, worldwide we find that the average is still above the replacement level – 2.7 births per woman in 2000 (down from 3.2 births per woman in 1990). This all makes sense because the global population continues to grow at a rate of 210,000 a day. The crucial issue is, once again, *where* that population growth is occurring.

As was pointed out in Chapter 14 ("Definition of Death"), religion can be a gigantic impediment in the campaign to widen contraceptive use. At the risk of being criticized for picking on just one faith, let's examine the Roman Catholic Church and its continued opposition to contraception. Catholicism is seeing its greatest growth in Africa, Asia and Latin America.[28] These are the regions of the world where population expansion poses the most significant risk. How rigorously will the church take a stand against contraceptives in these locations? Will it take a hard-line position in support of Pope Paul VI's *Humanae Vitae* encyclical, which says, "an action which either before, at the moment of, or after sexual intercourse, is specifically intended to prevent procreation" is "an unlawful birth-control method"?[29] Will the church choose to do what it does in more-developed countries – look the other way and allow its followers to use different methods of birth control (short of abortion)? Or will the church revise its policies to permit wider use of contraceptives?

There will always be a percentage of any population that will point to a literal interpretation of religious doctrine as a reason not to use contraception. Even in highly developed nations, there is no across-the-board acceptance of contraception. For those who cannot bring themselves to use, or advocate the use of, contraceptives, so be it. They should stand firm on their principles. But they should also step back from proselytizing the vast majority of people in the world who view contraception as permissible and acceptable, even if the practice is in conflict with religious doctrine. Furthermore, they should not impede the flow of contraception information and products in parts of the world where they are critically needed.

Religion is not the only impediment to contraceptive use. In some countries, the fear of domestic abuse keeps women from turning to contraceptives. According to a CNN report, a study in Ghana found that 43 percent of men take the position that a man is justified in beating his wife if she uses contraceptives without his expressed consent.[30] In Peru and Mexico, women are reluctant to discuss birth control with their husbands, fearing a violent reaction.[31]

Threats, coercion and punishment are too frequently the price a woman has to pay for using contraception in many places around the world.

These are serious barricades to any campaign to encourage wider contraception use. But the barricades need to be breached because if they are not, women will continue to endure unwanted pregnancies.

More to the point, contraception is crucial to slowing the rate of human reproduction in places where the number of births is clearly a problem. And foreign aid could be a valuable tool to ensuring that population-stressed countries have access to effective and affordable contraceptives.

Now let's look at the second requirement to achieving Goal #3: allowing for voluntary abortions and imposing no foreign-aid penalties on countries that permit voluntary abortions.

This will be the fork in the road for some people. Poll after poll reaffirms how deeply divided public opinion is over abortion. Religious or moral convictions usually push people to one side of the issue or the other. Less often considered in making judgments about abortion is how crucial a role the procedure plays in curtailing the growth of the world's population.

Of the 210 million pregnancies that occur each year worldwide, 132 million end in a live birth[32] and 22 percent, or 46 million, end in abortion.[33] (Miscarriages and stillbirths are responsible for another 15 percent, or 32 million, pregnancy terminations.)

In Chapter 14 ("Definition of Death"), we looked backward and calculated how large our population would be today if no abortions had been performed since 1973. Now let's look ahead. What would happen if over the next three decades we stopped all abortions and, as a result, *annually* added 46 million more people to the world's population? We would have *at least 1.7 billion more people by 2030* – over and above current population-growth projections. Equally important: Of those 1.7 billion, based on current reproduction behaviors, over 1.5 billion would be living in developing nations – places least able to handle this influx.[34]

For most of the world, abortion is a "sideline" exercise. Men do not experience the full effects or consequences of abortion the way women do. Many females are never confronted with having to make a decision about deliberately terminating a pregnancy.[35] Deciding where to come down on a complex issue like abortion is a lot easier if it is exclusively an intellectual exercise and not a decision that requires a woman to expel a part of her body.

But abortion is not a sideline issue if it is examined as part of an effort to limit population growth in places where a high concentration of humans spells trouble. The undeniable fact is that until there are other ways of preventing unintended births, abortion will continue to be a significant factor in keeping population growth under control. As with contraceptives, those who feel that they cannot compromise their religious or moral convictions regarding abortion should stick to their beliefs. However, it is hoped that they would not criticize or interfere with others who have concluded that while abortion is a difficult and usually troubling choice, giving birth to an unwanted child is even more disconcerting since it adds to a global problem that affects all of us.

Note that this Goal #3 does not call on governments to provide foreign aid for abortion services, although it leaves room for taking that action if a government should so choose. Rather, the provision calls on more-developed nations, at the very least, to stand neutral on abortion and not withhold foreign aid as a way of penalizing countries where abortion is permitted.

• • •

For those troubled by either or both of Goal #3's components, think about this declaration made in 1988 by a group called the Club of Earth, whose members all belong to both the U.S. National Academy of Sciences and the American Academy of Arts and Sciences:

> Arresting population growth should be second in importance only to avoiding nuclear war on humanity's agenda."[36]

Life demands that we make a lot of tough decisions. For some, Goal #3 is one of those decisions. We need that goal to help deter population growth in places where it can be ruinous. Without Goal #3, we risk sentencing billions of people to a life of misery and hardship – and leaving many more hopeless people to encourage and cheer on the next wave of terrorists.

So What Can We Do?

If we can find ways to move toward and ultimately reach these three goals, poverty and hopelessness will begin to wane, and the unstable atmospheric conditions that favor terrorism will become less threatening. Reaching these goals means tampering with the way foreign aid decisions are made. What could you and I possibly do that will have any meaningful impact on that decision-making process? Here's the answer:

**Put each and every candidate
running for national public office to a test.**

Virtually all the major players in the foreign-aid field are countries with representational forms of government. Foreign-assistance policies and guidelines are subject to the influence of duly elected officials. What you and I can do is place people in office who back the three goals presented in this chapter. That starts with screening out any candidate – regardless of political beliefs or party affiliation – who doesn't concur with what it will take to close the perilous gap between the world's rich and poor. It's the "ante up" part of the political process. Everyone who wants to be taken seriously as a candidate needs to answer "yes" to these few questions:

- Will you support allocating at least 0.7 percent of your country's annual budget to be used primarily for helping developing countries combat poverty at the grass-roots level? (As noted, 0.7 percent is the minimum level of foreign assistance targeted by the Organization of Economic Cooperation and Development.)

- Do you agree that grass-roots programs aimed at helping women should be given the highest priority when allocating foreign aid?

- Do you concur that foreign aid should be used to put the brakes on population growth in places where the addition of more people increases the probability of global problems?

- Will you sign and support enforcement of the Convention for the Elimination of All Forms of Discrimination Against Women (CEDAW)?

Getting candidates to give clear, unequivocal answers to these four questions will take more than a little pressure. You and I can attempt to squeeze out straightforward responses by confronting or contacting candidates on our own. What we may get back (if anything) are statements filled with loopholes and qualifiers. A much more productive way of shaking out unambiguous answers is to muster the resources of two powerful forces:

1. Women's organizations

2. The media

In countries making foreign aid payments, there are an extraordinary number of women's groups that could, if so inclined, put every candidate for national office to this test. These organizations represent a voting constituency that no candidate can afford to ignore. Just in the United States, for example, there are 27,000 large nonprofit organizations that devote all or much of their attention to women's interests and needs.[37] The U.S. also has 14,000 private and community foundations that single out women as a key interest area.[38] Of course, not every women's organization will be in favor of this screening test. The vast majority, however, are likely to see value in identifying individuals who are willing to use foreign aid to fuel a new and aggressive approach to countering global poverty.

The impact of media and its ties to women is also significant. First, there is a large and growing contingent of female writers, editors and TV/radio producers. A study by the International Women's Media Foundation of 71 countries and 40,000 journalists found 43 percent of those journalists are women.[39] Second, the assortment of women's magazines and TV/radio programs in the more-developed world is nothing short of staggering. Many of those publications and programs reach huge female audiences. To put numbers behind that statement, the 10 top-selling women's magazines in the world have a combined circulation of 39 million and a readership estimated to be *244 million women.*[40]

Not every individual running for election is going to be in sync with the three goals presented in this chapter. Thus, earmarking candidates who answer "yes" to the four questions on the test is only the first part of the battle. The second part is voting the right people into office. And who will make the call as to whether the right candidates get elected? Mainly…

Women.

Plenty of men will also join the ranks and support candidates who take a "yes" position on the test. However, it will take women voters (and there are a lot of them) to win the day.

So what can we do? We can encourage women's organizations and the media to press any candidate running for national office to answer the four questions, and then vigorously promote the names of those contenders who respond "yes" to each question. Next, we can vote into office only those policy makers who advocate using foreign aid to advance our three goals.

Some will criticize this plan of action as being overly simplistic and politically naive. Maybe they're right. On the other hand, maybe invoking simplicity and thinking outside the usual political box will get us moving in the right direction. As World Bank President James Wolfensohn reminded us, "any effort to fight poverty must be comprehensive."[41] *How Women Can Beat Terrorism* outlines a plan that needs to be a part of that comprehensive fight. Women *must* be a more integral part of the battle against poverty. As Thoraya Ahmed Obaid, a Muslim woman from Saudi Arabia who heads the U.N. Population Fund, told the BBC after the September 11 attacks:

> Women … are peacemakers who …cross geographical,
> tribal and geopolitical lines. Their work at the commu-
> nity level is an essential part of nation building. It is
> women who try to bridge differences and create the
> building blocks of reconciliation.[42]

Her words are worth heeding. The world doesn't have a short-age of women who have the capacity to help close the societal gap. What the world lacks – at least so far – is the resolve to unshackle women so they can become more instrumental in the world, and thereby make this book – and its casualty predictions– as off-target as Paul Ehrlich's *The Population Bomb* was some 30 years ago.

EPILOGUE

Great Transition: The Promise and Lure of the Times Ahead is a sobering book produced by the Stockholm Environment Institute. The group of economists, engineers, environmentalists and others responsible for the publication warned that if human development doesn't change course, "the nightmare of an impoverished, mean, destructive future looms."[1]

Even knowing that such a nightmare may not be that far off, humans have made no significant changes in their behavior. The 100 world leaders and 65,000 delegates who gathered in South Africa for the 2002 World Summit on Sustainable Development recognized where mankind is heading. That summit opened with the president of South Africa sounding this ominous warning:

> A global human society based on poverty for many
> and prosperity for a few, characterized by islands of
> wealth, surrounded by a sea of poverty, is
> unsustainable.[2]

The president's remarks came on the heels of a comment made by the U.N. official who headed up the summit. There is great danger, he said, in creating societies where people live "in a state of perpetual hopelessness."[3] That kind of hopelessness, he added, "is obviously going to hit back at you at some stage."[4]

For all the reasons listed in this book, terrorism is and will be the preferred recourse for any and all who are determined to "hit back." Between now and 2030, those of us living in the prosperous corners of the world are going to be targeted. Whether we experience a catastrophe or only minor events depends on what action we take today.

We need to liberate, educate, motivate, celebrate and elevate women in those regions of the world where people have been snared by dehumanizing poverty.

We need to do this fast.

We need to act now because it is the right thing to do for the billions of men, women and children who are not just poor but also hopeless.

We need to grasp the reality that in order to preserve and protect our own quality of life, we must make the world a better place for those less fortunate than ourselves.

NOTES

Prologue

1.   Sony Yee. "Nuclear Experts warn of threat from 'dirty bombs'." *Christian Science Monitor* (Nov. 5, 2001).

2.   A-Bomb, WWW Museum, Hiroshima, Japan, July 2000. Note: there are differing estimates as to the number of people killed outright or over time as a result of the atomic bombing of Hiroshima. Some sources note that 45,000 people died on Aug. 6, 1945 (most were civilians) and 19,000 over the next four months. The most frequently cited sources state that the bomb and its radiation effects killed 140,000 people by year-end 1945.

3.   "Patterns of Global Terrorism." *U.S. Department of State* (April 2001). Note: global terrorist attacks went up 8% from 1999 to 2000.

4.   "Recent Trends in Domestic and International Terrorism." *Center for National Security Studies* (April 1995).

5.   Gary Ackerman, and Cheryl Loeb. "Watch Out for America's Own Extremists." *The Christian Science Monitor* (Oct. 19, 2001).

6.   Abraham H. Maslow, Robert Frager, and James Fadiman. *Motivation and Personality.* New York: Addison-Wesley, 1987.

7.   "Population Growth Rate." *The World Bank* (2000).

8.   "State of the World Population 2001."

9.   "State of the World Population 2001."

10.   Ben Wattenberg. "The Population Explosion is Over." *New York Times Magazine,* November 23, 1997.

11.   Austin Ruse. "Global Monitor: Population control hurts elderly, UN Ambassador stuns pop controllers form." *PRI Review,* Population Research Institute, May/June 1998, p. 9, 15.

12.   Paul R. Ehrlich. *The Population Bomb.* New York: Ballantine Books, 1971.

13.   Ehrlich, *The Population Bomb,* p. 3.

14.   "The State of the World's Children 2002." *UNICEF* (September 2001).

15.   Hamlet's soliloquy upon contemplating suicide is a warning flag that could wave above this book: "To die, to sleep... To sleep, perchance to dream. Ay, there's the rub, for in that sleep of death what dreams may come when we have shuffled off this mortal coil, must give us pause..."

16.   As of the close of 2001, the list includes Iran, Sudan, Libya, North

Korea, Cuba, Iraq and Syria. Ref.: National Center for Policy Analysis, December 2001.

17. "Terrorist Group Profiles." *U.S. Department of State* (Oct. 11, 2001).
18. "Terrorism: Questions & Answers." Council on Foreign Relations. <http:www.terrorismanswers.com/causes/poverty2.html> January 2003
19. "Terrorism: Questions & Answers." Council on Foreign Relations. <http:www.terrorismanswers.com/causes/poverty2.html> January 2003
20. "Terrorism: Questions & Answers." Council on Foreign Relations. <http:www.terrorismanswers.com/causes/poverty.html> January 2003
21. "Terrorism: Questions & Answers." Council on Foreign Relations. <http:www.terrorismanswers.com/causes/poverty.html> January 2003
22. State of the World Population 2001.
23. State of the World Population 2001.
24. State of the World Population 2001.
25. "State of the World Population 1989." *United Nations Population Fund* (1989).
26. P.E. Hollerbach. "Power in Families: Communication and Fertility Decision-Making." *Journal of Population.* (1976).
27. Klaus M. Leisinger, Karin M. Schmitt, Rajul Pandya-Lorch. *Six Billion and Counting.* Washington, DC: International Food Policy Research Institute, 2002.
28. Taylor B. Seybolt. *Major Armed Conflicts. SIPRI Yearbook 2000: Armaments, Disarmament and International Security.* Oxford: Oxford University Press, 2000.
29. "Report to U.N. Agencies." *European Commission, Humanitarian Aid Office* (June 2001).

Part I – The Problem
Chapter 1: Where We're Heading

1. John B. Padgett. William Faulkner's Essays, Speeches, and Public Letters. William Faulkner on the Web, October 2000. <http//www.mcsr.olemiss .edu/~egjbp/Faulkner.html>
2. French Anderson. Leaving GATTACA. <http:www.biospace.com> January 2002.
3. The Total Solar Eclipse of 2030 November. <http:www.eclipse.za.net>
4. George Rathmann. Beyond Suspicion. <http:www.biospace.com> January 2002.
5. Patrick Collins. "The Space Tourism Industry in 2030." Proceedings of Space 2000, ASCE. Albuquerque, NM, March 2000. pp. 594-603.
6. "Major Quake Likely to Strike Between 200 and 2030." U.S. Geological

Survey Fact Sheet 152-99.

7.   *1997 Annual Report of the Social Security Trustees.* pp. 180, 115.

8.   Press Release. "Humans Running UP Huge 'Overdraft' with the Planet, Says New WWF Report." Geneva, Switzerland: World Wildlife Fund. July 9, 2002.

9.   Robert D. Kaplan. "The Coming Anarchy," *The Atlantic Monthly,* February 1994, pp. 44-76.

10.   "Water Crisis Predicted for China by 2030." *China Daily,* November 16, 2001.

11.   "Water Crisis Predicted for China by 2030."

12.   "Ambitious Chinese program will reroute water to arid north." Associated Press release, February 20, 2003.

13.   Bill Joy. "The Dark Side of Technology." Address to the Commonwealth Club of California (San Francisco), June 6, 2000.

14.   Bill Joy. "The Dark Side of Technology."

15.   Bill Joy. "The Dark Side of Technology."

16.   "Nuclear Power Plants May Generate a Third of Russia's Electricity by 2003." Interfax News Agency, May 25, 2000.

17.   Bulletin of the Atomic Scientists. <http:www.bullatomsci.org> May 3, 2001. Note: at the close of 2000, there were 438 nuclear-power plants operating around the world according to IAEA. Currently, nuclear power produces 16% of global energy with some countries such as France, Lithuania and Belgium dependent on nuclear power for over half their energy needs.

18.   "Bush decides on Nevada site for nuclear waste disposal." Associated Press release, February 16, 2002.

19.   Bulletin of the Atomic Scientists.

20.   "Bush decides on Nevada site for nuclear waste disposal."

21.   "Bush decides on Nevada site for nuclear waste disposal."

22.   Bruce G. Blair. "What If the Terrorists Go Nuclear?" Washington, DC: Center for Defense Information, Oct. 1, 2001.

23.   Physicians for Social Responsibility. <http//www.psr.org/conse-quences.htm> Note: the prediction assumed a total of 48 warheads would explode over Atlanta, Boston, Chicago, New York, Pittsburgh, San Francisco, Seattle and Washington, DC

24.   History of Bioterrorism. <http:www.ABCNews.com> Oct. 5, 2000.

25.   Miller, Engelberg, Broad, *Germs,* p. 314.

26.   Judith Miller et al. *Germs.* pp. 316-317.

Chapter 2: Five-Cluster Analysis

1.   Note: The World Bank includes territories (e.g. Puerto Rico) as coun-
     tries.
8.   John Donnelly. "A Deadly Family Feud." *The Boston Globe*, August 8,
     1999.
3.   John Donnelly. "A Deadly Family Feud."
4.   Michael Fleshman. Sharing Africa's Peacekeeping Burden.
     <http://www.un.org/ecosodev/geninfo/afrec/vol13no4/fpeacekp.ht
     m> December, 1999.
5.   Nuclear Power in the World Today.
     <http://www.uic.com.au/nip07.htm> March 2002.
6.   Nuclear Weapons Grade Fuel. <http://www.em.doc.gov/nuclear>
7.   Nicholas Krakev. "Havana Pursues Biological Warfare." *The Washington
     Times*, May 7, 2002.
8.   Theodor Herzl. *The Jewish State*. American Zionist Emergency Council,
     1946.
9.   "High Palestinian Birth Rate Seen as a 'Biological Bomb.'" *Knight
     Ridder Newspapers*, April 21, 2002.
10. "A Land Divided." *Newsweek*, April 1, 2002. pp. 40-41.
11. "The Future of Israel." *Newsweek*, April 1, 2002. p. 39.
12. Gail Foster. "*Straight Talk.*" The Conference Board. June 2002. p. 6.
13. Reuel Marc Gerecht. "They Live to Die." *The Wall Street Journal*, April
     8, 2002.
14. "Israel 'May have 200 Nuclear Weapons.'" *BBC News*, Aug. 23, 2000.
15. Carnegie Endowment for International Peace. "Nuclear Weapons in the
     Middle East." April 11, 2002.
16. Carnegie Endowment for International Peace.
17. Niall Ferguson. "Clashing Civilizations or Mad Mullahs: The United
     States Between Informal and Formal Empire." In *The Age of Terror* (edi-
     tors: Strobe Talbott and Nayan Chanda), New York: Basic Books, 2001,
     p. 137.
19. Niall Ferguson. "Clashing Civilizations or Mad Mullahs: The United
     States Between Informal and Formal Empire."
19. Andrew Higgins, and Alan Cullison. "Saga of Dr. Zawahri Illuminates
     Roots of al Qaeda Terror." *The Wall Street Journal*, July 2, 2002.
20. Phil Williams, and Paul N. Woessner. "The Real Threat of Nuclear
     Smuggling." *Scientific American*, January 1996.

Chapter 3: The Road to 2030

1.   Paul Kennedy. "Maintaining American Power from Injury to Recovery."
     In *The Age of Terror* (editors: Strobe Talbott and Nayan Chanda), New
     York: Basic Books, 2001, p. 70.
2.   John Lewis Gaddis. "And Now This: Lessons from the Old Era for the

New One." In *The Age of Terror* (editors: Strobe Talbott and Nayan Chanda), New York: Basic Books, 2001, p. 6.

3.   Paul Kennedy. "Maintaining American Power from Injury to Recovery." p. 59.

4.   There are many estimates as to the number of war deaths during the twentieth century. Matthew White says in "Wars and Democide of the Twentieth Century" <http://users.erols.com/mwhite28/war-1900.htm> that 180 million people died including those killed in battle as well as civilian casualties. In *The First Measured Century* (Theodore Caplow, Louis Hicks and Ben J. Wattenberg – Washington, DC: American Institute Press, 2000), the estimate is phrased this way: "... more than 100 million soldiers and civilians were killed in the wars of the twentieth century." The United Kingdom-based organization, Saferworld, uses the same language ("... armed conflict took the lives of over 100 million people ...) but adds that 170 million more deaths during the twentieth century could be attributed to political violence (see Hypertext: http://www.saferworld.co.uk/usefu.htm). James L Payne writes in the *Independent Review* (Winter 2002, pp. 447-455) that any claims that the twentieth century was the most violent in history is impossible to document. So, there are many figures to use in pegging deaths attributed to warfare during the past century. *Code Two* falls back on the loose estimate of "more than 100 million deaths" recognizing that this is probably a conservative calculation.

5.   "Sustainable Rural Development: Progress and Challenges." <http://www.fao.org/sd/Dodirect/DoengA01.htm>

6.   "Sustainable Rural Development: Progress and Challenges."

7.   Jonathan Rauch. "Firebombs Over Tokyo." *The Atlantic Monthly.* July/August 2002. p. 22.

8.   Jonathan Rauch. "Firebombs Over Tokyo."

9.   Royal College of Psychiatrists press release. "Plea to End Stigma of Mental Illness by WHO Director General." London: Royal College of Psychiatrists, July 2001.

10. Royal College of Psychiatrists press release. "Plea to End Stigma of Mental Illness by WHO Director General."

11. R. C. Kessler et al, "A Methodology for Estimating the 12-Month Prevalence of Serious Mental Illness," in *Mental Health*, United States, 1999, edited by R. W. Manderscheid and M. J. Henderson, Rockville, MD: Center for Mental Health Services, pp 99–109.

12. Pakistan Press Foundation. "Understanding Mental Illnesses." Seminar for journalists on August 8, 2001.

13. World Health Organization Director General Gro Harlem Brundtland statement to the Royal College of Psychiatrists. July 2001.

14. 4.5 million people in the U.S. have schizophrenia or manic-depression and 40% of them do not realize they are sick because the illness affects

the brain's frontal-lobe function. Source: E. Fuller Torrey and Mary Zdanowicz. "Kevin's Law Would Help Treat Mental Illness, Prevent Tragedy." *Detroit Free Press,* August 28, 2001.

15. "Takuma's trial must not be only about his mental state" *The Asahi Shimbun,* Japan, Dec. 28, 2000.
16. Sylvia Nasar. *A Beautiful Mind: A Biography of John Forbes Nash.* New York: Simon & Schuster, 1998.
17. Pakistan Press Foundation.
18. Ehud Sprinzak. "Rational Fanatics." *Foreign Policy Magazine,* September/October 2000.
19. Ehud Sprinzak. "Rational Fanatics."
20. The Worst Terrorist Attacks of the Past Quarter Century. <http:www.smh.com.au> Sept. 12, 2001.
21. Population Division, Department of Economic and Social Affairs, United Nations. *World Population Prospects – The 2000 Revision Highlights,* February 2001.
22. Kenneth V. Iserson, M.D. *Demon Doctors: Physicians as Serial Killers.* Tucson, AZ: Galen Press. 2001.
23. U.S. Warns of Doomsday Scenario. <http://www.cnn.com/2002/WORLD/asiapcf/south/05/31/kashmir.attack.toll> June 1, 2002.
24. Kenneth V. Iserson, M.D. *Demon Doctors: Physicians as Serial Killers.*
25. Niall Ferguson. "Clashing Civilizations or Mad Mullahs: The United States Between Informal and Formal Empire" in *The Age of Terror.* p. 118.
26. Strobe Talbott and Nayan Chanda. *The Age of Terror.* New York: Basic Books, 2001. Introduction – p. *x.*
27. L. Douglas Keeney. *Doomsday Scenario.* St. Paul, MN: MBI Publishing Company. 2002. p. 62.
28. Ira Helfand, M.D. Effects of a Nuclear Explosion. <http://www.psr.org/Helfand1.htm>
29. Bill Miller. "Study Urges Focus on Terrorism with High Fatalities, Cost." *The Washington Post,* April 29, 2002.
30. Emerging Infectious Diseases. <http://www.cdc.gov/ncidod/eid/vol7no6/lederberg.htm> November – December 2001.
31. Emerging Infectious Diseases.
32. America's Wars. <http://www.va.gov/pressrel/amwars01.htm>.
33. America's Wars.
34. Roland Wall. "War and the Environment." *Know Your Environment.* Philadelphia: The Academy of Natural Sciences. 2001.
35. Alexander Leaf, M.D. "Food and Nutrition in the Aftermath of Nuclear War." In *The Medical Implications of Nuclear War.* Washington, DC: National Academy of Sciences National Academy Press. 1986. pp. 284-289.
36. Alexander Leaf, M.D. *The Medical Implications of Nuclear War.* p. 285.

Part II: Poverty

Chapter 4: Ownership

1. *The State of World Population 2001.*
2. *The State of World Population 2001.*
3. *The State of World Population 2001.*
4. Largest Buddhist Populations. <http://www.buddhanet.net>.
5. Mellody Hobson. Credit Card Cleanup. <http://www.abcnews.go.com/sections/GMA/GoodMorningAmerica>.
6. James B. Twitchell. *Lead Us into Temptation.* New York: Columbia University Press, 1999.
7. Frank Pellegrini. "Person of the Week: The American Consumer." *Time,* August 30, 2001.
8. Juliet B. Schor. *The Overspent American: Upscaling, Downshifting and the New Consumer.* New York: Basic Books, 1998.
9. Juliet B. Schor. *The Overspent American: Up scaling, Downshifting and the New Consumer.*
10. R. J. Michaels. The Joy of Ownership. <http://www.*Asiaweek.com*> Jan. 12, 2001.
11. Mu'ammar al-Qadhafi. *Green Book.* Tripoli, Lybia: Public Establishment for Publishing, new edition – 1999.
12. Overview of World Religions. <http://www.philtar.ucsm.ac.uk/>. Note: estimates of the number of Buddhists in Japan range from 58% of the population to over 90%. Many Japanese claim to be both Buddhist and Shintoist – a factor that makes it difficult to pinpoint the exact number of Buddhists in the country.
13. Janet Wilson. "Refugees' Plight Extends Far Beyond Kosovo." *Los Angeles Times,* April 17, 1999.
14. *Toy Industry Fact Book – 2000-2001 Edition.* New York: Toy Industry Association, Inc. Information included in Chapter on "Industry Economics and Marketing."
15. *Toy Industry Fact Book – 2000-2001 Edition.*
16. James B. Twitchell. *Living It Up.* New York: Columbia University Press, 2002.
17. Press Release from Dr. Ing. h.c. F. Porsche AG, January 18, 2002.
18. "Important Series of Sales at Sotheby's Geneva." Sotheby's Holdings, Inc., (press release) November 2000.
19. "World Development Indicators." *The World Bank,* 2001.
20. J. Max Robbins. Increasingly, TV's a Mess of Messages. <http://www.tvguide.com/magazine/robins/020325.asp> *March* 23, 2002
21. "TV Viewing in Internet Households." *Nielsen Media Research* (May 1999).
22. Children & Television: Frequently Asked Questions.

<http://www.cme.org>. While the frequency of TV advertising aimed at children is high in the U.S., children-oriented ads in Australia average 34 per hour – that's more than double the frequency found in many European countries according to Consumers International in London (July 1999).

23. Children & Television: Frequently Asked Questions.
24. John Dougherty. "The Selling of ASU Football." *Phoenix New Times*, Sept. 17, 1998.
25. Facts and Figures about the Highway Beautification Act: Why It's Time for Reform. <http://www.scenic.org>.
26. United Nations: The Fourth World Conference on Women. <http://www.agora21.org/qcmf/qcmf-en10.html>.

Chapter 5: Control

1. "At a Glance, Genetic Code." *BBC News*, September 11, 2001.
2. *BBC News*.
3. Gary Cziko. *Without Miracles: Universal Selection Theory and the Second Darwinian Revolution*. Cambridge, Massachusetts and London, England: The MIT Press, 1995.
4. Ron Chepesiuk. In Bad Company. <http:// www.towardfreedome.com> December 2001.
5. Ron Chepesiuk.
6. "News and Resources – Sudan." *U.S. Committee for Refugees*.
7. "News and Resources – Sudan." *U.S. Committee for Refugees*.
8. "U.S. Ambassador Says Sudan Still Supports Terrorists." *Associated Press*, July 19, 1999.
9. Richard Waddington. "Sudan Government, Rebels Seal Nuba Ceasefire." *The Muslim News*, Jan. 19, 2002.
10. On Aug. 28, 1998, the United States bombed Sudan's Al Shifa pharmaceutical factory and stated the action was taken because the plant was manufacturing chemical weapons. The Sudan government and independent fact-finders charged that the factory was a legitimate pharmaceutical production facility and was not engaged in making weapons of mass destruction. The Sudan government has been accused of producing chemical weapons and using them in its war with southern rebels – although that charge has never been substantiated.
11. The Unabomber's Manifesto. <http:// www.courttv.com>.
12. United National Populations Fund.
13. United National Populations Fund.
14. United National Populations Fund.
15. GNP Per Capita. <http://www.worldbank.org>.
16. "2001 World Population Data Sheet." *Population Reference Bureau*.

17. Plea to End Stigma of Mental Illness by WHO Director General.
     London: *Royal College of Psychiatrists* (July 2001).
18. United Nations Public Inquiries Unit - From "FAQs".
     <http://www.un.org/geninfo/faq.html> 2000.
19. Thomas Carothers. "The Rule of Law Revival." *Foreign Affairs,* Vol. 77,
     No. 2, 1998.
20. Thomas Carothers. *Foreign Affairs.*
21. Theodore Kaczynski. "Industrial Society and Its Future." *Washington
     Post,* Sept. 19, 1995.
22. William T. Powers. *Behavior: The Control of Perception.* Chicago: Aldine
     Publishing Company, 1973, p. 271.
23. "Best-Selling Author and Business Strategist, Tom Peters, Speaks to
     Thousands at NAPM's 85th Annual International Purchasing
     Conference & Educational Exhibit." *Institute for Supply Management,*
     (April 30, 2000).
24. Mayra Buvinic. Women in Poverty: A New Global Underclass.
     <www.iadb.org/sds/ doc/767eng.pdf>.
25. Mayra Buvinic. Women in Poverty: A New Global Underclass.
     <www.iadb.org/sds/ doc/767eng.pdf>.
26. Mayra Buvinic. Women in Poverty: A New Global Underclass.
     <www.iadb.org/sds/ doc/767eng.pdf>.

Part III: Hopelessness

Chapter 6: Widened Societal Gap

1.   Joshua Robin. "Former President Carter makes his case for humanity."
     Seattle Times, Jan. 20, 2000.
2.   "Former President Carter makes his case for humanity." *Seattle Times.*
3.   Hendrick Hertzberg. "Essay on Jimmy Carter." from the Public
     Broadcasting Corporation program, *Character Above All,* 1996.
4.   P.J. O'Rourke. *"Closing the Wealth Gap." Cato Institute conference* (June
     18, 1997).
5.   Alan Beattie. "World Bank Calls for Private Aid in Attempt to Halve
     Poverty by 2015." *Financial Times,* Feb. 20, 2002.
6.   "World Bank Calls for Private Aid in Attempt to Halve Poverty by
     2015." *Financial Times.*
7.   "World Bank Calls for Private Aid in Attempt to Halve Poverty by
     2015." *Financial Times.*
8.   Peter Bauer. *From Subsistence to Exchange and Other Essays.* Princeton,
     NJ: Princeton University Press, 2000.
9.   "2001 World Population Data Sheet." Population Reference Bureau
     (2002).
10. "2001 World Population Data Sheet." Population Reference Bureau.

11. Andrew Johnston. "Disparities of Wealth Are Seen as Fuel for Terrorism." *International Herald Tribune,* December 20, 2001.
12. W. Michael Cox and Richard Alm. "Why Decry the Wealth Gap?" *New York Times,* January 24, 2000.
13. "Why Decry the Wealth Gap?" *New York Times.*
14. "Why Decry the Wealth Gap?" *New York Times.*
15. "49th Annual Executive Pay Survey." *Business Week,* April 19, 1999.
16. Lisa Collier Cool. "Fast Food. Junk Food. RV. Stress." *Good Housekeeping,* (May 2002): 119-124.
17. A Hot Dog Primer for Inquiring Minds. [electronic journal]. [cited May 2002]. Available <http://www.hot-dog.org/HotDogQandA.htm>. Note: the Council is a project of the American Meat Institute.
18. The State of the World Population 2001. [electronic journal]. Available <http://unfpa.org/swp/2001/english/tables.html>.
19. Thomas Friedman. "America's Self-Interest Will Best Be Served by Global Enlightenment." *New York Times,* March 21, 2002.
20. George Soros. *On Globalization.* [electronic journal]. Available <http://www.publicaffairsbooks.com/books/geo-sum.html>.
21. David Bank. "The Man Who Would Mend the World." *The Wall Street Journal,* March 14, 2002.
22. "The Man Who Would Mend the World." *The Wall Street Journal.*
23. "The Man Who Would Mend the World." *The Wall Street Journal.*
24. "The Man Who Would Mend the World." *The Wall Street Journal.*
25. Laurent Fabius. "Building Bridges in Ottawa: Laurent Fabius Proposes Some Steps that the Group of Seven Should Take to Tackle the Causes of World Poverty." *Financial Times,* February 8, 2002.
26. Larry Elliott and Charlotte Denny. "Top 1% Earn as Much as the Poorest 57%." *Guardian,* January 18, 2002.
27. "World Bank president urges big boost in development aid for Africa." *Associated Press,* June 5, 2002.
28. David C. Korten. *When Corporations Rule the World.* West Hartford: Kumarian Press, Inc. and San Francisco: Berrett-Koehler Publishers. 1995. p. 323.
29. "Internet Increases Global Inequality – U.N.," *BBC News,* July 12, 1999.
30. Susan Okie. "Genetic Gains Unlikely to Help World's Poor, Report Predicts." *Washington Post,* May 1, 2002.
31. "Genetic Gains Unlikely to Help World's Poor, Report Predicts." *Washington Post.*
32. Robert Wade. "Winners and Losers." *The Economist,* April 26, 2001.
33. Peter Ford. "Why do they hate us?" *The Christian Science Monitor.* September 27, 2001.
34. U.S. Census Bureau, Feb. 1, 2002.
35. Jeff Gates. "The Ownership Solution." *Boston Review,* December 1998/January 1999.

36.   United Nations Populations Fund. <http://www.unfpa.org/modules
      /6billion/facts.htm>.
37.   Bulletin of the Atomic Scientists.
      <http://www.thebulletin.org/media/022702pr.html>. February 27,
      2002.
38.   Bulletin of the Atomic Scientists.

Chapter 7: Hopelessness and Humiliation

1.   Eric Hoffer. *The True Believer*, New York: Harper & Row, Publishers,
      Inc. 1951. p. 15
2.   Dorhan Pamuk. "The Anger of the Damned," *The New York Review of
      Books,* November 15, 2001.
3.   Peter D. Bell. "Where the End of Poverty Begins." Speech to Princeton
      University, Feb. 22, 2003.

Part IV: Population Growth

Chapter 8: Introduction

1.   "Sustainable Urban Environments." *United States Environmental
      Protection Agency,* August 25, 1998.
2.   Jerry Brown. *A Brave New World of Environmental Destruction,* 1998.
3.   Denis L. Meadows, Donella H. Meadows, Jorgen Randers, and William
      W. Behrens III. *The Limits to Growth.* London: Earthscan Publications.
      Ltd., 1972.
4.   Keith Suter. "Fair Warning? The Club of Rome Revisited," *Australian
      Broadcasting Corporation,* 1999.
5.   Bjorn Lomborg. *The Skeptical Environmentalist.* Cambridge: Cambridge
      University Press, 2001. (Note: originally published in Danish as *Verdens
      Sande Tilstand* in 1998)
6.   Lomborg. *The Skeptical Environmentalist,* p. 4.
7.   Lomborg. *The Skeptical Environmentalist,* p. 4.
8.   Chris Lavers. "You've Never Had It So Good." *The Guardian,*
      September 1, 2001.
9.   "Population Explosion Now a Birth Dearth." *Orange County Register,*
10.   Michael S. Berliner, Ph.D. (April 16, 2001). On Earth Day Remember –
      If Environmentalists Succeed, They Will Make Human Life Impossible.
      In Ayn Rand Institute [electronic journal]. [cited January 2002].
      Available http://www.aynrand.org/medialink/environ.shtml.
11.   John Carlisle. "The Campaign Against Urban Sprawl: Declaring War on
      the American Dream." *National Policy Analysis #239* National Center for
      Public Policy Research (April 1999).
12.   Carlisle. "The Campaign Against Urban Sprawl: Declaring War on the

American Dream."

13. Tom Burke. *Ten Pinches of Salt.* London: Green Alliance, August 2001.

14. Life on Earth. In Overpopulation Group [electronic journal]. [cited January 2002]. Available http://www.aynrand.org/medialink/environ.shtml.

Chapter 9: People and Land

1. *"Food shortages imperil 3 million in southern Sudan." United Nations Food and Agriculture Organization* (Jan. 5, 2001).

2. Lomborg. *The Skeptical Environmentalist,* p. 61.

3. Lomborg. *The Skeptical Environmentalist,* p. 61.

4. N.A. Mujumdar (Nov. 27, 2001). Food distribution and growth-equity linkages. In Yahoo Finance Business Line [electronic journal]. Available <http://www.hinduonnet.com/businessline /2001/11/27/stories/042720ju.htm>.

5. From California Integrated Waste Management Board, 2001.

6. Willy H. Verheye. "Food Production or Food Aid?: An African Challenge." *Finance & Development.* December 2000.

7. Lewis Wolpert. *"Genetics Can Provide Food to The Starving Millions." University College London* (November 12, 1999).

8. Lomborg. *The Skeptical Environmentalist,* p. 250 (cited from sources: Jonathan Baille and Brian Groombridge, *1996 Red List of Threatened Animals,* 1997; K.S. Walter and H. J. Gillett – eds., *1997 Red List of Threatened Animals,* 1998; Robert M. May, John H. Lawton and Nigel E. Stork, *Assessing Extinction Rates,* 1995; and W. V. Reid, "How Many Species Will There Be?" a chapter in a book by T.C. Whitmore and J.A. Sayer, *Deforestation and Species Extinction,* Chapman and Hall, 1992).

9. James R. Craig, David J. Vaughan and Brian J. Skinner. *1996 Resources of the Earth: Origin, Use and Environmental Impact.* Upper Saddle River, NJ: Prentice Hall, 1996

10. Lomborg. *The Skeptical Environmentalist,* p. 109.

11. G. Tyler Miller, Jr. *Living in the Environment – 12th Edition.* Belmont, CA: Wadsworth/Thomson Learning, 2002.

12. G. Tyler Miller, Jr. *Living in the Environment – 12th Edition,* p. 269.

13. G. Tyler Miller, Jr. *Living in the Environment – 12th Edition,* p. 267.

14. Vernon M. Briggs, Jr. "Malthus: The economist." *The Social Contract* (Spring 1998): 213.

15. Lomborg. *The Skeptical Environmentalist,* p. 62.

16. Lester R. Brown et al. *State of the World 2001.* New York: W.W. Norton & Company, 2001. p. 44.

17. Lester R. Brown et al. *State of the World 2001.* p. 45.

18. Lester R. Brown et al. *State of the World 2001.* p. 45.

19. David L. Levy and Peter Newell. "Oceans Apart." *Environment* 42(9): 8

– 20; Terry Hennessy, "Produce in Progress," *Progressive Grocer,* 79(12): 69-72. Note: *The Skeptical Environmentalist* excerpts from these publications noting that in the EU, 59% of consumers view GM foods as risky. In the U.S., however, 60% are positive about food biotechnology.

20. Madeleine J. Nash and Susan Horsburgh. "The Fury of El Nino." *Time,* March 2, 1998.

21. Lomborg. *The Skeptical Environmentalist,* p. 5.

22. Andrew Goudie. *The Human Impact on the Natural Environment.* Cambridge, MA: MIT Press, 2000.

23. Nikos Alexandratos (ed.). *World Agriculture: Towards 2010. FAO Study.* Food and Agriculture organization of the United Nations, Rome, 1995.

24. "Saving the Earth." *Food and Agricultural Organization of the United Nations,* Nov. 8, 2001.

25. Julio Henao and Carlos Baanante. "Nutrient Depletion in the Agricultural Soils of Africa," from *A 2020 Vision for Food, Agriculture, and the Environment – Brief 62,* Washington, DC: International Food Policy Research Institute, October 1999.

26. Conservation Agriculture: Economic Benefits. <http://www.ecaf.org> February 2002.

27. Conservation Agriculture: Economic Benefits.

28. "Worldwide Forest/Biodiversity Campaign News." <http://www.forests.org/recent/ 2000/stdesfor.htm> November 1, 2000. Note: Through 2002, Staples opened 1,400 stores in the U.S – 400 more retail outlets than its closest competitor. However, in 2002, Staples began to slow down its growth rate and even closed 22 previously-opened stores. "We pushed the envelope a little too aggressively," Staples CEO Ronald Sargent told *The Wall Street Journal* (March 13, 2002).

29. Lomborg. *The Skeptical Environmentalist.* p. 117.

30. Lomborg. *The Skeptical Environmentalist.* p. 117.

31. Lester R. Brown et al. *State of the World 2001.* p. 11.

32. G. Tyler Miller, Jr. *Living in the Environment – 12th Edition,* p. 592.

33. G. Tyler Miller, Jr. *Living in the Environment – 12th Edition,* p. 593.

34. Corruption, Lawlessness Fuel Epidemic of Illegal Logging in Indonesia. <http://www.usnewswire.com> Feb. 20, 2002.

35. Population Reference Bureau, Washington, DC, 2002.

36. Population Reference Bureau, p. 592.

37. U.S. Newswire.

38. The statement has been credited to a number of people including one of the founding fathers of OPEC.

39. "Mission/Vision Statement." *National Energy Technology Laboratory Combustion Technologies, Morgantown, WV:* U.S. Department of Energy (October 2001).

40. Drilling to the Ends of the Earth – The Case Against New Fossil Fuel Exploration. <http://www.ran.org> 2001.

41. Drilling to the Ends of the Earth – The Case Against New Fossil Fuel Exploration.
42. "Monthly Energy Review." *U.S. Department of Energy*, Energy Information Agency (March 2000).
43. "Realizing the Potential of Fusion Energy." *Physics in Action* (December 1999).
44. "Oil Supplies – Are We Really Running Out of Oil?" *The American Petroleum Institute* (October 1996).
45. Lomborg. p. 130. Extracted from Energy Information Agency data – 1998.
46. Lomborg. *The Skeptical Environmentalist.*
47. Petroconsultants U.K. Ltd., *World Petroleum Trends*, 1996.
48. Stuart Baird. "Energy Fact Sheet – Coal." *Energy Educators of Ontario* (1993).
49. Stuart Baird. *Energy Educators of Ontario.*
50. "Fact Sheet OMS-5: Automobile Emissions: An Overview." *Environmental Protection Agency.* EPA National Vehicle and Fuel Emissions Laboratory (August 1994).
51. "Fact Sheet OMS-5: Automobile Emissions: An Overview."
52. Oil, Our Untapped Energy Wealth. <http://www.doe.gov> Feb. 22, 2002.
53. Fred Guterl. "When Wells Go Dry," *Newsweek*, April 15, 2002, pp. 32B-F.
54. Adam Piore. "Hot Springs Eternal," *Newsweek*, April 15, 2002, pp. 32H-L.
55. James R. Craig, David J. Vaughan and Brian J. Skinner. *Resources of the Earth: Origin, Us and Environmental Impact*, Upper Saddle River, NJ: Prentice Hall, 1996.
56. James R. Craig, David J. Vaughan and Brian J. Skinner. *Resources of the Earth: Origin, Us and Environmental Impact.*
57. Lomborg. *The Skeptical Environmentalist.* p. 144.
58. Lynn Scarlett. *Earth Report, 2000.* New York: McGraw-Hill, 2000. p. 54.
59. Lomborg. *The Skeptical Environmentalist.* p. 148.
60. Lomborg. *The Skeptical Environmentalist.* p. 138.
61. Ohio Department of Natural Resources Division of Recycling and Litter Prevention (December 1999).
62. *"Aluminum Industry Analysis Brief."* U.S. Department of Energy (1999).
63. Ohio Department of Natural Resources Division of Recycling and Litter Prevention.
64. Ohio Department of Natural Resources Division of Recycling and Litter Prevention.
65. *"Aluminum Industry Analysis Brief."*
66. Lomborg. *The Skeptical Environmentalist* United States – 1999 Facts and Figures. <http://. p. 147.
67. Municipal Solid Waste in the www.epa.gov/epaoswer/non-

hw/muncpl/msw99.htm>.

68.   Lomborg. *The Skeptical Environmentalist.* p. 207.

69.   William Rathje and Cullen Murphy. "Five Major Myths about Garbage and Why They're Wrong." *Smithsonian Magazine* (July, 1992) pp. 113-122.

70.   Waste & Recycling: Data, Maps & Graphs. http://www.zerowasteamerica.org/statistics.htm.

71.   "*Consumer Handbook for Reducing Solid Waste.*" *U.S. Environmental Protection Agency* (1992).

72.   William P. Cunningham and Barbara Woodworth Saigo. *Environmental Science, a Global Concern – Fifth Edition.* New York: McGraw-Hill Higher Education, 1999. Hazardous waste is a discarded material that is known to be (a) fatal to humans or lab animals in low doses; (b) toxic; (c) ignitable with a flash point lower than 60 degrees Centigrade; (d) corrosive; or (e) explosive or highly reactive.

73.   William P. Cunningham and Barbara Woodworth Saigo. *Environmental Science, a Global Concern – Fifth Edition.*

74.   Lester R. Brown et al. *State of the World 1999.*

75.   Lester R. Brown et al. *State of the World 1999.*

76.   "Nuclear War." *The Wall Street Journal,* April 9, 2002.

77.   Lynn Scarlett. *Earth Report, 2000.* p. 42.

78.   Lynn Scarlett. *Earth Report, 2000.* p. 60.

79.   Gary Gardner. "Accelerating the Shift to Sustainability." *State of the World 1999.* (Lester R. Brown et al), New York: W.W. Norton & Company, 1999. p. 198.

80.   Trends in Species Loss in the United States. <http://www.sierraclub.org>.

81.   Sweet Home. <http://www.sweet-home.or.us>.

82.   Sweet Home. In the 1980s, the Sweet Home Ranger District in Oregon annually produced 86 million board feet of timber until the Northern Spotted Owl controversy forced much of the logging to stop. In 1992, the height of the owl fight, the district produced only 100,000 board feet.

83.   Rowan B. Martin. "Biological Diversity," in *Earth Report, 2000.* New York: McGraw-Hill, 2000, p. 208.

84.   Trends in Species Loss in the United States.

85.   Trends in Species Loss in the United States.

86.   Trends in Species Loss in the United States.

87.   Lester R. Brown et al. *State of the World 2001.*

88.   "Significant biodiversity loss across North America, NAFTA body's State of the Environment report says." *North American Commission for Environmental Cooperation* (Jan. 7, 2002).

89.   Significant biodiversity loss across North America, NAFTA body's State of the Environment report says." *North American Commission for Environmental Cooperation.*

Chapter 10: People and Water

1.   Meredith Wilson. *The Music Man,* 1950.
2.   Payal Sampat. "Uncovering Groundwater Pollution." in Worldwatch
     Institute's *State of the World 2001.* New York and London: W.W.
     Norton, 2001. p. 31.
3.   Payal Sampat. *State of the World 2001.* p. 22.
4.   Payal Sampat. *State of the World 2001.* p. 23.
5.   Tushaar Shah, David Molden, R. Sakthivadivel, and David Seckler. *The
     Global Groundwater Situation: Overview of Opportunities and Challenges.*
     Sri Lanka: International Water Management Institute, 2000.
6.   Alex Kirby. "Silt behind dams worsens water shortage." *BBC report,*
     Dec. 4, 2001.
7.   William Finnegan. "Leasing the Rain." *The New Yorker,* April 8, 2002,
     p. 44.
8.   Lomborg. *The Skeptical Environmentalist.* p. 6.
9.   Sandra Postel and Linda Starke. *Pillar of Sand: Can the Irrigation
     Miracle Last?* New York: W.W. Norton & Company, 1999.
10. "Emerging Water Shortages Threaten Food Supplies, Regional Peace."
     Worldwatch Institute (July 17, 1999).
11. "Emerging Water Shortages Threaten Food Supplies, Regional Peace."
     Worldwatch Institute.
12. *World Resources 1996-97.* World Resources Institute, New York: Oxford
     University Press, 1996.
13. B. R. Hanson, G. Fipps, and E.C. Martin. *Drip Irrigation of Row Crops:
     What Is the State of the Art?* Abstract – Kansas State University, 2000.
14. *The State of the World Population 2001.* New York: United Nations
     Population Fund, 2002.
15. *The State of the World Population 2001.*
16. *The State of the World Population 2001.*
17. *The State of the World Population 2001.*
18. "Desalination – Producing Potable Water." *California Resources Agency*
     (1997).
19. "Desalination – Producing Potable Water." *California Resources Agency.*
20. Lomborg. *The Skeptical Environmentalist.* p. 154.
21. Russell Smith. "Africa's Potential Water Wars." *BBC News,* Nov. 15,
     1999.
22. Russell Smith. *BBC News.*
23. Lomborg. *The Skeptical Environmentalist.* p. 136.
24. "The Poor Pay Much More for Water ... Use Much Less – Often
     Contaminate." *World Water Council* (Aug. 5, 1999).
25. "The Poor Pay Much More for Water ... Use Much Less – Often
     Contaminate." *World Water Council.*
26. "The Poor Pay Much More for Water ... Use Much Less – Often
     Contaminate." *World Water Council.*

27. "Similar Patterns of Ground Water Pollution Found in United States and China." *U.S. Geological Survey, U.S. Department of the Interior* (Feb. 6, 2002). The report studied ground water in the U.S. (California's Central Valley and the Delmarva Peninsula of Maryland, Virginia and Delaware) and Hebei Province near Beijing, China.

28. "*Soil and Water Quality: An Agenda for Agriculture.*" *National Academy Press* (1993).

29. Lomborg. *The Skeptical Environmentalist.* p. 197.

30. Lomborg. *The Skeptical Environmentalist.* p. 202.

31. "A River Runs Through It." *Time,* March 25, 2002, p. 59.

Chapter 11: People and Air

1. "Dreaming of white Christmas? Dream on, study says." *Associated Press,* (December 22, 2001).

2. Global Warming. <http://www.epa.gov/global-warming> Aug. 29, 2001.

3. Seth Dunn. "Decarbonizing the Energy Economy," in Worldwatch Institute's *State of the World 2001.* New York and London: W.W. Norton, 2001. p. 87.

4. James K. Glassman. "Turning Green." *The Wall Street Journal,* February 14, 2002.

5. "Pollution Cloud Threatens Asia." *BBC News.* June 11, 1999.

6. "Respirators issued to fight snowmobile fumes." *Associated Press* (February 16, 2002).

7. "Global Warming Poses Severe Threat to the 'Richest' Natural Areas." *World Wildlife Fund* (Feb. 7, 2002).

8. The Larsen B ice shelf disintegrated between Jan. 31 and Mar. 7, 2002, according to the National Snow and Ice Data Center at the University of Colorado.

9. Michael Llanos. "Staggering End to Antarctic Ice Shelf." *MSNBC News,* March 19, 2002.

10. Michael Llanos. *MSNBC News.*

11. Michael Llanos. *MSNBC News.*

12. Michael Llanos. *MSNBC News.*

13. Michael Llanos. *MSNBC News.*

14. Philip Stott. "Cold Comfort for 'Global Warming.'" *The Wall Street Journal,* March 22, 2002. Note: Stott is emeritus professor of biogeography at London University.

15. Philip Stott. *The Wall Street Journal.*

16. Philip Stott. *The Wall Street Journal.*

17. "Towards a Sustainable America: Advancing Prosperity, Opportunity, and a Healthy Environment for the 21st Century." *President's Commission on Sustainable Development,* May 1999.

18.   Representative Dana Rochrabacher. Statement to the U.S. House of
       Representatives on June 13, 2001.
19.   Alex Kirby. "Human Effect on Climate 'Beyond Doubt'." *BBC News,*
       Jan. 22, 2001. Note: the Intergovernmental Panel on Climate Change
       was created by the U.N. in 1998 to examine global warming. The panel
       includes hundreds of scientists. IPCC is sponsored by the U.N.
       Environment Programme and the World Meteorological Organization.
20.   Richard S. Lindzen. Global Warming: The Origin and Nature of the
       Alleged Scientific Consensus.
       <http://www.cato.org/pubs/regulation/reg/15n2g.html>.
21.   Seth Dunn. *State of the World 2001. p.* 85.
22.   Seth Dunn. *State of the World 2001. p.* 85.
23.   Seth Dunn. *State of the World 2001. p.* 85.
24.   John Carlisle. "Carbon Dioxide is Good for the Environment."
       *National Policy Analysis #334 (*April 2001).
25.   "Climate Change 1995 – the Economic and Social Dimensions of
       Climate Change." *From working group report of Intergovernmental Panel
       on Climate Change.*
26.   Lomborg. *The Skeptical Environmentalist.* p. 322.
27.   Lomborg. *The Skeptical Environmentalist.* p. 324.
28.   Global Warming: 4 – 7 Degree Temperature Rise by 2100.
       <http://www.ucar.edu> August 2, 2001.
29.   Lomborg. *The Skeptical Environmentalist.* p. 324.
30.   Christopher Cooper. "Kyoto Pact Offers Opportunities to Crow." *The
       Wall Street Journal,* Nov. 1, 2001.
31.   Katherine Ellison. "The Voice from the Pew." *Worth,* July/August
       2001, p. 96.
32.   Laurent Belsie. "Firms Climb Toward 'Climate Neutral.'" *The Christian
       Science Monitor,* August 20, 2001, p. 15.
33.   Thomas Gale More. *Climate of Fear: Why We Shouldn't Worry about
       Global Warming.* Washington, DC: Cato Institute, 1998.

Chapter 12: People and Poverty

1.   Lomborg. *The Skeptical Environmentalist.* p. 4.
2.   Roger Thurow. "Poisonous Legacy – 'Black Village' Testifies to
       Communism's Toll on the Environment." *The Wall Street Journal,* Jan.
       9, 2002, p. 1.
3.   Lomborg. *The Skeptical Environmentalist.* p. 177.
4.   Thurow. *The Wall Street Journal.* p. 1.
5.   Lomborg. *The Skeptical Environmentalist.* p. 7.
6.   "Food and Agricultural Organization of the United Nations." *FAO
       Statistical Databases (*May 2001).
7.   Payal Sampat. p. 29.

8.   Mike Grunwald. "In Dirt, Water and Hogs, Town Got Its Fill of PCBs." *Washington Post,* January 1, 2002. P. 1A.
9.   Cat Lazaroff. "Replacing Grass with Trees May Release Carbon." Release: Environmental News Service, August 8, 2002.
10.   Joel Best. *Damned Lies and Statistics.* Berkeley and Los Angeles, California: University of California Press, 2001.
11.   World Wide Fund for Nature. <www.panda.org/resources/publications/forext/report97/index.htm>.
12.   Lomborg. *The Skeptical Environmentalist.* p. 114.
13.   <http://www.guidestar.org>.
14.   AAFRC. *Giving USA 2001.* Indianapolis, IN: AAFRC Trust for Philanthropy, 2001.
15.   Lomborg. *The Skeptical Environmentalist.* p.352.
16.   See N. Birdsall. "*A Cost of Siblings: Child Schooling in Urban Columbia,*" in J. Davanzo and J.L. Simon (eds.) *Research in Population Economics,* Greenwich, CT: Blackwell, 1980.
17.   *The State of World Population 1991.*
18.   See: World Bank. *World Development Report 1997,* New York: Oxford University Press, 1997
19.   David Smith. Too Many People. <http://news.nationalgeographic.com/ news/2000/07/0728_population.html>.
20.   Amartya Sen. "Population and Gender Equity." *The Nation.* July 24/31,2000.

Part V – Three Forces

Chapter 13 Introduction

1.   R.L. Sivard et al, *World Military and Social Expenditures,* 1993, Washington, DC: World Priorities, 1993. p. 21.

Chapter 14: Definition of Death

1.   Yeshivat Hakotel. The Jewish People's Secret Weapons. <http://www.hakotel.org> 2002.
2.   Kate Milner. "Who Are the Suicide Bombers." *BBC News,* Dec. 2, 2001. Note: An Associated Press report (March 24, 2002) reported that in Palestine, the suicide bomber pool has widened to include more secular, nonpolitical and even female volunteers.
3.   Religions of the World: Numbers of Adherents; Rates of Growth. <http://www.religioustolerance.org>.
4.   Religions of the World: Numbers of Adherents; Rates of Growth.
5.   Richard Ostling. Researcher tabulates world's believers – World

Christian Encyclopedia.
<http://www.sltrib.com/2001/may192001/saturday/98496.htm>
2002.

6. Richard Ostling. Researcher tabulates world's believers – World
    Christian Encyclopedia.

7. Adelle M. Banks. "Religion's Influence, After Sept. 11 Spurt, Bank to
    Normal Levels." *Religion News,* March 20, 2002. The nationwide poll of
    2,002 adults has a margin of error of 2.5%.

8. Adelle M. Banks. *Religion News.*

9. Adelle M. Banks. *Religion News.*

10. Leonard Peikoff. Abortion Rights are Pro-Life.
    <http://www.religion.aynrand.org> 2000.

11. See *The Encyclopedia of Women and World Religion,* Serinity Young et al.
    (eds.), Macmillan, 1999. Much of the information about contraception
    and religion has been culled from Kathleen O'Grady's material included
    in that publication.

12. *Britannica Book of the Year, 1999,* Chicago: Encyclopedia Britannica,
    Inc.

13. *Britannica Book of the Year, 1999.*

14. Kathy Coffey. "It's time to end the hypocrisy on birth control."
    Uscatholic.org, June 1998.

15. "Brazilian Women Use Contraceptives Despite Catholic Church." *New
    York Times,* Sept. 2, 1994.

16. Jean-Claude Carriere. "Human Life Threatens All Life: The Dalai Lama
    Speaks Out." *Zero Population Growth of Greater Boston Newsletter,* Vol.
    7, No. 2, March/April 1997.

17. *"Fertility and Contraceptive Use." UNICEF Statistics,* March 2001.

18. Note: emergency contraception (the "morning-after pill") tends to raise
    louder protests within certain religious circles.

19. "Facts in Brief." *Alan Guttmacher Institute* (February 2000).

20. The projection takes into account the reproduction rates of 15 to 44
    year-old women including those offspring of women who gave birth in
    the 1970s and early 1980s.

21. Bible: Numbers 31:15-18.

22. Stanley Henshaw and Kathryn Kost. "Abortion Patients in 1994-95;
    Characteristics and Contraceptive Use." *Family Planning Perspectives*
    (July/August 1996).

23. *"Clandestine Abortion: A Latin American Reality." Alan Guttmacher
    Institute* (1994).

24. Jane Hurst. *The History of Abortion in the Catholic Church. Washington,
    DC: Catholics* for a Free Choice, 1983.

25. "World Life League: New European 'Black Death' "Now Comes in Pill
    Form." *World Life League* (July 7, 1999).

26. "Reform Jewish Movement Appalled by Comparison between Holocaust and Abortion Pill." *Religious Action Center of Reform Judaism.*

27. Rabbi Raymond A. Zwerin and Rabbi Richard J, Shapiro. Judaism and Abortion. <http://www.*rcrc.org*> 2000. Note: the concept infers that a fetus is a part of a woman's body and that, as such, the woman's life takes precedence over a potential life. Abortion becomes permissible if a woman elects to sacrifice part of her body (in this case, a fetus) as a means of assuring her overall well-being. However, most Judaic teachings do not extend this right to the use of abortion as a means of birth control; as a means of avoiding the responsibility of bearing children.

28. Choosing Judaism: The Universalism of Judaism and Personal Freedom. <http://www.joi.org> 2002.

29. Zwerin and Shapiro.

30. Daniel C. Maguire. *Sacred Choices: The Right to Contraception and Abortion in Ten World Religions.* Minneapolis, MN: Augsburg Fortress, Publishers, July 2001. Chapter 9.

31. *"The World's Abortion Laws 1999." Center for Reproductive Law and Policy* (wall chart).

32. "Religious Voices Worldwide Support Choice." *Center for Reproductive Law & Policy* (2002).

33. Kuala Lumpur. *"Islam and Family Planning." Sisters In Islam* (2000).

34. Vasu Murti and Mary Krane Derr. Abortion is Bad Karma: Hindu Perspectives. <http://www.fnsa.org> Fall 1998.

35. Vasu Murti and Mary Krane Derr.

36. Religious Voices Worldwide Support Choice. <crip.org/pub_fac_atkrel.html> March 20.

37. Religious Voices Worldwide Support Choice. Note: mental health impairment includes the aftereffects of rape and contraceptive failure.

38. "60% of Abortions Unsafe: OGSH." *The Hindu,* July 13, 2001.

39. Rebecca Wind "Access to Abortion Still Under Fire after Three Decades of Legality in the U.S." *Alan Guttmacher Institute* (Jan. 17, 2002).

40. How Buddhists feel about abortion is often determined by whether or not they consider a fetus to have attained "personhood."

41. Daniel P. Horigan. "Of Compassion and Capital Punishment: A Buddhist Perspective on the Death Penalty." *American Journal of Jurisprudence* (1996).

42. *The World's Abortion Laws. <http://www.crlp.org> February 1999.*

43. James J. Hughes and Damien Keown. "Buddhism and Medical Ethics: A Bibliographic Introduction" *Journal of Buddhist Ethics.* Vol. 2, (1995). Note: information about the three Buddhist responses to abortion are drawn from this article.

44. Daniel C. Maguire. *Sacred Choices: The Right to Contraception and Abortion in Ten World Religions.*

45. Leonard Peikoff. Abortion Rights are Pro-Life.
46. "Levels and Trends of Contraceptive Use in 1998." *United Nations Population Division* (2000).
47. "Facts in Brief." *Alan Guttmacher Institute* (February 2000).
48. "Religious Intolerance Cited Around World" *Associated Press* (Sept. 10, 1999).
49. "Religious Intolerance Cited Around World" *Associated Press*.
50. Religiously-Based Civil Unrest and Warfare. <http://www.religioustolerance.org>.
51. *"Geneva Spiritual Appeal." Office of the United Nations High Commissioner for Human Rights* (1999).

Chapter 15: *Organizations*

1. Mary E. Clark. "The Backward Ones." *PCDForum Column* no 51 (June 25, 1993).
2. Mary E. Clark. "The Backward Ones."
3. R. B. Mason. Let Us Organize for Safety in Chicago, proclamation – Oct. 11, 1871 <http://www.chicagohs.org>.
4. *"1998 Data Book".* U.S. Department of the Treasury: Internal Revenue Service, *Publication 558.*
5. Charles Hill. *A Herculean Task: The Myth and Reality of Arab Terrorism.* New York: Basic Books, 2001, p. 99.
6. Charles Hill. *A Herculean Task: The Myth and Reality of Arab Terrorism.* p. 100.
7. Charles Hill. *A Herculean Task: The Myth and Reality of Arab Terrorism.* p. 106.
8. Sigmund Freud. *Group Psychology and the Analysis of the Ego.* New York: W.W. Norton, 1959.
9. Gustave Le Bon. *Psychologie des foules.* Minneola: Dover Publications, 2002 as quoted in Freud's *Group Psychology and the Analysis of the Ego,* p. 12.
10. Sigmund Freud. *Group Psychology and the Analysis of the Ego.* p. 70.
11. William McDougall. *The Group Mind.* Manchester: Ayer Company Publishers, 1973. Note, this book was originally published in 1920 by Cambridge University Press.
12. Sigmund Freud. *Group Psychology and the Analysis of the Ego.* p. 23.
13. Sigmund Freud. *Group Psychology and the Analysis of the Ego.* p. 77.
14. William McDougall. *The Group Mind.*
15. Sigmund Freud. *Group Psychology and the Analysis of the Ego.*
16. Gregg Zoroya. "Woman describes the mentality of a suicide bomber." *USA Today,* April 22, 2002.
17. "Woman describes the mentality of a suicide bomber." *USA Today.*
18. Sigmund Freud. *Group Psychology and the Analysis of the Ego.* p. 12.

19.   Sigmund Freud. *Group Psychology and the Analysis of the Ego.* p. 12.
20.   John Moore. (October 4, 2001) The Evolution of Islamic Terrorism: an Overview. <http://www.pbs.org/wgbh/pages/frontline/shows/target/>.
21.   Sigmund Freud. *Group Psychology and the Analysis of the Ego.* p. 13.
22.   Sigmund Freud. *Group Psychology and the Analysis of the Ego.* p. 13 - 15.

Chapter 16: Technology

1.   W. Brian Arthur. "How Fast Is Technology Evolving?" *Scientific American,* (Feb. 1997).
2.   W. Brian Arthur. "How Fast Is Technology Evolving?"
3.   In 1999, six new planets were discovered bringing the number of extra solar planets to around 30.
4.   "World Cultural Report." United Nations Educational, Scientific and Cultural Organization (1998).
5.   "TV Basics – Television Households." Television Bureau of Advertising (2002) cites Nielsen Media Research as source of information.
6.   (2002). Don't Buy It – Get Media Smart. [electronic journal]. Available <http://www.pbskids.org>.
7.   *"TV Basics – Time Spent Viewing – Persons."* Television Bureau of Advertising (2002) (cites Nielsen Media Research as source of information). An earlier reference in this book notes that the typical U.S. family has one or more TV sets turned on seven-plus hours a day. An explanation for the apparent discrepancy – different people within the same household are glued to the TV at different times. According to Nielsen Media Research, children and teens watch television a little over three hours a day; women are in front of the set four hours forty-six minutes a day – men: four hours eleven minutes per diem.
8.   "TV Basics – Time Spent Viewing – Persons."
9.   Mark Sappenfield. "Mounting Evidence Links TV Viewing to Violence." *The Christian Science Monitor,* March 29, 2002.
10.   Mark Sappenfield. "Mounting Evidence Links TV Viewing to Violence."
11.   John Whitfield. (March 29, 2002). Blow for Teens' TV Time. [electronic journal]. Available <http://www.nature.com/nsu/020325/020325-9.html>.
12.   Mark Sappenfield. "Mounting Evidence Links TV Viewing to Violence."
13.   It's Four Hours of TV Daily for Most Youths. Available <http://strait-stimes.asia1.com/sg/singapore/story/0,1870,120049,00.html>
14.   "Reality TV Still a Hit." *BBC NEWS* (April 4, 2002).
15.   *World Culture Report.*
16.   *World Culture Report.*

17.   Leila Conners Petersen. "The Wired World Atlas." *Wired Magazine* (November 1998).

18.   "Al-Jazeera Goes It Alone." *BBC News,* October 8, 2001.

19.   "Al-Jazeera Goes It Alone." *BBC News.*

20.   "US urges curb on Arab TV channel." *BBC News.* October 4, 2001.

21.   Barry M. Leiner, Vinton G. Cerf, David D. Clark, Robert E. Kahn, Leonard Kleinrock, Daniel C. Lynch, Jon Postel, Larry G. Roberts, Stephen Wolff. A Brief History of the Internet. Available <http://www.isoc.org/Internet/history/brief.html>.

22.   How Many Online? [electronic journal]. [cited February 2002]. Available <http://www/nua.ie/surveys/how_many_online>.

23.   Christopher Flavin. "*Rich Planet, Poor Planet.*" from The Worldwatch Institute, *State of the World 2001*, New York, London: W.W. Norton, 2001, p. 6.

24.   Christopher Flavin. *State of the World 2001.* p. 6.

25.   Google search engine.

26.   (2001) How to Make a Bomb from a Battery. [electronic journal]. Available <http://www.totse.com>.

27.   Michael Robbins (1997). How to Make a Bomb. [electronic journal]. Available <http://www.ohscanada.com>.

28.   Atomic Bomb Design. [electronic journal]. Available <http://www.accutek.com>.

29.   "The Reality of Pornography on the Internet." Operation Kids, Inc., (December 2002).

30.   Internet proves vital communications tool. [cited Sept. 12, 2001]. Available <http://www.cnn.com/2001/TECH/Internet/09/12/attacks.Internet/>. Note: Prodigy Communications Corporation and the University of California at Berkeley were credited for being the first to go online with websites dedicated to tracking Sept. 11 victims.

31.   Jay Lyman. How Terrorists Use the Internet. [cited Sept. 12, 2001]. Available <http://www.newsfactor.com/perl/story/7731.html>.

32.   ISOC Around the World: Thinking Globally, Acting Locally. [electronic journal]. Available <http://www.isoc.org>.

33.   ISOC Around the World.

34.   Nicholas Negroponte. The Next Billion Users. [electronic journal]. [cited June 1996] Available <http://wired.com/wired/archive/4.06/negroponte_pr.html>.

35.   The Next Billion Users.

36.   The Next Billion Users.

37.   Energy Emerges as a Key Issue for Johannesburg." [electronic journal]. [cited May 8, 2002]. Available <http://www.johannesburgsummit.org>.

38.   Robert Wade. "Winners and Losers." *The Economist,* (April 26, 2001).

39.   Lloyd J. Dumas. *Lethal Arrogance.* New York: St. Martin's Press, 1999. p. 22.

40.   "Bulletin of the Atomic Scientists." The Education Foundation for Nuclear Science (Feb. 27, 2002).

41.   "Bulletin of the Atomic Scientists."

42.   "Bulletin of the Atomic Scientists."

43.   "Bulletin of the Atomic Scientists."

44.   "Bulletin of the Atomic Scientists."

45.   "Russian Weapons Security Found Lax." *Knight Ridder Newspapers* release. April 6, 2003.

46.   Edward J. Markey. "The Threat of Nuclear Terror." *The Washington Post,* Feb. 28, 2002.

47.   "Bulletin of Atomic Scientists." One hand of the "clock" was moved from nine to seven minutes to midnight on Feb. 27, 2002. This is the third time since 1991 that the Doomsday Clock has been advanced. The clock has been a symbolic device used by the Bulletin of Atomic Scientists (founded by scientists in 1945) to warn the world about nuclear danger.

48.   "Bulletin of Atomic Scientists."

49.   Steve Sternberg. "Germ Warfare: New Threat from Terrorists." *Science News,* (May 18, 1996), p. 311.

50.   Peter Passell. "Flimsy Accounting on Nuclear Weapons." *New York Times,* July 9, 1998.

51.   Henry F. Cooper. "Limited Ballistic Missile Strikes. GPALS Comes Up with an Answer." *NATO Review,* Web Edition, No. 3 (June 1992): 27-30.

52.   Mark Carson, Theodore Taylor, Eugene Eyster, William Maraman, and Jacob Wechsler (1987). Can Terrorists Build Nuclear Weapons? [electronic journal]. Available <http://www.nci.org>.

53.   George Harper. "A Do-It-Yourself A-Bomb." *New Scientist,* (March 27, 1980): 998.

54.   Phil Williams, and Paul Woessner. "The Real Threat of Nuclear Smuggling." *Scientific American,* (January 1996).

55.   Can Terrorists Build Nuclear Weapons? Hyptertext.

56.   "Indo-Pak Nuclear War Would Stop Short of Total Destruction." *Associated Press,* January 26, 2002. Statement made by M.V. Ramana who noted that many variables – weather, positioning of the bomb, etc. – would determine final death toll.

57.   Rorber Lull. Experts Answers Questions about Radiation Exposure. [electronic journal]. {cited January 23, 2002]. Available http://www.uscf.edu>.

58.   Ira Helfand, M.D., Effects of a Nuclear Explosion. [electronic journal]. Available <http://www.psr.org>.

59.   Effects of a Nuclear Explosion.

60.   Walter Pincus. "Bush Urged to Abolish Nuclear War Plan." *The Washington Post,* June 20, 2001. Note: the information included in the news story is from the National Resources Defense Council.

61.   L. Douglas Keeny. *The Doomsday Scenario.* St. Paul: MBI Publishing

Company, 2002.

62.   Elizabeth M. Whelan. "Don't Have a Meltdown Over Dirty Nukes."
       The Wall Street Journal, June 11, 2002.

63.   David Whitehouse. Analysis: Making a 'Dirty Bomb.' [electronic jour-
       nal]. [cited June 10, 2002]. Available <http://news.bbc.co.uk/hi/eng-
       lish/world/americas/newsid_2037000/
       2037056.stm>.

64.   Mark Thompson. "What Is a 'Dirty Bomb'?" *Time,* June 10, 2002.

65.   Analysis: Making a 'Dirty Bomb.' Hyptertext.

66.   Khidhir Hamza. "The Dirty Secret of 'Dirty Bombs.'" *The Wall Street
       Journal.* June 12, 2002.

67.   Charles J. Hanley. "Specialists Work to Reduce 'Dirty Bomb' Threat."
       Associate Press, July 5, 2002.

68.   Charles J. Hanley. "Specialists Work to Reduce 'Dirty Bomb' Threat."

69.   "Germ Warfare: New Threat from Terrorists." *Science News.*

70.   Peter Landry. Historical Biographies, Nova Scotia: Jeffrey Amherst
       (1717-97). [electronic journal]. [cited march 2000]. Available
       <http://www.bluepete.com>.

71.   Note: Amherst College goes out of its way to clarify the origins of its
       title. The college was named for the town of Amherst and not the British
       General.

72.   Peter d'Errico. Jeffrey Amherst and Smallpox Blankets. [electronic jour-
       nal]. [cited March 2001]. Available <http://www.nativeweb.org>.

73.   Thomas W. McGovern, and George W. Christopher. Biological Warfare
       and Its Cutaneous Manifestations. *The Electronic Textbook of
       Dermatology,* New York: The Internet Dermatology Society, Inc.

74.   David Abel. "Beyond Anthrax: Are There Other Threats?" *Boston
       Sunday Globe's,* November 14, 2001.

75.   David Abel. "Beyond Anthrax: Are There Other Threats?"

76.   David Abel. "Beyond Anthrax: Are There Other Threats?"

77.   David Abel. "Beyond Anthrax: Are There Other Threats?"

78.   "Health Aspects of Chemical and Biological Weapons," *World Health
       Organization.* 1970.

79.   Judith Miller, Stephen Engelberg, and William Broad. *Germs.* New
       York: Simon & Schuster, 2001, p. 298.

80.   Judith Miller et al. *Germs.* p. 39.

81.   David Abel. "Beyond Anthrax: Are There Other Threats?"

82.   Descriptions of the BWs are a compilation of information extracted
       from several books and articles about biological agents (many of which
       are referenced elsewhere in these endnotes).

83.   Nuclear, Biological, Chemical Warfare. [electronic journal]. Available
       <http://www.N-B-C—Warfare.com>.

84.   David Abel. "Beyond Anthrax: Are There Other Threats?"

85.   Bruce W. Nelan. "Germ Warfare." *Time World,* Dec. 1, 1997.

86.   "Germ Warfare." *Time World.*

87.   Jon Cohen. "Designer Bugs." *The Atlantic Monthly,* July/August 2002.
88.   John Barry, Mark Hosenball, and Adam Rogers. "In the Germ Labs." *Newsweek,* February 25, 2002.
89.   Robert Block. "Bitter Researchers Are Big Question In Germ Warfare." *The Wall Street Journal,* May 20, 2002. Note: Quote is from Amy Sands, deputy director of the Center for Nonproliferation Studies at the Monterey Institute of International Studies. She appeared before the U.S. Senate Foreign Relations Committee in March 2002.
90.   Judith Miller et al. *Germs.*

Part VI: Negative Envy

Chapter 17: Pulling Down vs. Pushing Up

1.   Robert Andrews, Mary Biggs, Michel Seidel et al, *The Columbia World of Quotations.* New York: Columbia University Press, 1996. (Quotation from Aristotle's *The Art of Rhetoric,* section 6, chapter 2:11).
2.   Dante Alighieri. *The Divine Comedy.* New York: Everyman's Library – Alfred A. Knopf, April 1992.
3.   Ayn Rand. *Return of the Primitive: The Anti-Industrial Revolution.* New York: Plume, 1999.
4.   Ayn Rand. *Return of the Primitive: The Anti-Industrial Revolution.*
5.   Daniel C. Maguire. *Sacred Choices.* Minneapolis, MN: Fortress Press, 2001, p. 58.
6.   "Global Financial Profile." *Report of the High-Level Panel on Financing for Development* (June 2001).
7.   Samuel P. Huntington. *The Clash of Civilizations and the Remaking of World Order.* New York: Simon & Schuster, 1996.
8.   Samuel P. Huntington. "The Age of Muslim Wars" *Newsweek,* Dec. 17, 2001.
9.   Slamic Summit Opens with Slap at West. <http://www www.cnn.com/WORLD> Dec. 9, 1997.
10.   Slamic Summit Opens with Slap at West.
11.   Jonah Goldberg. Civilization Envy – On Muslims, Israel and McDonald's. <http://www.nationalreview.com> September 28, 2001.
12.   Jonah Goldberg. Civilization Envy – On Muslims, Israel and McDonald's.
13.   Jonah Goldberg. Civilization Envy – On Muslims, Israel and McDonald's.
14.   2001 World Population Data Sheet, Population Reference Bureau. <http://www.prb.org/content/navigationmenu/other_reports/2000-2002/2001_world_population-data-sheet.htm> 2001.
15.   Helmut Schoeck. *Envy: A Theory of Social Behavior.* Indianapolis, IN: Liberty Fund, Inc., 1987.

Chapter 18: What It All Means

1.   "Al-Qaida terror manual recommends targets." *Associate Press*, Feb. 2, 2002.
2.   "Al-Qaida terror manual recommends targets." *Associate Press*.
3.   John Kelsay. "Fighting the 'Good' Fight: The Return of the Religious War." *Research in Review*, Florida State University, fall/winter issue, 1999.

Part VII: The Solution

Chapter 19: Liberate, Educate, Motivate and Celebrate Women

1.   Stephan Paulus. *Nostradamus 1999*, St. Paul, MN: Llewellyn Publications, 2000.
2.   Associated Press Release. "Powell: U.S. Fight Targets Poverty Along with Terrorism." Feb. 2, 2002.
3.   *Brussels Declaration*. Third United Nations Conference on the Least Developed Countries. May 14-20, 2001.
4.   Associated Press Release. "Powell: U.S. Fight Targets Poverty Along with Terrorism."
5.   Associated Press Release. "Powell: U.S. Fight Targets Poverty Along with Terrorism."
6.   "Women are Natural Peace Keepers." *The Namibian*, March 9, 2001.
7.   United Nations Office of the High Commissioner for Human Rights. "Fact Sheet No. 22, Discrimination against Women: The Convention and the Committee." June 25, 1993.
8.   Michael Fathers. "Second-Class Citizens." *Time Asia*, April 2, 2001.
9.   Lewis Machipisa. Zimbabwe: Power for Women. <http://www.ips.org/womenleaders/wo=ll.html>
10.   Ilene B. Prusher. "Small Steps, but the Pace Quickens." *The Christian Science Monitor.* August 7, 2000.
11.   Fast Facts on Gender Issues. <http://www.unfpa.org/gender/facts.htm>
12.   "Women are Natural Peace Keepers." *The Namibian*.
13.   Convention on the Elimination of All Forms of Discrimination against Women. <http://www.un.org/womenwatch/daw/cedaw,htm>
14.   George F. Will. "Another Pose of Rectitude." *Newsweek*. September 2, 2002.
15.   Education for All Year 2000 Assessment Results. <http://www.uis.unesco.org/uisen/know/know_p/centre3.htm>
16.   Education for All Year 2000 Assessment Results.
17.   Carol Bellamy. "The Role of Employment and Work in Poverty

Eradication: the Empowerment and Advancement of Women." United
Nations Childrens Fund. July 6, 1999.

18.   Eradicating Feminized Poverty.
      <http://www.unifem.undp.org/ec_pov.htm>

19.   United Nations Development Fund. <http://www.
      un.org/Pubs/ourlives /undp.htm>

20.   Carol Bellamy. "The Role of Employment and Work in Poverty
      Eradication: the Empowerment and Advancement of Women."

21.   "Women and Poverty." United Nations Population Fund.

22.   Press Release. "UNFPA Executive Director Asks World Leaders to
      Invest in Greater Role for Women in Development." United Nations
      Populations Fund. March 18, 2002.

Chapter 20: The Test

1.   Geoff Winestock. "For Egypt's Terrorists, Fertile Ground Lay in
      Widespread Poverty." *The Wall Street Journal,* Jan. 18, 2002.

2.   Geoff Winestock. "For Egypt's Terrorists, Fertile Ground Lay in
      Widespread Poverty."

3.   Niall Ferguson. "Clashing Civilizations or Mad Mullahs: The United
      States Between Informal and Formal Empire," in *The Age of Terror* (edi-
      tors: Strobe Talbott and Nayan Chanda), New York: Basic Books, 2001,
      p.137.

4.   George McGovern. The Real Cost of Hunger.
      <http://www.un.org/chronicle> November 3, 2001

5.   In 1983, the Grameen Bank was established in Bangladesh. The bank has
      become world famous for its micro-lending mainly to women throughout
      the country. The average bank loan to a woman is around $150 and its
      borrowers include over two million people – mostly women. The bank
      has found that female loan recipients are excellent risks and end up using
      the money to develop income-producing enterprises that ultimately
      improve their family's living conditions (e.g. enhance the control of their
      lives and expand their ownership capabilities).

6.   Andres Oppenheimer. Small Donors Show Up U.S. Aid.
      <http://www.miami.com/mld/
      miamiherald/news/columnists/andres_oppenheimer/3729418.htm>

7.   "America's Shame: Foreign Aid Should Be a U.S. Priority." *The
      Guardian,* March 18, 2002.

8.   "Ranking the Rich." *Foreign Policy.* <http://foreignpolicy.com>.

9.   "Ranking the Rich." *Foreign Policy.* <http://foreignpolicy.com>.

10.   Grameen – Banking for the Poor. <http://www.grameen-info.org>.
      Much of the information about the Grameen Bank has been extracted
      from the organization's website.

11.   Rebecca N. Fonkem. "In Cameroon, a Female-Centered Organizaiton

works to conquer the Poverty of Rural Women." *United Nations Chronicle*. November 1, 1999.

12.   Mayra Buvinic. "Women in Poverty." *Foreign Policy*. Fall 1997.

13.   Speech by Peter D. Bell. "Where the End of Poverty Begins." Princeton University Woodrow Wilson School of Public and International Affairs. Feb. 22, 2003.

14.   Frank Gardner. "Saudi Women Defy Business Curbs." BBC News Online. Jan. 21, 2001.

15.   "Birthrates in Developing Nations May Be in Decline." *New York Times*, March 12, 2002.

16.   United Nations Development Program: China, China Human Development Report, Beijing, 1998.

17.   China's population is now nearly 1.3 billion people with its census increasing by 12 million people a year.

18.   Hannah Beech. "China's Baby Bust." *Time Pacific*, August 6, 2001.

19.   Note: particularly in rural areas throughout China, boys are valued more highly than girls because they are important labor resources for farm families. Consequently, it is not uncommon for female fetuses to be aborted or even for newborn daughters to be killed. Two decades later, this practice has created another problem – a shortfall of nearly 50 million females, according to the World Health Organization. "The first wave of children born under the policy is reaching marriageable age and there are far too few brides to go around," says *Time* magazine. "The most desperate bachelors have taken to marrying relatives. In a few places, the practice has become so common, the communities are referred to as 'incest villages.'" See: Hannah Beech. "With Women So Scare, What Can Men Do?" *Time*. July 1, 2002. p. 8.

20.   "With Women So Scare, What Can Men Do?" *Time*.

21.   China Population Information and Research Center, Beijing. <http:www.cpirc.org>

22.   Elisabeth Rosenthal. "For One-Child Policy, China Rethinks Iron Hand." *New York Times*, Nov. 1, 1998.

23.   United Nations Population Division, "Global Database on Contraceptive Prevalence," New York: United Nations, as of March 2001.

24.   United Nations Population Division, "Global Database on Contraceptive Prevalence."

25.   United Nations Population Division, "Global Database on Contraceptive Prevalence."

26.   United Nations Population Division, "Global Database on Contraceptive Prevalence."

27.   United Nations Population Division, "Global Database on Contraceptive Prevalence."

28.   Philip Jenkins. "The Catholic Church's Culture Clash," *The Wall Street Journal*, March 26, 2002.

29.   Pope John Paul VI. Humanae Vitae.
       <http://www.vactican.va/holy_father/paul_vi/encyclicals/docu-
       ments/hf_p-vi_enc_25071968>_
       humanae-vitae_en.html.
30.   CNN Report. September 20, 2000.
31.   CNN Report. September 20, 2000.
32.   Induced Abortion Worldwide. <http:www.gutmacher.org>
33.   <http://www.gutmacher.org>
34.   <http://www.gutmacher.org> 78% of the world's abortions are cur-
       rently performed in developing nations.
35.   <http://www.gutmacher.org> Annually, 3.5% of women in their child-
       bearing years have an abortion (estimate).
36.   Franck Amalric. "Population Growth and the Environmental Crisis:
       Beyond the 'Obvious.'" In *The North and the South and the
       Environment*. London: Earthscan Publications Ltd. 1955.
37.   GuideStar. http://www.guidestar.org/controller/search.gs>.
38.   The Foundation Center.
       <http://12.39.246.37/custom/redesign/query.html?
       col=privfdn&col=corp&col=commfdn&ht=0&qp=&qt=women&qs=&q
       c=&pw=100%25&ws=0&la=en&qm=0&st=1&nh=10&lk=1&rf=0&oq=
       &rq=0&si=0.>
39.   International Women's Media Foundation. < http://www.medi-
       awatch.ca/research/gmmp/ Default.asp?pg=4>.
40.   Magazine World.
       <http://www.fipp.com/Data/Top%2050%20Womens.pdf>.
41.   Speech by James D. Wolfensohn to the World Bank Group, March 21,
       2002.
42.   Anna McDermott. "Women's Vital Peace Role." BBC News Online.
       Nov. 8, 2001.

Epilogue

1.   Paul Raskin, Paul, Tariq Banuri, Gilberto Gallopín, Pablo Gutman, Al
       Hammond, Robert Kates, and Rob Swart. *Great Transition: The Promise
       and Lure of the Times Ahead*. A report of the Global Scenario Group.
       SEI PoleStar Series Report no. 10. Boston: Stockholm Environment
       Institute. 2002.
2.   Associated Press Release. "Summit Opens with Focus on Poverty." Aug.
       27, 2002.
3.   Andrew C. Revkin. "Forget Nature. Even Eden is Engineered." *The
       New York Times*, August 20, 2002.
4.   Andrew C. Revkin. "Forget Nature. Even Eden is Engineered."